Dedicated to the spiritual master of the entire world, His Divine Grace A. C. Bhaktivedanta Swami Prabhupāda, who worked tirelessly to give us the treasure of Vedic wisdom and showed us practically how to live a Kṛṣṇa conscious lifestyle, even in childhood.

"If we train children by developing and encouraging their propensity to love Kṛṣṇa, then we shall be successful in educating them to the topmost standard."

His Divine Grace
A. C. Bhaktivedanta Swami Prabhupāda

If you are interested in purchasing or distributing this book, please contact the author at

1615 Martha St.
Boise, ID 83706
USA
aruddha108@yahoo.com
www.krishnahomeschool.com

Homeschooling Krishna's Children

Aruddha Devi Dasi

Krishna Homeschool

ISBN 978-1-7369610-9-4

Grateful acknowledgment is given to Gannett Co., Inc. for their kind permission to reprint two articles from *The Idaho Statesman*, "A Temple Opens" and "Wise Guys".

All names in the book have been changed in order to protect the families' privacy.

Contents

Appendices

Foreword

Conscientious *gṛhasthas* naturally want to provide the very best educational opportunity they can for their children. Options in the realm of children's education, and particularly the social environment in the public school system, are often too compromised for caring parents to confidently or comfortably send their children into them.

A natural and suitable option for conscientious parents to consider when evaluating options regarding their children's primary and secondary education is homeschooling. Some parents feel intimidated by this option because they lack clear guidelines on how and what to teach. They don't want to find themselves experimenting on their own children.

This book, compiled by Aruddhā Devī Dāsī, provides an enormous treasury to such parents. It tells them *how* to homeschool their children without sacrificing the quality of their children's academic development, and it maximizes character development, the primary fruit of an effective educational experience. Aruddhā Dāsī's writing presents a method of homeschooling that is based on Śrīla Prabhupāda's books and his overall instructions for children's education. The book is drawn largely from her own experience with homeschooling, but it can easily be adapted according to individual circumstances.

I have had a lot of experience over the years and throughout the US how Aruddhā Dāsī, after pioneering homeschooling with her own family, has extended her homeschooling model to scores of others, guiding and supporting them. Inspired and empowered by both her model and her example, many other families have also been successful.

Romapāda Swami

Acknowledgments

This book is a tribute to the efforts of our great teacher and the spiritual master of the entire world, His Divine Grace A. C. Bhaktivedanta Swami Prabhupāda, who worked untiringly to give us this treasure of Vedic knowledge through his translations and purports. Where would we be without these pristine Bhaktivedanta purports that enlighten and inspire us every day, answering our doubts and guiding us on how to serve Kṛṣṇa and His creation? The recitation of the Sanskrit verses brings auspiciousness to the readers, and their explanations bring peace to the heart and mind. Śrīla Prabhupāda's books have a way of talking to us like a compassionate friend, guiding us through our difficult journey in the material world while showing us the path back to Godhead.

Śrīla Prabhupāda not only gave us wisdom through his books but also showed us practically how to live a Kṛṣṇa conscious lifestyle. If this spiritual training starts from childhood, the results can be wonderful.

My most humble obeisances at the lotus feet of my spiritual master, His Holiness Gopāla Kṛṣṇa Goswami, who inspired me to share my experiences in educating my sons with others. He has been a constant source of guidance and encouragement. An untiring preacher, he works hard to please Śrīla Prabhupāda without expecting anything in return. I beg for his mercy so that I may always serve his instructions and follow in his divine footsteps.

I would like to offer sincere thanks to His Holiness Candramauli Swami, His Holiness Dānavīr Goswami, His Holiness Hanumatpreṣaka Swami, His Holiness Rādhānātha Swami, His Holiness Romapāda Swami, and Her Grace Rukmiṇī Devī Dāsī for their generous guidance and encouragement while I was writing this book and delivering my homeschooling seminars.

My heartfelt gratitude goes to my dear husband, Ananta-rūpa Prabhu. Without his help, counsel, and support, homeschooling our children would not have been possible. On a day-to-day level he took a keen interest in how and what I was teaching, ensuring that our sons received a well-rounded education based on practical service and the study of Śrīla Prabhupāda's books. Most of all, he worked hard to give us a stable home so that we could carry on our homeschooling without anxiety.

My blessings to my sons, Rādhikā Ramaṇa and Gopal Hari, who encouraged and inspired me to record my experiences in this book. They spent countless hours traveling with me around the world to offer seminars. I am also grateful to Rādhikā Ramaṇa for editing my articles for the ISKCON Education website, and to his wife, my dear daughter-in-law, Amrita Keli, for her assistance in preparing slides for the seminars.

I am thankful to Gary Thomas, my main editor, who patiently and meticulously edited this ever-expanding book. He taught the boys Sanskrit during their homeschooling years and thus naturally understood the purpose and content of this book. His expertise in Sanskrit and English were a great help in the project.

Profound thanks go to Varṣānā Devī Dāsī from London for her guidance in finding a publisher; Rādhākaṇṭha Dāsa from Bangalore, Mañjarī Devī Dāsī from Bangalore, and Kelsey Gilbert for spending many hours transcribing our seminar recordings on a tight deadline; and to Anantshesh Dāsa from Pune for sending me information on the current legal status of homeschooling in India.

I would like to give thanks to all the devotees in Boise, particularly Amṛtā Devī Dāsī and her family, for helping with temple services so I could spend more time writing; Śrīnivāsācārya Dāsa and Sundarī Rādhikā Devī Dāsī for helping me troubleshoot computer problems even at odd times during the day; and Jayashree Narayan and Jennifer Lawrence for typing up my early, handwritten essays.

Several people helped with the production costs of this book. They are Śyāma Vilāsinī Devī Dāsī and Ācārya Ratna Dāsa from Mauritius, Kalyana Raman and Vijayalakshmi Gada Raman from Washington State, Viṣṇucaraṇa Dāsa from Tennessee, Baskar Dhanagopalan and Akhila Baskar from Georgia, and Kṛṣṇa Kumārī Devī Dāsī from Washington State. My heartfelt thanks to all of them for their generous assistance.

The ISKCON GBC Ministry for Educational Development gave its blessings to my seminars, and their ISKCON Education website published my first articles on homeschooling, creating the basis of this book. I am grateful to the Ministry for facilitating me in this way, and especially to Anupamā Devī Dāsī at the Ministry office.

Finally, I offer sincere thanks to all the parents and children who have given substance to this project by their questions, suggestions, corrections, and appreciation. Thank you for tolerating my shortcomings and allowing me to serve you in some small way.

Background

How This Book Came To Be

As our children reached school age, my husband and I began seriously considering our options for their formal education. Like many devotee parents, our aspirations were straightforward: we wanted to instill deep Kṛṣṇa conscious values in our children while giving them a solid academic education. We investigated area public schools and tried a private school for a while, but we were disappointed in one way or another. We then considered sending our children to a *gurukula* boarding school in another city, but there were few of these schools to choose from, and the ones that existed were too far away.

Besides, we needed each other as a family. Boise is a small town, and when we moved to Boise in 1986, there was no temple or devotee community here. So my husband and I started a small center in our home, hosting regular programs on Sundays. It was then that we came upon the concept of homeschooling, which was becoming increasingly popular in the United States. We purchased a readymade homeschooling curriculum, but soon gave it up and put together our own lesson plans, using Śrīla Prabhupāda's books as the main textbooks. After several years of homeschooling in this way we had no doubt: the process was working and our children were doing well both academically and spiritually. The small center grew into a beautiful midsize temple for their

Lordships Śrī Śrī Rādhā-Baṅkebihārī – our protectors and proprietors. The temple became the focus of many of our homeschooling activities.

Soon after the boys graduated from university, I began receiving calls from young devotee parents who had heard of homeschooling and wanted guidance in teaching their own children. They were determined to give their children a Kṛṣṇa conscious education grounded in strong

The ISKCON temple in Boise

spiritual, moral, and academic values, but they were unsure how to go about it. I helped them the best I could. Soon these queries led to homeschooling seminars, where I could offer a more systematic presentation and personally interact with more parents. As interest grew among devotee communities, I was invited for seminars in cities throughout the United States, India, and England. As more parents adopted homeschooling to educate their children, I found satisfaction in their success.

Wherever I went, parents asked me to write a book to systematically explain the method of homeschooling I had developed using Śrīla Prabhupāda's books. Five years ago I began writing down my own homeschooling experiences, researching Śrīla Prabhupāda's instructions on education, and listening to parents' questions, ideas, and experiences. This book is the result of that process.

I pray this book will please Śrīla Prabhupāda and the community of devotees in some small way. It was Prabhupāda's strong desire that children born into devotee families be trained as exemplary Vaiṣṇavas: "If we are able to make a whole generation of our children into fine Kṛṣṇa conscious preachers, that will be the glory of our movement and the glory of your country as well. But if we neglect somehow or other and if we lose even one Vaiṣṇava, that is very great loss." (Letter to Stokakṛṣṇa Dāsa, June 20, 1972)

I hope this book will give parents the encouragement and confidence they need to homeschool their children and raise them as exemplary Vaiṣṇavas. This book should be used as a guide to the basic principles, motivations, and methods of Kṛṣṇa conscious homeschooling. Every family is unique, so it's important to apply these principles to your individual circumstances. We need to do what is best for our children while remaining fixed in our determination to follow Śrīla Prabhupāda's instructions.

I have written this book as a series of short essays so that busy parents can read it in chunks. Although it may be tempting to skip around to one chapter or another, I encourage you to read the chapters in order so you see how the various aspects of homeschooling work together to provide a well-rounded education. Once you have finished reading it through, the book's format will allow you to come back to a particular chapter when it becomes relevant to your own homeschooling. There is also a "Frequently Asked Questions" chapter in the back.

I ask my readers to forgive the faults and shortcomings of this book. I am neither a śāstric scholar nor a professional educator; my only desire is to share what I have learned from my personal attempt at Kṛṣṇa conscious homeschooling. This book is only a beginning; I hope there will be many more guides, curriculums, and resources for home-schoolers in the future.

Aruddhā Devī Dāsī
Nṛsiṁha-caturdaśī, May 26, 2010
New Biharvan, Boise, Idaho

Basic Principles of Kṛṣṇa Conscious Homeschooling

Homeschooling can be part of a Kṛṣṇa conscious lifestyle, but it is a mistake to think Kṛṣṇa consciousness is simply an aspect of homeschooling. A Kṛṣṇa conscious lifestyle should be the focus of homeschooling. That is, we should be inspired to raise our children as good devotees rather than focusing only on their scholastic achievements, with Kṛṣṇa consciousness taking second place. Śrīla Prabhupāda's books are of a high spiritual caliber, so if we base our curriculum on his books, academic achievement will follow naturally.

What does it mean for children to live a Kṛṣṇa conscious life? Prabhupāda explains this in simple terms: "Simply follow the program of the elders, let the children associate as much as possible with the routine Kṛṣṇa conscious program, and when the others go out for working and business matters, the children can be given classes." (Letter to Aniruddha Dāsa, March 7, 1972)

This is what we tried to do in our own homeschooling. The children lived at home just as they would in a *gurukula* – with a few adjustments. We held our own morning program, and after breakfast *prasāda* we studied the *Bhāgavatam* for two or three hours every day. This study became a major part of our homeschooling curriculum, and through the *Bhāgavatam* we covered a number of subjects. Then after our study we applied what we were learning in our practical daily activities. For example, we would go out preaching, giving classes on Kṛṣṇa consciousness at local schools. We also wrote and rehearsed devotional plays, organized devotional festivals, performed Deity worship, distributed books at local events, and went out on *harināma*. There was never a dull moment for us; homeschooling was so filled with Kṛṣṇa conscious activities that there was no time for anything else.

Śrī Śrī Rādhā-Baṅkebihārī, presiding Deities in Boise, Idaho, USA

Śrīla Prabhupāda's idea for the education of our children was to make them well-rounded devotees who are expert in *śāstra,* eager to give Kṛṣṇa to others, and steady in their personal practice. He once said, "We are interested to open [a] school if there is education for Kṛṣṇa consciousness ... But we are not interested in so-called godless education. That is not our business." (Lecture, November 13, 1973, Delhi)

Since Kṛṣṇa is the source of all knowledge, if we understand and love Him, then all sorts of knowledge will follow. Everything material and spiritual comes from Kṛṣṇa. This is why Śrīla Prabhupāda emphasized spirituality as the goal of education; he knew that *Śrīmad-Bhāgavatam* has everything in it needed to understand both the material and spiritual worlds. Śrīla Prabhupāda envisioned our children receiving not only an academic education but developing godly character as well. To have good character one must have God in the center of his or her life; otherwise, there is no impetus to check one's actions. Kṛṣṇa has many wonderful qualities, such as kindness, wisdom, peacefulness, and forgiveness, and a godly person can develop these same qualities. Good character comes from living a pure and simple life dedicated to hearing and chanting the holy names, the basis of all learning. Since the main purpose of homeschooling is to raise a Kṛṣṇa conscious child, a Kṛṣṇa conscious lifestyle must be the basis for home education.

Why We Homeschooled Our Children

When my two sons, Rādhikā Ramaṇa and Gopal Hari, each turned five, I enrolled them in private school, hoping for wonderful results. They both studied there for the first two years of their schooling. I felt as though I was being responsible with their academic education, but I also wanted to train them to be good devotees. I wanted to read them stories from the *Kṛṣṇa* book and *Śrīmad-Bhāgavatam* and teach them to play the *mṛdaṅga*. I thought I would do this teaching after they came home from school, but I was soon disappointed to realize there was no time. They were tired when they got home, and it was difficult after they had been out for a full day to get them into a devotional frame of mind. I also found I had to spend time undoing some of what they were experiencing in school.

Gopal once told me how his class teacher, out of frustration, had spent the entire day talking about good behavior, because some of the children were misbehaved and disruptive. I felt so much academics time had been wasted. Good behavior and character come from being God conscious. Kṛṣṇa teaches us our values and standards through the scriptures and the examples of saintly persons. Yet public and private schools are secular institutions where any talk of spirituality is discouraged.

The school turned out not to be a healthy environment for my children. When Gopal was in kindergarten he had a young teacher whose boyfriend would come to class and openly kiss her in front of the children. She also neglected to stop his classmates when they teased him

Ananta-rūpa Dāsa, Aruddhā Devī Dāsī, Gopal Hari Dāsa, and Rādhikā Ramaṇa Dāsa

about his *śikhā* and his lunch menu, which was generally *capātīs* and *sabjī*. He was mortified, but the teacher never took any action.

In this school the teachers would heat all the lunches in a microwave oven before handing them out to the students. One time the teacher accidentally exchanged the contents of another box with the contents in Rādhikā Ramaṇa's lunch box. He found himself biting into a chicken leg instead of the broccoli *pakorās* I had packed for him. Fortunately, he spit it out before swallowing it, finding the taste strange since he had never eaten meat.

Another time, I went to sit in on Rādhikā Ramaṇa's math class, and I noticed how he had finished his math work before everyone else and was sitting bored, with nothing to do. The teacher had twenty students, so of course she could not spend individual time with him to challenge him further. Most schools cater to the needs of average students; if children are above average they are bored, and if they are below average they are frustrated. These are just a few of the reasons why we decided to homeschool our children.

Even more to the point, Prabhupāda said that children who are born into devotee families are not ordinary and should be given great care. These children are fortunate. Even those of us who were born in India and brought up in vegetarian families and with Vedic culture and habits did not have the good fortune of hearing the holy name and *kṛṣṇa-kathā* from the day we were born. Taking birth in a family of devotees means the children have performed at least some devotional service in their past lives. They are here to finish their purification and go back to Godhead. If we neglect this important point and fail to give them the proper training by which they can advance to the topmost level, they can easily fall back. Birth alone will not save them from taking another body or help them go back to Godhead.

The purpose of education is to understand who God is, our relationship with Him, and the nature of the material world. This body belongs to Kṛṣṇa, and the purpose of life is to use it in His service and recover our lost relationship with Him. When Lord Caitanya asked Rāmānānda Rāya to define the highest standard of education, he replied that it is knowledge of the science of Kṛṣṇa. In a society where there is no philosophy of God consciousness, there are no values. For example, we see that today in the name of material advancement there is no protection of women, children, old people, or cows or other animals, and no respect for brahminical culture. Both crime and mental and physical disease are increasing daily.

Material education aims at sense gratification – how to live and enjoy this world. This may give an apparent immediate benefit, but spiritual education aims at enjoyment in its pure form in our relationship with Kṛṣṇa, which is both immediately and ultimately beneficial and auspicious. Therefore as parents we should also tend to our children's spiritual needs and protect them from this endless cycle of birth and death. Homeschooling can be an ideal way to give our children the atmosphere and training they need to lead a life of service to Kṛṣṇa.

The Benefits of Homeschooling

Prabhupāda listed two things that are great blessings for anyone: to have the guidance of a spiritual master and to be born in a family of devotees. In this chapter, let's examine the second blessing. Great spiritual stalwarts such as Parīkṣit Mahārāja, Yudhiṣṭhira Mahārāja, Mīrā Bāī, Uddhava, and our own Śrīla Prabhupāda had the great fortune to be born in families of devotees and receive good training from early childhood.

Śrīla Prabhupāda mentions the benefits of such training in his purport to *Śrīmad-Bhāgavatam* 2.3.15: "By the grace of Lord Śrī Kṛṣṇa, we had the chance of being born in a Vaiṣṇava family, and in our childhood we imitated the worship of Lord Kṛṣṇa by imitating our father … Our spiritual master, who also took his birth in a Vaiṣṇava family, got all inspirations from his great Vaiṣṇava father, Ṭhākura Bhaktivinoda. That is the way of all lucky Vaiṣṇava families."

I can hardly overemphasize how much our children need good training from the beginning of their lives. To help with this training Prabhupāda encouraged devotees to send their children to *gurukula*. But if there is no *gurukula*? The parents must become the guru and the home the *kula* (*āśrama*). We can please Śrīla Prabhupāda by giving our children a Kṛṣṇa conscious education at home.

Homeschooling Makes Better Devotees

There are at least three reasons why homeschooling is able to help our children become good devotees. First, homeschooled children avoid the negative influences found in so many schools and experience far less pressure to adopt the values of their peers.

Second, it is difficult for teachers who do not understand the value of devotional service to serve as appropriate role models. Not following the four regulative principles prohibiting meat eating, illicit sex, gambling, and intoxication has a detrimental effect on their character. Children learn by example, and it is difficult for them to find good examples in nondevotee schools.

Third, at home parents *can* serve as good role models for their children. Prabhupāda refers to the importance of a teacher's moral qualifications in his purport to *Śrīmad-Bhāgavatam* 1.9.26: "For learning Vedic knowledge, one must approach a person who is cent percent engaged in devotional service. He must not do things which are forbidden in the *śāstras*. A person cannot be a teacher if he drinks or smokes. In the modern system of education the teacher's academic qualification is taken into consideration without evaluation of his moral life. Therefore, the result of education is misuse of high intelligence in so many ways."

Good Association Through Homeschooling

Homeschooling inculcates moral character and values in children through good devotee association and reading from Śrīla Prabhupāda's books. *Śrīmad-Bhāgavatam* is a wonderful book to teach from because it gives the philosophy of the *Bhagavad-gītā* through stories, and children love stories. These stories are not fictitious; rather, they tell of the histories of great saints and of Kṛṣṇa and His *avatāras*. By reading such histories, one directly associates with these great personalities and their teachings, and by such association one begins to develop the character of these very same personalities. As children grow older they learn to appreciate the instructions given by Queen Kuntī, Prahlāda Mahārāja, Dhruva Mahārāja, Kapila-deva, and so many others. In fact, a number of the devotees described in the *Bhāgavatam,* such as Prahlāda and Dhruva, are children themselves, so our own children have perfect examples and heroes to follow.

The scriptures tell us that Śrī Caitanya Mahāprabhu heard the stories of Dhruva Mahārāja and Prahlāda Mahārāja hundreds of times while growing up, but still was not satiated. The instructions of these saints are so valuable that no other moral book can compare with them. Children develop good character and saintly qualities by reading *Śrīmad-Bhāgavatam.*

The Home Environment

Character Training

The most important part of a child's education is character training, not accumulating degrees to get good jobs and money. After all, money cannot buy happiness. The Vedic scriptures say that real happiness comes when we link ourselves to the whole, to the Supreme Lord.

Prabhupāda often mentions that the world is full of debauchees, rogues, and thieves. Because these classes of men can be found even among the rich and educated, we know that education by itself does not necessarily provide knowledge of how to be a better person or a gentleman. But Vedic education is different because its goal is to make us godly so we can find true happiness. When we give such education to our children, Kṛṣṇa becomes pleased and will also take us, the parents, back to Godhead for our devotional service.

Cāṇakya Paṇḍita says the quality of an education is measured by whether or not the student has learned to see others' wives as his own mother, others' property as clods of dirt, and other living entities as the same as himself. Prabhupāda explains how in Vedic society influential citizens sent their children to *gurukula* to learn good character. Parents understood the value of good *gurukula* training in terms of character development, sense control, and the development of qualities like tolerance, humility, and detachment.

In his *Śrīmad-Bhāgavatam* purport to 6.5.25, Prabhupāda gives an example of how much a father should value character education:

> Prajāpati Dakṣa sent his second group of sons to the same place where his previous sons had attained perfection. He did not hesitate to send his second group of sons to the same place, although they too might become victims of Nārada's instructions. According to the Vedic culture, one should be trained in spiritual understanding as a *brahmacārī* before entering household life to beget children. This is the Vedic system. Thus Prajāpati Dakṣa sent his second group of sons for cultural improvement, despite the risk that because of the instructions of Nārada they might become as intelligent as their older brothers. As a dutiful father, he did not hesitate to allow his sons to receive cultural instructions concerning the perfection of life; he depended upon them to choose whether to return home, back to Godhead, or to rot in this material world in various species of life. In all circumstances, the duty of the father is to give cultural education to his sons, who must later decide which way to go. Responsible fathers should not hinder their sons who are making cultural advancement in association with the Kṛṣṇa consciousness movement. This is not a father's duty. The duty of a father is to give his son complete freedom to make his choice after becoming spiritually advanced by following the instructions of the spiritual master.

Unfortunately, most parents today do not train their children in Kṛṣṇa consciousness; they simply train them in sense gratification: how to earn money and accumulate material things. Parents make sure their children have the material facilities and education that will bring good jobs, but they will not let them join a spiritual organization or read the *Bhagavad-gītā* because they think these things a waste of time. And once their children are entangled in material love it is difficult for them to develop spiritual love, because they think the purpose of life is to enjoy.

"Therefore education of Kṛṣṇa consciousness should be given from the very childhood, *kaumāra,* from the age of fifth year up to the tenth year ... Children, as you teach them, they learn. They are innocent. Unfortunately, we do not give them training about Kṛṣṇa consciousness. We give them education for sense gratification, how you can earn money, economic development." (Lecture, April 10, 1974, Bombay)

In a lecture on *Bhagavad-gītā* 4.16, Prabhupāda described the results of this miseducation: "Although India is the land of spiritual culture, our small children, even though they go to school and college, have no connection with *Bhagavad-gītā.* They have no connection with *Bhagavad-gītā.* They are simply trained up for sense gratification. In Western countries also – for sense gratification. The very thing which is to be suppressed, sense gratification, education for that is given. They do not know what is *karma* and what is *vikarma.* Now, when the students become disobedient and they create riots and set fire in the buses, then they lament. But why have you educated the students like that? Who is responsible for this? The rascals, they do not know. Here is Kṛṣṇa prescribing: *kiṁ karma kim akarmeti/ kavayo 'py atra mohitāḥ.* Even learned men, they become bewildered." (Lecture, April 5, 1974, Bombay)

Therefore it is the duty of parents to train their children in Kṛṣṇa consciousness from the beginning of their lives. The first part of the training is how to be an ideal *brahmacārī,* which teaches children how to control sexual attachment. "Everyone should be trained up to give service. That is *gurukula.* And *brahmacārī,* this sex impulse should be controlled. That ruins the whole character." (Lecture, July 31, 1976, New Mayapur)

Prabhupāda said that to send our children to school just to learn to be better at eating, sleeping, mating, and defending is foolish, because all four of these are innate in every child. He gave the example of how babies immediately put food in their mouths when they are given something to eat. They require no training. The same is true for mating, defending, and sleeping. These propensities are already in us; we don't need to be educated in them. However, we do require training in how to control these activities so that we can advance spiritually. For this *brahmacarya* training, a *gurukula* is essential, because such training must start from the beginning of a child's life.

"Our prescription is that in the beginning of life the child should be taught self-restraint (*brahmacarya*), and when he is past twenty he can marry. In the beginning he should learn how to restrain his senses. If a child is taught to become saintly, his semen rises to his brain and he is able to understand spiritual values. Wasting semen decreases intelligence. So from the beginning, if he is a *brahmacārī* and does not misuse his semen, then he will become intelligent and strong and fully grown. For want of this education, everyone's brain and bodily growth are being stunted. After the boy has been trained as a *brahmacārī,* if he still wants to enjoy sex he may get married." (Letter to Śyāmasundara Dāsa, October 5, 1971)

Prabhupāda was not impressed by scholarship if the scholars had no character. It does not matter what *varṇa* or *āśrama* our children adopt, they must have good character. Prabhupāda said children can serve in the area for which they are most suited, whether teaching, administrative work, business or farming, or work under an employer. For all of them the most important thing to train is their character. This training comes with good spiritual *sādhana* and engagement in devotional service, which is why Prabhupāda stressed so much the importance of a Kṛṣṇa conscious lifestyle for our children: he wanted them to be able to develop saintly qualities from the beginning of their lives.

As children chant and dance with the elders in the home and temple, their hearts are cleansed and they develop an attraction for Kṛṣṇa. They start to relish Kṛṣṇa's pastimes and His remnants and gradually lose their taste for mundane things. As they read the scriptures, the characters of spiritual heroes rub off on them and they themselves become saintly. Raised in such an environment they know nothing but Kṛṣṇa. We can see this from the examples of our previous *ācāryas,* including King Parīkṣit and Yudhiṣṭhira Mahārāja, Uddhava, and Mīrā Bāī, all of whom were raised in Kṛṣṇa consciousness from birth and developed exalted devotional qualities.

Morning Program

An enthusiastic daily morning program at home is important when we are homeschooling our children. We are all creatures of habit, and if we inculcate good spiritual discipline in children they will maintain it throughout their adult lives. Also, there is great benefit to starting the day with remembering the Lord, chanting His holy name, and reading His books. These practices make the mind peaceful and happy. Our children can then think intelligently about spiritual matters. The morning program will also help them control their restless minds and reduce misbehavior. If we attend our morning program with sincerity and faith and then maintain a Kṛṣṇa conscious mood throughout the day, we can actually have little saints running around the house – naughty like all children, but oftentimes in a transcendental way.

To establish a morning program at home we need to maintain a home altar with devotional pictures or Deities, preferably Gaura-Nitāi. We also need an *ārati* tray with all the items of worship, along with a whisk, peacock fan, and conch. Try to put the children to bed early enough that they can wake up at a reasonably early time. After they have had sufficient sleep according to their age, wake them up and help them shower and dress for the morning program. Try to never miss a day. If the children are late in waking because of a late-night festival or some other occasion, then when they do wake up, conduct the entire morning program of *maṅgala-ārati, tulasī-pūjā,* Deity greeting, and *guru-pūjā,* even if you have already held all these events earlier. The children can take turns dressing as *pūjārīs* or leading the *kīrtana.* Always be enthusiastic at the morning program, and dance and chant loudly.

Dānavīr (age 9) and Damayantī (age 7) lead the morning program in Budapest, Hungary.

After the *ārati* is over, encourage your children to offer food to the Deities so they understand the importance of offering and eating only *prasāda.* If they are old enough they can chant mantras or they can say their own sweet prayer asking Kṛṣṇa to please eat so that everyone can benefit from His *prasāda.* After breakfast we can read them stories from *Śrīmad-Bhāgavatam.* Choose a story like the one about Prahlāda Mahārāja, and read only the translations. Discuss with them the finer points of the story, gauging the depth of your discussion by their maturity.

The length of the morning program can be adjusted depending on the age of the children. You can shorten the program to ten or fifteen minutes or do whatever is practical. It is important to keep the children's experience of Kṛṣṇa consciousness positive and enjoyable. Simplifying the program (*ārati* with only incense and a flower, for example) is all right for small children, who generally have short attention spans. However, we should not dispense with the morning program altogether simply because it is too troublesome or the children are reluctant to participate. We should be determined to start the day with chanting and hearing about Kṛṣṇa. Besides being spiritually beneficial, the morning program keeps the family together. Among nondevotees it is common to plan family weekends around activities such as watching a favorite show on television together, bowling, or going to church, but for devotees such togetherness can be accomplished twice a day, every day. The family that chants and reads together stays together!

Children and the Holy Name

I believe the holy name is the essence of our children's education. The scriptures say that Kali-yuga is full of quarrel, hypocrisy, anxiety, and temptation, and thus it is difficult to approach the Lord through the processes of meditation, temple worship, and sacrifice – methods that were easier in previous ages. But Kṛṣṇa and the holy name are nondifferent, and in the age of Kali Kṛṣṇa incarnates as the holy name to make it easy for us to approach Him.

Understanding the perils of Kali-yuga, Śrīla Prabhupāda asked his followers to chant sixteen good rounds of the Hare Kṛṣṇa *mahā-mantra* every day. He knew that without daily chanting of the holy name it would be practically impossible for people to follow the four regulative principles. In the 1960s when Prabhupāda first came to America, people were unwilling to give up their sinful habits. They saw free sex and drugs and other forms of intoxication as a way to achieve peace and spirituality. Prabhupāda simply introduced the chanting of the holy name, and as their hearts gradually became purified, they gave up sinful habits and became *sādhus*. Even today people are surprised to see the transformation chanting the holy name brings about.

Chanting is like a detergent that scrubs the heart clean of all misgivings. The holy name alone has the power to overcome the degraded aspects of today's society. This was why Lord Caitanya came five hundred years ago – to kill people's demonic mentality with the weapon of *saṅkīrtana,* the congregational chanting of the holy name. Chanting has the power to infuse in the hearts of even the most fallen souls stirrings of *bhakti.* Imagine the power the holy name can have on the hearts of devotees and their children, who have good association and training.

Even though we train our children to become devotees with good character, as they get older, mundane association in schools, colleges, and the workplace can still affect them. Śrīla Prabhupāda was well aware of this, so he decreed that of all his instructions the daily chanting of sixteen good rounds is the most important. Chanting has the power to protect us from *māyā's* subtle intrusions and keep us fixed on the *bhakti* path.

The story of Ajāmila in the Sixth Canto of *Śrīmad-Bhāgavatam* provides a good example of how *māyā* can affect us in subtle ways, even if we are trained in brahminical culture. This story is relevant for us as we homeschool our children and try to instill in them good character. Even with this training, will our children always remain safe from the lures of illicit sex, drug abuse, and other temptations?

As Ajāmila was walking back from the forest one day, he saw a prostitute engaged in sex with a man. His mind became agitated, and he left his chaste wife and went after the prostitute, bringing her into his home. He then engaged in abominable activities and tried to satisfy the prostitute with material things, which he acquired by dishonest means. Śrīla Prabhupāda explains that *māyā* in the form of attraction to the opposite sex is so strong that anyone who does not take shelter of the holy name is apt to fall down:

> When Cupid attacks somebody and one becomes too much attracted by lust, all his education, all his culture, all his knowledge, becomes stunned. Therefore one has to avoid this society.... Therefore, from the very beginning of life a boy is sent to *gurukula* for good association. Still there are many *gurukulas* in India, a spiritual master training some boys in spiritual life. That has also become polluted. So many things ... This is Kali-yuga.

> Therefore the only way of deliverance from this bewilderment is chanting Hare Kṛṣṇa, Hare Kṛṣṇa, Kṛṣṇa Kṛṣṇa ..." (Lecture, January 3, 1971, Surat)

Prabhupāda explains in the same lecture that even though Ajāmila was properly trained, he was still attracted to illicit sex because of his spiritual immaturity: "So these things are being shown regularly in the cinema. What character will be formed of the young men? By seeing once, this Ajāmila, he fell down so much, and our boys and girls are seeing these things every day in the cinema. So what kind of character you can expect from them? These are the instruction to be taken from *Śrīmad-Bhāgavatam*."

Is proper training simply a waste of time, then, given the cultural climate in which our children are growing up and the immorality to which they are exposed? Not if we train them to chant the holy name. Again, we see this in Ajāmila's case. Although he succumbed to immoral behavior in his youth, he was saved at the end of his life when he called for his son, Nārāyaṇa. Even though Ajāmila was calling for his son, the Lord's name is so powerful that Viṣṇu's agents immediately arrived on the scene to protect him, and they stopped the Yamadūtas from taking him to hell for punishment.

As parents, then, we should not only be concerned with giving our children a good academic education; we should also give them a taste for and attachment to the holy names. Kṛṣṇa is the source of both material and spiritual knowledge, so if we teach our children to serve Kṛṣṇa, they will naturally and effortlessly receive the opulences of knowledge, wealth, fame, strength, and renunciation. *Śrīmad-Bhāgavatam* (5.18.12) tells us:

> All the demigods and their exalted qualities, such as religion, knowledge, and renunciation, become manifest in the body of one who has developed unalloyed devotion for the Supreme Personality of Godhead, Vāsudeva. On the other hand, a person

> devoid of devotional service and engaged in material activities has no good qualities. Even if he is adept at the practice of mystic yoga or the honest endeavor of maintaining his family and relatives, he must be driven by his own mental speculations and must engage in the service of the Lord's external energy. How can there be any good qualities in such a man?

In other words, material qualifications naturally follow spiritual qualities, not the other way around. We know this from the examples of Sudāmā Brāhmaṇa, Dhruva Mahārāja, and many other great devotees.

So how can we develop in our children an attraction for chanting the holy names? Śrīla Prabhupāda's formula was simple: If children simply follow their elders and rise early for the morning program of *japa, kīrtana,* reading *Śrīmad-Bhāgavatam,* and eating *prasāda,* they will become pure devotees. Here are some ways we can infuse our children with love for the holy name.

Daily Practice

A daily morning program is essential to developing a taste for chanting. When we come before the Deities and sing for Their pleasure, we become purified and naturally develop attraction for Their names. We are creatures of habit, and our minds can be disciplined to think about Kṛṣṇa all day and not about temptation by following a routine program. Śrīla Prabhupāda said that rising early every day and singing the Lord's names are the only austerities that can be expected of children. Other than this, they should be allowed to play, eat as much *prasāda* as they like, and study.

Both good association and training are necessary to help children chant nicely. Bad association in the form of television and video games should be avoided at all costs because they distract the mind from Kṛṣṇa. The spiritual progress our children make through chanting will have less effect or even be counteracted by bad association. We should be careful what we expose them to.

Chanting Japa

I gave my sons bead bags when they were three years old, and when they turned six I encouraged them to chant one or two rounds a day. We always chanted together. I did not let them chant *japa* on their own because they could develop bad habits, and chanting could become a chore or burden to them. As we chanted our *japa,* I would inspire them to chant better, explaining to them that Kṛṣṇa would dance on their tongues if they chanted purely. This fascinated them and they tried to chant better.

Śrīla Prabhupāda did not want children to be forced to chant *japa.* They should not see *japa* as a punishment but rather as a fun way to talk to Kṛṣṇa and develop a personal relationship with Him. In other words, when children misbehave, we should not punish them by making them chant an extra round. Similarly, we should not threaten them with extra chanting: "If you don't do this, you will have to chant an extra round."

However, Prabhupāda did want children to be encouraged to chant *japa* – even small children. One time he became upset when small children were not allowed to use *japa* beads while chanting because they were disrespecting them: "I have just been informed by my servant, Śrutakīrti, that the young children, under twelve, are not allowed to use their *japa* beads while chanting. This policy is not good. Why this change has been made? I never said they should not use their beads. That is our business. They must be taught how to respect their beads. How they can learn unless they use them?" (Letter to Yadunandana Dāsa, May 14, 1975)

One good way to encourage children to chant is to have them participate in *japa* get-togethers with friends. In Boise on each Ekādaśī, devotees get together to chant *japa* for one hour and then honor *prasāda.* This encourages even small children to chant because it is a friendly, intimate setting, and they see other children chanting.

Similarly, every year on January 1 we celebrate a "Japathon," when all the devotees and congregational members come together to begin the new year by chanting as many rounds as possible. We held our first New Year's Japathon festival in 1998 for the spiritual benefit of the citizens of our community. In the beginning years, our goal was to chant as many holy names as there were people in the city of Boise, but gradually we increased our goal to the population of the state of Idaho. In 2010, about eighty participants, including twenty children, chanted over 1,500 rounds – 2.5 million names – far exceeding our goal of 1.25 million names. Shyam, age eleven, chanted sixty rounds, and other children such as Sarah, Angela, and Vrinda chanted thirty-five, thirty, and twenty-five rounds respectively. For some children, the Japathon provides their very first experience with *japa,* and they begin chanting regularly after the event.

Over the last few years, several other temples have picked up on the idea and are conducting their own New Year's Japathons. The atmosphere is very sweet, and everyone starts the year feeling encouraged.

A family in Mauritius who are homeschooling their two boys, Kartik, thirteen, and Uddhava, ten, have been successful in introducing *japa* in their home. Every Ekādaśī the family members wake at 2:30 A.M. and start chanting *japa,* continuing until 2:30 P.M., with breaks for *maṅgala-ārati* and *prasāda.* When the parents first started this program, they were hesitant to wake their children so early, but the children insisted, so the following Ekādaśī they all chanted together. Kartik and Uddhava each chanted forty-eight rounds, and their parents each chanted sixty-four rounds. Pleased with the success of chanting *japa* as a family, they have now opened their home for other devotees to come and do the same.

Small children who are encouraged in a positive way will learn to chant *japa* by imitating the adults around them. Although they may start slowly, once they are twelve or thirteen years old, they will increase the number of their rounds and begin thinking about accepting initiation from a spiritual master. It is valuable for our children to have the shelter of a spiritual master before they live away from home for the first time.

Underlying the rules and regulations of good chanting, the most important principle is to approach Kṛṣṇa with love and devotion. If we miss this spirit of chanting, then the rules become a burden. As parents, we should give our children unconditional love and then encourage them to give that love to Kṛṣṇa. In this way, they will grow up to become strong devotees, fixed in their relationship with the holy names.

Teaching Our Children to Eat Only Prasāda

Another thing we can do in our homes conducive to learning and to keep our children pure is to serve and eat only *prasāda,* avoiding all unoffered foods cooked by nondevotees. Lord Caitanya, the *yuga-avatāra* for this age, emphasized the chanting of the holy name as the only means of achieving love of God. Unlike other incarnations who came to annihilate demons, this most merciful form of the Lord instead used a secret weapon to subdue the demonic mentality of Kali-yuga: chanting the holy name and distributing *prasāda,* food offered to Kṛṣṇa with love and devotion. Just as we can tame an animal by feeding it, so we can tame all demonic tendencies in ourselves and others by serving *prasāda*. Eating and distributing *only prasāda* is so important that in many cases it may be the only way of melting cold hearts that have forgotten Kṛṣṇa since time immemorial.

Devotees have many stories to tell in this regard. No amount of philosophical discussion can equal the power of a plate of *prasāda* when it comes to changing people's hearts. This is especially true with children, for whom eating is an important activity.

So a devotee homeschooling family should keep plenty of nutritious *prasāda* available at all times. A standard menu can consist of *dāl,* rice, *sabjī,* and *capatīs,* but other options are available according to the needs and desires of the family. Children are easily attracted to all kinds of food, and if we want them to avoid unoffered food, we have to replace those foods with a variety of *prasāda* at home.

By keeping our children, during their early years, satisfied with delicious *prasāda,* we will help them become peaceful, with their senses controlled. When they grow older and discover other interests, they won't need as much variety and will remain happy even with simple *prasāda.* Śrīla Prabhupāda said that children should be given as much to eat as they want because they don't need to exercise control in honoring *prasāda:* "Let them … eat as much *prasāda* as they like. … It is nice if they eat often – if children overeat it doesn't matter, that is no mistake." (Letter to Aniruddha Dāsa, January 10, 1972)

Prabhupāda wanted parents to take good care of their children as their first duty. "If they are not healthy, then how they can prosecute their education? If they are undernourished it is not good for their future activities. They must have sufficient quantity of milk, and then *dāl, capātīs,* vegetables, and a little fruit will keep them always fit. There is no need of luxurious fatty foods, but milk is essential." (Letter to Satsvarūpa Dāsa, October 9, 1971)

"Outside" Food

What about pizza parties at friends' homes or even restaurants? We should definitely avoid any food that has been purchased outside or cooked by nondevotees, and we should certainly never give it to our children. The consciousness of the cook enters the food as it is prepared. Lord Caitanya tells us in the *Caitanya-caritāmṛta* (*Antya-līlā* 6.278), "When one eats food offered by a materialistic man, one's mind becomes contaminated, and when the mind is contaminated, one is unable to think of Kṛṣṇa properly."

So what can we do when invited out? We can make our own pizza or cake and take it to the party. If we explain our dietary guidelines to the hosts, they will usually understand. (We can tell them that as strict vegetarians, we don't eat anything that is cooked in a kitchen where meat is prepared. This is similar to the kitchen rules for a kosher diet.) If that's not possible, better to skip the party altogether. Instead we can make pizza at home and offer it to Kṛṣṇa, then enjoy the *prasāda* with our family. When children are too young to understand why they cannot eat at restaurants or the homes of nondevotees, it is good to offer them something better at home – *prasāda*, of course – so that they will not feel deprived. When they are older, ten years old and up, it is not necessary to substitute so often, as they are then old enough to understand why the austerity is necessary and even come to enjoy it.

My son Gopal told me years later that he had always enjoyed the feeling of avoiding unoffered foods at parties and other occasions as though he had a secret pact with Kṛṣṇa that we would not eat anything unless He ate it first. Often little children will use these occasions as an opportunity to innocently tell their friends about Kṛṣṇa or vegetarianism. Children can be quite bold and confident when they know that they have the support of their parents and Kṛṣṇa.

Parents often ask what they should do when other devotees in their community do not follow the same standard in eating only *prasāda*. Perhaps they order vegetarian food from restaurants or buy ready-made meals from grocery stores. How do we explain such differing standards to our children?

Actually, children can benefit from encountering different devotees at different levels of understanding, because they learn to negotiate differences. Children need to realize that everyone – devotee and non-devotee – has to be respected regardless of their standard of practice. Yet respect doesn't necessarily mean we emulate the habits of those who have lower standards than our own.

We should not underestimate children's ability to understand and adapt to their surroundings. Growing in Kṛṣṇa consciousness means seeing things with the eyes of discernment, and this task is not too complicated for children. Although initially children tend to see things in black and white, they gradually learn that the world comes in many shades of gray.

The strongest influence children have is their parents, and children naturally aspire for whatever standards their parents set. The early years of careful cooking and feeding our children only *prasāda* will pay off later in their lives because their hearts will be purified and they will always want to please Krsna by eating His remnants. When they are adults and venture out on their own, thanks to the good training you have given them, they will be able to follow the principle of eating only *prasāda* in spite of any difficulties they may encounter.

A Student's Perspective on Eating "Only Prasāda"

Rādhikā Ramaṇa shares memories of the examples set for him in his childhood and how they affected his determination to eat only prasāda

One of the things I remember most about growing up is the example my father set us. He was employed as a product manager for a multinational electronics firm, and he used to travel all over the world. He was always very strict on this point of eating only *prasāda,* whether he was at work in Boise, traveling, or attending some social function. My mother used to spend a couple of days cooking before he left on a long trip, preparing as many dishes as possible to last while he was gone.

Of course, there were occasions when the trip might not cooperate with these plans. I remember once when he went to East Asia for two or three weeks – the *prasāda* from home ran out and he couldn't find a local source. For several days he survived on nuts and fruits. This made a strong impression on me because I realized it was possible to keep such vows. If we are determined, Kṛṣṇa will help us follow our principles.

Sticking to What We Know Is Right

Growing up with this example, then, I wanted to be able to do the same thing when I reached adulthood. When I was at Oxford University, there were times when it was necessary to go out with a particular faculty member, or I would be invited to an important occasion, and in situations like these I would call the restaurant in advance and make special arrangements. I would ask, "Could you please make me a nice fruit plate? Just cut the fruit and arrange it on a plate, and that's all I'll have. Give me salad for the first course, and the fruit platter for the main course, and for dessert you can give me strawberries and cream." They would say, "That's all you can eat?" and I'd answer, "Yes, that's okay."

And every time it would work out very, very nicely. The servers would bring my plateful of mangoes and other fruit – I think the cooks felt sorry for me, so they always went out of their way to make the plate especially nice – and everyone at the table would be envious of what I had: "Wow, someone really likes you in the kitchen!" I'd say, "It's just fruit," but my friends would be impressed and quite happy for me as well.

Sometimes we're afraid that if we don't act exactly like our colleagues we'll be seen as "strange" or "weird" and lose our chance for promotion, but the fact is people respect someone who is able to stand up for his principles. In the beginning, of course, people will tease, pushing a little to test us, and if we give in, we become a laughingstock. But if we apply our principles consistently right from the start, from the time we get the job, we make it clear that we have certain standards. In the end people respect people who are prepared to live according to their values.

Change in Consciousness

There are very few things in this world that have as direct and long-lasting an impact on our consciousness as the food we eat. Things that go into our mouths hit right to the soul. We'll notice the difference if we're sensitive. Those who eat nondevotee food on a regular basis may not. But if we eat only *prasāda* and then accidentally eat something cooked by nondevotees, the difference in our consciousness is immediately noticeable.

Even a simple thing like eating a slice of store-bought bread can have an effect. Who cooked that bread? Who stirred the dough? Who showed up in the morning and turned on the proofing machine? Those people's consciousness is in the bread, and the bakery's customers take that consciousness into their systems. If devotees also take it in, it will be like trying to light the fire of Kṛṣṇa consciousness while pouring water on it.

Setting an Example for Children

It might seem counterintuitive, but I think that when children are given the option to eat only *prasāda* they're more open to it than their parents imagine. As adults we tend to become weak and say, "Oh, just go ahead and eat that." If children are supported by their parents, they themselves don't hesitate so much. It's often our own weakness as adults that creates obstacles for our children. If as adults we set a good example, our children will learn from us. My father's behavior is a good case in point.

Good Association

It's said that "Example is better than precept." Even though we need both, Śrīla Prabhupāda often stressed the importance of example over precept, because if one cannot show by example, then the verbal precept has little value. "Unless one is firmly convinced about Kṛṣṇa consciousness, I don't think the children will learn properly from such a person." (Letter to Satsvarūpa Dāsa, February 16, 1972) "Whatever the elder members are doing, the children should do if possible. But for teaching the teachers themselves should be fixed-up initiated devotees. Otherwise how the children can get the right information and example?" (Letter to Aniruddha Dāsa, March 7, 1972)

According to the Vedic system, the teacher must not only be learned about spiritual matters but also have good character. Therefore parents who are homeschooling their children must be initiated devotees – or at least aspiring to be initiated – and follow the four regulative principles, namely, no gambling, no intoxication, no meat eating, and no illicit sex. Why are these conditions necessary?

Prabhupāda gives the example of Tarzan: "Children imitate whoever they associate with. You all know the movie *Tarzan*. He was brought up by monkeys and he took on the habits of monkeys. If you keep children in good association, their psychological development will be very good. But if you keep them in bad association, they will turn out bad." (Lecture, October 5, 1971, Calcutta)

Prabhupāda compared children to a soft dough that can be molded into different types of pastry. Children are born innocent, but as they grow and associate with bad influences, they acquire bad habits. If they associate only with *sādhus* or devotees, they are unlikely to develop these bad habits. To clarify this point further Prabhupāda gives the example of a person who smokes or drinks. In the beginning nobody likes to smoke or drink. These habits are learned – and given up – simply by association.

If children live in the association of Kṛṣṇa conscious parents and other devotee elders, they will quickly advance spiritually due to their exposure to these persons' good habits.

What steps can we take to give our children good association at all times?

Making Sure We as Parents Have Kṛṣṇa Conscious Association

As parents it is helpful to first secure ourselves in devotional qualities before we take up the task of educating our children. By following the regulative principles, rising early for *maṅgala-ārati,* chanting sixteen rounds of the *mahā-mantra* daily, and reading Śrīla Prabhupāda's books, we can actually develop these qualities quickly and easily. We will then be inspired to help our children do the same. Otherwise there will be no inspiration, and our instruction will have little effect on them. We need to give our children both practical and theoretical knowledge.

Lord Caitanya Mahāprabhu showed by His own example how to be an ideal devotee of Kṛṣṇa. He asked His disciples to write wonderful literature on the philosophy of Kṛṣna consciousness, but first He personally came to show them how to live the philosophy in a simple and sublime way: by the process of hearing about and chanting the pastimes of the Supreme Personality of Godhead. When we take up this process of hearing and chanting enthusiastically, our children will do the same and receive the same benefit.

Association with Senior Devotees

Great souls are like living scriptures, so associating with and serving them is an important aspect of homeschooling and should not be underestimated. When our children serve and associate with spiritually advanced devotees who have detached themselves from family and material acquisitions, those devotees' character traits rub off and the children develop humility and a good service attitude. This has an eternal impact on their young, impressionable minds.

We all need heroes and heroines in our lives, leaders we can emulate and feel confident about. We see in today's world how children have disappointing heroes – rock stars, actors, and athletes who may possess special talents but too often are of questionable character. Because of a lack of proper guidance, children emulate these people, and the result is detrimental or even hazardous. But if given exemplary heroes, our children will feel confident about who they could become when they grow up.

When my sons were children their heroes were three *sannyāsīs* who visited us regularly in Boise and gave us spiritual guidance. The boys grew up admiring these *sannyāsīs'* qualities and trying to emulate them, and later they several times traveled with them to offer service. Gopal recently wrote a thankful letter to Gaṇapati Swami, with whom he had close association during his childhood. It was only when I read his letter that I really understood the impact this kind of association has on a child. Here is an excerpt from Gopal's letter:

> Recently I was greatly missing you. I was thinking how wonderful you are and how kind and merciful you have been to me. I was feeling bad that I have not written to you in such a long time. I am very sorry. This year was my first year as a D.Phil student, and it was quite demanding.
>
> I read your Vyāsa-pūjā offering to Śrīla Prabhupāda this year, and somehow it really touched me. It also brought back many memories of your visits to Boise, and your selfless preaching in Boise, both in the university and to our family. Some of the best

memories of my life are being with you in Boise – when I had the chance to go with you to the book tables, *harināmas,* and evening home programs. I also remember the time when you took my brother and I to Vṛndāvana, Māyāpur, and the Science and Religion conference in Calcutta. All these things continue to stay with me, and I continue to hanker for your association again.

When I read your Vyāsa-pūjā offering, I was thinking that maybe, if Kṛṣṇa is merciful, in my next life I could once again assist you in some small way in your *saṅkīrtana.*

Your insignificant servant,
Gopal Hari Dāsa

A Student's Perspective on Good Association

Rādhikā Ramaṇa shares his thoughts on the importance of association in homeschooling

In America right now the big headlines are all about a certain golf champion. He's famous, and of all the athletes in the world he had an especially clean image. Because of that he was hired by a number of companies to do advertisements and endorsements. But even though it seemed he was completely focused on the game, completely dedicated, and clean and pure in his habits, just recently a scandal has come out and we discover that he's actually been having extramarital affairs for the last several years. His wife, family, and fans are devastated, and his image has crumbled around him – a lot of the companies that hired him for endorsements are now letting him go because they don't think he presents the role model they're looking for.

But one thing that has been overlooked in the media is the impact this has on children. There's a whole generation of children who've grown up looking up to this athlete as a role model for focus, dedication, purity, and a certain moral uprightness, and now that's finished.

Children now see that even the people they most admire are no longer worthy of their emulation. Or worse, it's possible that children continue to emulate these persons, and that the misbehavior of an athlete like this one can then have an even more detrimental impact on society. This is the reason Prabhupāda continuously emphasized the importance of good role models – because too often we believe that a person can be a good role model even without being a devotee of God. No matter how much goodness an individual has, we still know that the mode of goodness is never found in its pure form in this world. It's always mixed with passion and ignorance. Even if we find someone who's in the mode of goodness and seemingly worthy of emulation, it's only a matter of time before the modes of passion and ignorance appear and sully his or her purity.

The only way to maintain the mode of goodness in its pure form is to rise to the transcendental level, the level of *śuddha-sattva*. This is why ultimately we have to look for Kṛṣṇa conscious role models. And this is the wonderful thing about a Kṛṣṇa conscious education – at a young age children accept as role models pretty much anyone placed in front of them, and if these role models are appropriate, then the first few years of a child's life can set a proper direction for his or her entire lifetime. People variously say that everything we need to learn in life we learn in kindergarten or in the first five years of life, because so many impressions are created during those early years. By the age of five most children have learned at least a few nursery rhymes, and we never forget them! I could recite several nursery rhymes right now. Even though it's been years since I learned them, I still know them by heart. Why? Because they were taught to me at just the right time.

If we give children good association when they are young, it won't matter as much which direction they decide to go as they grow up, because the Kṛṣṇa conscious role models they had during those first few years will stay with them. It may be that at some point in our children's lives they may wander away from Kṛṣṇa consciousness, perhaps become a little distracted or somehow fall into *māyā*. But the essential habits, principles, and impressions we have helped them learn in childhood will never be completely lost, and it will only be a matter of time before their education shows its true power again.

My mother has presented Gopal's letter in these pages. I'd like to also share a few memories of my own of Gaṇapati Mahārāja. Gaṇapati Swami mostly travels in the western United States, going from one university to another, bringing Śrīla Prabhupāda's books. He's ideal in his practice of *sannyāsa*. He used to come to Boise regularly – he likes to go to out-of-the-way places, where no one else visits, and when I was young we were practically all alone there in Idaho. When Gaṇapati Swami came he always gave a lot of personal attention to my brother and I.

These visits impacted us deeply, as you can see from Gopal's letter. Gaṇapati Swami trained us in practical ways. I remember one time when we were eight and ten years old, it was Prabhupāda's appearance day, the day after Janmāṣṭamī. At that time, our family was managing the whole Janmāṣṭamī festival alone, so we were exhausted the next day, waking for Prabhupāda's appearance day and preparing for his feast. So here it was, Śrīla Prabhupāda's appearance day, and the temple was still a mess from Janmāṣṭamī. It was almost noon, and we knew we had to proceed with the program.

But Gaṇapati Swami stopped everything: "No, no, we can't have Vyāsa-pūjā like this. Śrīla Prabhupāda's appearance day cannot happen in unclean surroundings." He said, "You two boys have to help me. Clean everything." He put us to work cleaning. I have never in my life received such a lesson in cleaning as I received from him that day. He made us clean every single spot – the temple room, the kitchen, everywhere – and he would say, "I'll give an award to the boy who collects the most dirt." So we were pulling out books from bookshelves and looking under things, and all these areas we thought were clean we discovered were all so dirty.

Looking back, it was such powerful training. At the University of Florida in Gainesville, they have a nice *prasāda* lunch distribution program on campus. They've distributed over a million plates of *prasāda* to students over the last ten or twelve years – since Prabhupāda's time, actually. Once a week they hold a community cleanup of the kitchen, and when I was teaching there I would join in. All the devotees were surprised that a PhD would know how to clean, because in their experience most PhDs were a little impractical, with their heads in the clouds. What could a professor know about real life? But no matter what area of life we go into, whatever we do, the training we receive from senior devotees, from Vaiṣṇavas, leaves a very special mark inside and is also of practical use.

We can and should always try to seek out that kind of association for our children as far as possible. Sometimes we think that *sannyāsīs* and gurus don't have time – there are so many children. How many of them will they actually engage? But you'd be surprised. Every senior devotee has special time for young, up-and-coming devotees, whether they are infants or teenagers. Senior devotees all give special time, because they know the importance of a little bit of training. That training I received from Gaṇapati Swami lasted only an hour, but it made an impact on my entire life. A little bit can go a long way when it comes to association.

Purity is the Force

In ISKCON we often hear the wonderful motto: "Books are the basis, purity is the force, preaching is the essence, and utility is the principle." In this section I will concentrate on purity.

There are many things we can do to make the home pure and thereby conducive to our children's learning. For example, we can keep an altar with Deities so that God can be the center of our lives, we can vibrate spiritual sounds by chanting the *mahā-mantra,* we can cook and honor *prasāda,* and we can always associate with likeminded devotees.

But even after we introduce these auspicious things into our homes, we must still be careful to avoid things that would pollute the body, mind, and home atmosphere. The one activity that most single-handedly destroys serenity, purity, and good sense is watching television. Countless reports, statistics, and studies have shown that television has bad effects on any human being. From the Vaiṣṇava point of view, all the principles of religion are broken while watching television because almost all the programming displays violence, illicit sex, gambling, and intoxication as acceptable ways of life.

One might argue that it is all right to watch good programs on television – the Discovery channel, if you live in North America, or other similar educational programs. Many people feel such programming helps children improve academically.

But this is a false argument because even if children pick up a few facts about nature or science, they do not become more intelligent or creative as a result. Television encourages passive learning – the "tube" is a one-way download from the screen to the mind. Reading and hearing, on the other hand, encourage active learning; the child has to make an effort to gain information and to create a mental picture of what's being written about. As a result, the benefits and joys of reading are much greater than those of watching TV.

Even if one accepts the educational value of certain shows, does any child stop watching TV once the Discovery program ends? For example, studies show that drinking one glass of wine is good for health. This may be true, but who stops at one glass? A little educational TV inspires children to watch more TV, and they won't necessary discriminate between educational and noneducational programming. Furthermore, even the educational programs are littered with dozens of commercials, which are full of undesirable elements designed to lure – meat, sex, intoxicants. Studies show that children are very impressionable in their early years and are easily influenced by their environment and association.

And watching television wastes so much time. Statistics have shown that the average child in America watches four hours of television daily. In contrast, parents spend around four minutes *per week* in meaningful conversation with their children. What then can the child accomplish in life? All the available leisure time is spent watching television or playing computer games. Hobbies such as music, art, cooking, and gardening take time. If a child goes to school eight hours a day, sleeps eight hours a day, and sits in front of a screen four hours a day, there are only four hours left – most of which is spent in eating, bathing, and other daily necessities.

Besides creating a physically lazy child, a TV lifestyle also destroys creativity and imagination – children who watch a lot of television become mentally lazy from not having to think. Television is a one-sided transmission from the "box" to the mind of the child. Watching television is so mentally easy that the child loses his or her taste for things that are intellectually challenging, such as reading and mathematics. The same is true of computer games. Children who spend hours in front of a computer or television screen often lack social skills and find it difficult to focus on other things. This is why so many teachers have problems getting their students to study.

Creative activities such as music, carpentry, sculpture, painting, drama, dance, handicrafts, and sports all expand the talents of children. If time is spent on these pursuits, by the time they grow up children will possess a wealth of talents and skills they can be proud of and use in Kṛṣṇa's service. On the other hand, if they spend their time watching television – for ten or fifteen years – by the time they are adults their minds will be "TV conditioned" and they will have nothing permanent to show for their investment.

The Key to Limiting Television

The most effective way to have our children avoid television is simply not to own a TV set. We had a television, but it did not receive a signal, so we could only use it as a VHS player for Kṛṣṇa conscious videos. Parents and the devotee community need to support this effort as a whole by coming together and engaging the children in Kṛṣṇa conscious worship and social activities.

Kṛṣṇa conscious training is a complete package. The more we practice *sādhana* – the morning program, regular chanting, reading Prabhupāda's books – the stronger our children will grow and the easier it will be for them to give up their bad habits. Devotional service is so wonderful that when we engage our children in Krsna's service, they naturally develop a higher taste and lose their taste for the dull material pleasures. Try it and see.

A Student's Perspective on Television

Rādhikā Ramaṇa shares his thoughts on the problems with television – both its content and as a medium

What People Watch

Television's content typically breaks all four regulative principles, glorifying exactly those things we are trying to get our minds off. If we spend time chanting and associating with devotees and trying our best to purify the mind – to focus it on Kṛṣṇa and control the senses – why, then, would we want to sit for an hour and allow all this garbage to enter our system?

Ūrmilā Dāsī, a well-known ISKCON educator with decades of experience running a *gurukula,* once wrote an article for *Back to Godhead* in which she called television the "one-eyed guru." In our temples we place the guru on the seat of honor in the center of the room and sit patiently and listen as he enlightens us. In our homes we treat the television in the same way, giving it the highest place of honor in the house. When we walk into almost any living room the television is the centerpiece. Practically speaking, a *vyāsāsana* is given to this one-eyed guru, and everyone gathers around daily for at least an hour but usually more, morning and evening, to listen and learn.

But most of what is shown on television is intended to glorify the body in one way or another. Some shows are subtler and some more direct, but too many of them include scenes that place the characters in compromising situations.

In America movies are rated, but even a PG movie (which many parents consider okay for young children) can include illicit sex and violence. Activities we all speak against in the temple are glorified on the big and small screens in our homes. We hear one thing from the guru in the temple and then go home and hear the opposite from the other guru in our living room. Unfortunately, the main difference between the two teachers is that the one-eyed guru has more direct access to us than our spiritual master. We might see our spiritual master only once or twice a year, and then only in the temple. The one-eyed guru, on the other hand, is present in our bedrooms, our living rooms, and our dining rooms, and he speaks to us in our most intimate and relaxed moments. We give television open access to our hearts and minds around the clock, but the spiritual master is restricted to designated places and times – usually only a few times a week at the most.

How People Watch

As for television as a medium, there have been numerous studies demonstrating that because of the way it works, television breaks down our ability to think critically, so that the more immediate tendency takes over: to accept whatever is presented to us. This is especially serious when we are talking about children and their minds. Naturally they're ready to accept anything in such a vivid and realistic fashion. The more television children watch, the more they believe the world is actually what they see on TV.

The mind is by nature imaginative and creative, but television saps these energies. If we read a description of a beautiful forest scene or a passage decrying injustice, or we find a sudden twist in a plotline, we have to make the effort to comprehend what is being said and then create a picture in our minds. If we listen to the same story on the radio, we may not have to decode the words, as we would if we read them, but we are still forced to use our imagination.

The problem with television is that we don't have to make any effort at all – not to gain information or visualize scenes. Everything is served up on a plate. A steady diet of this spoonfed pap turns the mind into mush. When we watch television we sit there drooling. I wish I were being facetious, but recent studies have measured the level of brain activity while subjects watch television and basically, because everything is flowing only in one direction, the brain activity level is zilch – no imagination, no creativity, no conscious thought.

This is especially disturbing in an age when businesses demand that schools produce a particular type of graduate. Everywhere we turn we are told that the twenty-first century needs creativity, problem-solving abilities, innovation, and critical-thinking skills. Aren't these exactly the qualities destroyed by television?

What If We Don't Watch?

It's not difficult to understand how watching television is detrimental, whether we examine the question from the perspective of an academic researcher or a Kṛṣṇa conscious parent. Sometimes, though, we have a nagging fear that if our children don't watch they'll somehow miss out on something. Will they be stupid – not knowing what's going on in the world? Will they miss some sort of enjoyment?

This last question comes up because for many people, television is the only source of *rasa* in the material world. What they don't know is that this is perverted *rasa*. Devotees are trying their very best to replace mundane *rasa* with transcendental *rasa*. Watching television, then, is like trying to light a fire while pouring water on it. It is counterproductive.

Simply by avoiding television we can make a huge difference in our own lives and in the lives of our children. In the United States, the average home has the television turned on for six hours and forty-seven minutes per day. Imagine all the activities one could do in that time, whether it's spending time with family, engaging in a hobby, learning a new language, reading Prabhupāda's books, visiting the temple – all opportunities lost.

Not only is precious time wasted, but so much junk is introduced into our minds. According to A. C. Nielsen, in a sixty-five-year life, the average person will have spent nine years staring at a television. The average child who watches television has witnessed 8,000 murders before finishing elementary school, and sees 20,000 commercials every year. The school year totals up to about 900 hours, but the average child watches 1,500 hours of television during the same year. It's no wonder that homeschooling can be so competitive and efficient. Look at how much time can be saved just by turning off the TV.

But turning it off can be difficult, even for devotees. If we're trying to limit television in our own home but the children go to another devotee's house and watch TV for an hour there, it's going to cause problems. We have to be strong as a community to successfully accomplish the goal of saving time and putting our energies to better use. We can't just blame the children for watching television! They struggle if they see other devotees, especially adults, following different standards, and because of this they become attached to television. Television is very difficult to give up.

Parents often fear that if their children don't watch television they'll become misfits, unable to relate to others and the world around them. Naturally, we don't want our children to feel out of place, but it actually takes very little work to become informed about what's going on in the world. Our children don't have to sit and watch every serial or even every newsreel television offers simply to stay informed.

If any of you do watch the news regularly, you know that the broadcasters repeat the same news again and again throughout the day. If you watch a twenty-four-hour news channel, all you'll hear are the same five news stories until the broadcaster runs across something new, and then all you get is a lot of blabbering before the full information is available.

If you read the headlines of the next day's newspaper, you'll learn about as much as you would have had you watched the previous day's news on television. The front page has all the most important news, and the rest of the paper is mostly extraneous information for people who need something else to engage their minds. I know from my own experience that a homeschooling education devoid of television does not hold students back. I used to feel nervous that I might not know enough, but it's just a matter of being out in the world and talking to people, and we all pick up enough to come across properly.

It doesn't matter whether you're working a job every day or attending a university, the fact is that devotees always appear very intelligent to the general populace because we have vision and integrity. And what if someone tells us something we don't know? Tiger Woods has been in the news lately, for example. If we don't know the details of his story, still, as soon as we hear it we are capable of giving a Kṛṣṇa conscious perspective on it. We know how to see events. We can have faith that our children will not appear unintelligent or foolish or socially inept just because we have limited their television and given them a proper education. Of course, our children will feel out of place in some social circles, but that's okay. No child feels included in every social circle. As devotees, we have made certain choices about our lifestyle that set us apart. Actually, everyone does that.

I would go so far as to suggest that children who grow up with a constant bombardment from television and other mind-distracting media are the ones who are socially incapable. I see nowadays that students can barely maintain a conversation without glancing constantly at their mobile phone. I've been talking to people who, as soon as there's a break in the conversation, don't know how to fill it, so they pull out their cell phone and punch buttons – I think mainly to fill the silence.

We don't have to worry about our children. As devotees, they'll know how to go about the world. Kṛṣṇa promises in the *Gītā* that He will give us whatever intelligence we need.

A Student's Perspective on the Internet

We've discussed television, but the real problem these days is the Internet. The Internet is available all the time and almost everywhere. Rādhikā Ramaṇa probes the new problems created by easy access to the Internet

Sometimes people who avoid watching television believe the Internet a safer source of information. But the Internet is more addictive than television. Many people who use the Internet daily suffer from a psychological disorder, whether they realize it or not, called Internet addiction. In the United States ninety percent of children over twelve go online every day. They include chat rooms, Facebook, MySpace, and other social networking sites as part of their regular social fabric to an extent previous generations cannot even imagine.

Unfortunately, much of the Internet is nothing but a huge repository of junk. If everyone took all the worthless things in their house and put them in one place, that's something like the Internet. It used to be that no one would listen to you unless you had something worthwhile to say, but now you can have an instant audience whenever you want. It's the nature of the Internet that as soon as you put up a website, there are people willing to read what you have to say whether your ideas are worthwhile or not.

Ninety-nine percent of websites fail to list the author of their "information." So who's giving the knowledge? A person pontificating on religion might be someone who is morally fallen. A writer with medical advice might know nothing about medicine. (Even worse, as Alexander Pope said, "A little learning is a dangerous thing," and people who diagnose themselves on the Internet risk their health even if the source gives valid information.)

The source of information is important in any line of work. When I assign research papers to my students, I expect them to actually visit the library and read books! The tendency of today's students, on the other hand, is to type keywords into Google, cut and paste a few paragraphs from the first ten hits, and hand in the result. Teachers want their students to learn how to evaluate the source and accuracy of information, but the Internet seems to work on the opposite principle.

In Kṛṣṇa consciousness we believe the source is more important than the content because if the source is reliable, we know the content will also be reliable. Śrīla Prabhupāda often gives the example of the mother as a reliable source. Why? Because a mother will never cheat her children. She has only their best interest in mind. Even if she doesn't have all the knowledge in the world, whatever she gives will be for their benefit. On the other hand, we sometimes meet people who know a lot, but because of their impure intent their knowledge can actually cause harm. Just because something is true doesn't make it beneficial.

The source of information is critically important. In a Kṛṣṇa conscious education our first task is to find the right source and then respectfully ask for content. The Internet functions in exactly the opposite way. Content – information – is what matters; the source has little relevance. As Kali-yuga progresses, *māyā's* tools for entering our life become more and more sophisticated, and if we look carefully we'll see that the Internet is one of *māyā's* largest tools. Everything on the Internet is fluctuating, changing, ephemeral. Even a site with actual information on it might disappear within a day. There is no stability, only an illusion prepared by *māyā*.

Internet Content

Way too much of the content on the Internet is pornographic, so no matter how careful we are, if our children spend enough time on the Internet they will eventually find themselves in sexual association. Naturally, for a curious child it's tempting to look at such pages. In this respect there is little difference between television and the Internet. Television, at least, is limited to the number of channels available, and as parents we can usually restrict those channels. The Internet, though, is unlimited in content, and there's no good way to limit a child's access. Even sites with accurate information and unobjectionable content are supported by advertising. The site may be safe, but the ad content may present problems.

Today many children are addicted to the Internet, partly because of peer pressure at school. Children create their own identities through networking sites such as Facebook, MySpace, and Twitter. Lonely children might think the Internet can end their isolation, but the Internet is not about relationships. Everything about it changes. A boy I know who was spending hours on Facebook had his account deleted by Facebook because he was spending too much time on it. He had a mental breakdown.

Does this mean we should go back to the Stone Age and not allow our children to use the Internet at all? How will they compete for jobs or even learn to use the Internet to aid their Kṛṣṇa conscious research? We should use the Internet as a tool the way we would use any tool. We use hammers and chisels in the ways they are intended, but don't carry them around with us everywhere or try to have a relationship with them.

There are a few basic policies we can follow for using the Internet:

First, don't use the Interent as a substitute for real community. Children especially need to learn how to build and negotiate relationships face to face. Rather, use the Internet as a substitute for the postal service – to send and receive email.

Second, don't try to study a subject through the Internet. Better to go to the library and find a book. Do use the Internet, if you like, to look up facts – to find a statistic or to get directions to an unfamiliar address.

Third, avoid the "always-on" mode of Internet surfing, whether at home, work, or wherever you are on your mobile phone. Better to go online, get the information you need, and log off.

No Substitute for Books

My students know I want them to go to the library and actually study, but they also know there are a variety of books online, and they might believe they can use a search engine to find the nuggets of information they need faster than reading the books themselves. We have to remember that there is no substitute for books. The process of patiently sitting with a book and working through it, extracting its knowledge and seeing that information in context – this generates a different level of knowledge than what online searching can provide.

Searching a book with a computer and finding hits on a particular topic give us "sound bites" of information, but it doesn't give us knowledge, because knowledge depends on putting that information in context. Knowing the answer to a problem isn't the same thing as being able to solve the problem and apply the answer properly. Understanding the context of knowledge and having the patience to understand the full picture an author presents gives a different level of understanding than a "search and hit" function.

In ISKCON there are devotees who prefer the VedaBase to reading Prabhupāda's books, and certainly the VedaBase is a useful tool for certain tasks, such as preparing quotations for a class or a book. But the VedaBase's search capabilities are useful only if we already understand the point Prabhupāda is trying to make. If we don't read the chapter surrounding the quote, we might miss something vitally important. We might know the chapter-and-verse reference to something Kṛṣṇa said in the *Bhagavad-gītā,* but we can truly understand what He is saying only if we look at the verse in context – the verse in question might be a summary or an objection to the three verses that preceded it.

For example, in *Gītā* 6.47 Kṛṣṇa says, *yoginām api sarveṣāṁ, mad-gatenāntar-ātmanā/ śraddhāvān bhajate yo māṁ, sa me yuktatamo mataḥ:* "Of all the different *yogīs,* the one who is attached to Me in devotion, who worships Me with full faith, he is the best in My opinion." A useful verse – one we quote often. But if we remember the context, this verse is much more powerful and effective. In the preceding verse Kṛṣṇa says *tapasvibhyo 'dhiko yogī:* the *yogī* is better than the *tapasvī,* who is better than the *jñānī,* who is better than the *karmī.* Out of all these classes of transcendentalists the *yogī* is better. And then He says in 6.47 that of all the *yogīs,* His devotee is the best. Once the verse is placed in context, the pinnacle of an entire chapter, we see how Kṛṣṇa has actually placed the *bhakta* on top of every single category of transcendentalist. That realization is not available through an Internet search function but comes only through handling the book.

We have to try hard not to lose the culture of reading books. Especially in India, there is a new tendency to jump from an agricultural economy straight into the information age, skipping industrialization and the mass printing of books that went along with it. There are Indian publishers, of course, but before some people have had the opportunity to develop the habit of reading books the Internet is available to them. India is progressing into the information age faster than any Western country ever did, so we have to be very, very careful, or we can lose a lot by missing that intermediate stage.

Respect for Elders

A growing problem in Kali-yuga is that even after spending their entire lives taking care of their children, the elders in society are neglected by those same children, sometimes even abused or left in nursing homes. Śrīla Prabhupāda blames this disrespect on improper education: "In the modern society, even a boy thinks himself self-sufficient and pays no respect to elderly men. Due to the wrong type of education being imparted in our universities, boys all over the world are giving their elders headaches. Thus *Śrī Īśopaniṣad* very strongly warns that the culture of nescience is different from that of knowledge." (*Śrī Īśopaniṣad,* mantra 10, purport)

To bring back the culture of knowledge one has to train children from the beginning of their lives to give proper respect to the elders both within the family and in the greater community. The family is an essential element in maintaining social stability and promoting spiritual values. Respect for and protection of the spiritual master, parents, teachers, elders, women, children, weak and dependent living beings, and persons dedicated to the welfare of others and the service of God are all important elements in the development of a healthy and secure society.

Prabhupāda says these feelings of respect are an important goal of proper family life: "Ajāmila repented his negligence in performing his duty to his wife, father, and mother. It is the duty of grown-up children to render service to their aged parents. This practice should be reintroduced into present society. Otherwise, what is the use of family life? Proper family life means that the husband should be protective, the wife chaste, and the children grateful to their father and mother. Children should think, 'My father and mother gave me so much service. When I was unable to walk, they carried me. When I was unable to eat, they fed me. They gave me an education. They gave me life.' A bona fide son thinks of ways to render service to his father and mother. And just as a woman is expected to be faithful to her husband, so the husband should be grateful for her service and protect her. Because of his association with a prostitute, however, Ajāmila had abandoned all his duties. Regretting this, he now considered himself quite fallen." (*A Second Chance: The Story of a Near-Death Experience,* p. 131)

Respecting Elders in the Family

Scriptures such as *Śrīmad-Bhāgavatam,* the *Mahābhārata,* and the *Rāmāyaṇa* are full of stories that capture the imagination of children and teach important lessons in Vaiṣṇava etiquette. A good example of proper respect was shown just before the Battle of Kurukṣetra. After Kṛṣṇa had finished speaking the *Bhagavad-gītā* to Arjuna, Yudhiṣṭhira Mahārāja stepped down from his chariot and went over to the Kauravas' side to receive the blessings of his grandfather and teachers there. This was quite shocking to all who witnessed it, because Yudhiṣṭhira went unarmed and unprotected. The *Mahābhārata* explains how even the cruel Duryodhana and others on his side were moved by Yudhiṣṭhira's etiquette: "Witnessing the respect and honor he paid to his elders, even the Kauravas praised him. Cries of 'Excellent! Bravo!' were heard among the soldiers on both sides. As they thought on the noble qualities of Yudhiṣṭhira and his brothers, the soldiers wept aloud." (*Mahābhārata,* trans. Kṛṣṇa Dharma Dāsa, p. 568)

In the same book Kṛṣṇa Dharma Dāsa gives us a contrasting instance where such etiquette was not followed. He writes: "Aśvatthāmā heard Karṇa insulting his maternal uncle. Droṇa's son had never had much time for Karṇa, who showed little respect for his elders. Now he had gone too far. Kṛpa was a brahmin and the Kurus' teacher. He did not deserve to be mistreated by the charioteer's son. Aśvatthāmā took out his sword and jumped from his chariot, roaring at Karṇa. "How dare you speak like that, fool! The *ācārya* spoke the truth about Arjuna and his brothers, but because you are envious you could not tolerate it." (p. 724)

Śrīla Prabhupāda tells how Yudhiṣṭhira was just as respectful toward his elders after the battle had ended: "A good example of this practice of respecting elders is Yudhiṣṭhira Mahārāja, the great saintly Pāṇḍava king. After the battle of Kurukṣetra, Yudhiṣṭhira and his four brothers would go every day to offer their respects to their paternal uncle, Dhṛtarāṣṭra.… This story from *Śrīmad-Bhāgavatam* illustrates the system of offering respects to the elderly members of the family. After the morning's duties are performed, next one must go and offer obeisances to the spiritual master and the elderly persons in the family. One must also offer respects to a guest. Usually we know when a certain guest is coming to our home and can make preparations beforehand, but sometimes it happens that someone comes unexpectedly, and he too must be received with respect." (*A Second Chance: The Story of a Near-Death Experience,* p. 73)

In the *Rāmāyaṇa,* Lord Rāma's etiquette toward his mother, father, and other seniors in his kingdom is unparalleled, and children can learn important lessons from it. Kṛṣṇa Himself showed respect toward His parents, Vasudeva and Devakī, and foster parents, Nanda Mahārāja and Yaśodā Mātā. When He entered Dvārakā He offered His obeisances to all the senior members of His family and friends according to protocol. He paid His respects to His aunt, Queen Kuntī, even though she knew about His Godhood.

In *Śrī Caitanya-caritāmṛta* (*Ādi-līlā* 10.49, purport) Śrīla Prabhupāda tells how Lord Caitanya advised others to respect His elders: "When Śrī Caitanya Mahāprabhu and Nityānanda Prabhu were sitting together in the house of Śrīvāsa Ṭhākura, Murāri Gupta first offered his respects to Lord Caitanya and then to Śrī Nityānanda Prabhu.

Nityānanda Prabhu, however, was older than Caitanya Mahāprabhu, and therefore Lord Caitanya remarked that Murāri Gupta had violated social etiquette, for he should have first shown respect to Nityānanda Prabhu and then to Him."

Respect Toward the Lord and His Devotees

Scriptures such as the *Hari-bhakti-vilāsa* and *The Nectar of Devotion* talk about the proper activities of a Vaiṣṇava, such as offering respect and obeisance to the guru, to the Lord, and to His devotees. So they can show proper respect to the Lord, we must teach our children about the Lord and His many opulences and how to avoid offenses in the temple and while worshiping the Deity. When children learn to respect Kṛṣṇa they automatically learn to respect all living entities, because they see them as part and parcel of Kṛṣṇa. We can teach our children how to show respect to the guru by serving him ourselves and inquiring from him with submission. When *sannyāsīs* and senior Vaiṣṇavas visit, we can teach our children how to give proper respect and service by setting an example.

Respecting Devotees

Viṣṇujana Swami stressed how respecting devotees leads to spiritual advancement: "So I think it would behoove all of us if we just try to fulfill this one injunction – and that is to offer respect to the devotees. If you don't offer respect to devotees, then you become what is called a *vaiṣṇava-aparādhī,* an offender of the devotees. Just for neglecting the devotees you become an offender of the devotees, and by doing so your attachment for Kṛṣṇa wanes. It becomes less and less. And you can know this because your mind will be more and more agitated for materialistic fulfillment. So you have to be very, very careful of fault-finding, a peer type of feeling among your godbrothers and godsisters, and you have to treat everyone that, 'Oh, they are the personal property of Rukmiṇī and Dvārakādhīśa.' Then, if you think like that and you touch their feet, offer obeisances, then automatically your mind will be clear just like the high sky, and you won't be able to have impure thoughts because you'll always be protected by Kṛṣṇa, being a friend of the devotees."

The best way to teach children to respect others is by our own example. When parents themselves respect family elders, children easily follow their example.

I used to take the boys to India every year so they could connect with their grandparents and other family elders. The love grandparents give grandchildren is special. My parents and my husband's spoiled our sons in every way. They also appreciated that the boys were devotees in ISKCON. Initially they were apprehensive when they heard we had adopted a Kṛṣṇa conscious lifestyle. They felt insecure because they thought we were going to leave them for Kṛṣṇa. However, our regular visits assured them, and they became amazed to see their grandchildren entrenched in the Vedic way of life, and found them better and more respectful than many children in India nowadays. They were inspired to become serious devotees themselves, and eventually adopted the Kṛṣṇa conscious path.

The value of showing respect was especially beneficial in the case of my father-in-law, a university professor who could not at first be convinced of the superiority of the devotional path. He loved the boys, of course, and would listen to them talk about Kṛṣṇa consciousness even though he wouldn't listen to anyone else speak about spiritual topics. The conversations he had with my sons made a deep impression on him, and eventually he embraced the Vaiṣṇava path. Some years later he left his body chanting the *mahā-mantra,* with his family chanting around him. Everyone in my family gave credit to our children for his change of consciousness. As parents we do the hard work of training our children, but they in turn can affect hundreds of people during their lifetime.

My sons also loved and respected my father, who was so impressed by their material and spiritual accomplishments that he started to regularly attend the ISKCON Allahabad temple. Soon after, he was chanting sixteen rounds daily and offering service, helping to raise funds for the new temple. He also helped in the construction of the new temple there and sponsored its first full-size Rādhā-Kṛṣṇa Deities from Jaipur. He was very close to our children, and by Kṛṣṇa's arrangement at the time of his unexpected death, Rādhikā Ramaṇa was the only one near him and was chanting the *mahā-mantra* in his ear. This was also a powerful experience for my son.

Not only do our children benefit spiritually by learning these important values but they continue to take care of their elders materially and spiritually as they grow older. Our children will be grateful for all the hard work we have done for them and will be eager for advice and encouragement. They will be good examples in a society that too often lacks respect for elders.

Homeschooling During the Early Years

Children up to the age of five are strongly influenced by the behavior of their elders at home and imitate whatever happens around them. These early years lay the foundation for their entire lives, and one can almost predict what quality a child will have as an adult by looking at the training he or she received during these crucial first five years. We have many examples in ISKCON of children who were raised in a Kṛṣṇa conscious environment from the beginning of their lives and who are now sources of inspiration for others.

Children's formal training begins at five, whether they go to a public school, *gurukula,* or are taught at home by their parents. But what about the years before formal education? How do we create a Kṛṣṇa conscious environment for infants, toddlers, and preschoolers?

Because children in this age group learn mostly by imitation, the first step is to create a home atmosphere surcharged with Kṛṣṇa consciousness. There should be constant vibration of the holy name and *kṛṣṇa-kathā,* as well as devotional activities like Deity worship, *prasāda* distribution, and preaching. In this way all the senses of our children will be engaged in Kṛṣṇa conscious activities – hearing them, observing them, and participating in them. Without a doubt they will make advancement quickly and effortlessly.

Dovetailing Their Desire to Play

Prabhupāda said young children are innocent and have a tendency to play. If we channel their play in Kṛṣṇa conscious ways, they will make advancement quickly.

With infants we can surround them with Kṛṣṇa conscious sights and sounds, such as the chanting of the holy name (live or on CD) and pictures of Kṛṣṇa strategically placed so they can look at them easily. We can also dress as Vaiṣṇavas, with *tilaka* and neck beads, and talk to them about Kṛṣṇa, even though they may be too young to comprehend everything. We can find toys for them related to Kṛṣṇa consciousness. We can feed them with our mother's milk and, when they are ready for solid foods, we can cook for them rather than feed them store-bought baby foods.

For toddlers and preschoolers, besides keeping the home peaceful, clean, and Kṛṣṇa conscious, we can devise Kṛṣṇa conscious indoor and outdoor games for them. For example, for indoor games we can give blocks, Play-Doh, toy cooking sets, and some other safe items, and then inspire them to imitate a temple lifestyle with play worship, cooking, and offering. We can also engage them in various art projects, such as making cards for festivals and props for plays, or making jewelry or doing beadwork. We can tell or read stories about Kṛṣṇa from children's story and picture books or Prabhupāda's *Kṛṣṇa* book and *Śrīmad-Bhāgavatam*. We can chant and play simple instruments with them, and observe festivals by engaging them in decorating, cooking, and giving them small roles in plays.

Toddlers can also imitate Deity worship with their Kṛṣṇa dolls. In Boise, we have a four-year-old devotee girl named Vrinda who plays all day long with her Kṛṣṇa and Balarāma dolls. Her mother does not buy her any other toys but instead shops with her once a week to find things to decorate her dolls. I have gone to her house and seen the dolls decorated and ornamented differently every day. Vrinda's mother

Chaitanya Chandra (age 1) plays with a mṛdaṅga in Boise, USA.

helps her make bead necklaces, anklets, and bracelets for Them. She has many different types of clothes, turban covers, jewelry, and beautiful bows. Every morning Vrinda performs *maṅgala-ārati* for Kṛṣṇa and Balarāma, then decorates Them profusely with flowers and other paraphernalia and makes an offering of food. Then she goes around the devotee community to invite mothers and children for *śṛṅgāra-ārati* and *guru-pūjā* at her home. She plays the recording of the "Govindam" prayers, shows her Deities a mirror, and performs another *ārati* with *kīrtana*. Both mother and daughter tell me they experience the same feelings they have in the temple. Every day when Vrinda walks over to the "big temple" to see Rādhā-Baṅkebihārī she looks at the temple Deities closely, scanning for ideas on how to make her dolls as beautiful. Occasionally she asks me for a peacock feather or a new piece of cloth so she can make turbans. Sometimes she plays Dāmodara-līlā with me (she is Mother Yaśodā and I am Kṛṣṇa – since she takes care of Kṛṣṇa and Balarāma, she sees herself as Their mother). The rest of the day she listens to stories about Kṛṣṇa (she can describe some of these stories quite elaborately), learns her numbers and letters, plays with other devotee children in the community, or participates in temple programs. When she wants to eat snacks, cookies, cakes, or even candy, her mother immediately satisfies her desire by making them at home and offering them first to Kṛṣṇa.

Children raised in this kind of environment know nothing but Kṛṣṇa and are happy and peaceful. Prabhupāda emphasized that to give our children Kṛṣṇa consciousness is actually "real education." In an arrival lecture in Dallas on March 3, 1975, he remarked: "If we simply learn how to worship Kṛṣṇa, how to please Him, how to dress Him nicely, how to give Him nice foodstuff, how to decorate Him with ornaments and flowers, how to offer our respectful obeisance unto Him, how to chant His name, in this way, if we simply think, without any so-called education we become the perfect person within the universe. This is Kṛṣṇa consciousness. It doesn't require A-B-C-D education. It requires simply change of consciousness. So if these children are being taught from the very beginning of their life ... We had the opportunity of being trained up by our parents like this."

Outdoors, children can be inspired to play Kṛṣṇa conscious games. In a letter to his disciple Stokakṛṣṇa Dāsa (June 13, 1972) Prabhupāda wrote: "The children should always be instructed by taking advantage of their playful mood and teaching them to play Kṛṣṇa games like pretending to be cowherd boys, cows, peacocks, or demons, and in this way if they always think of Kṛṣṇa by playing just like they are actually present in association with Kṛṣṇa then they will become Kṛṣṇa conscious very quickly."

Sports like swimming and wrestling are also good and can be made Kṛṣṇa conscious by reminding children of Kṛṣṇa's pastimes in Vṛndāvana, such as His sports in the river Yamunā or His wrestling match with Kaṁsa's men in Mathurā. They can also enact sword, bow and arrow, or club fights from the *Mahābhārata* or *Rāmāyaṇa* or from Kṛṣṇa's pastimes.

Don't Let Them Waste Their Time

We can find many other creative ways to engage our children in serving Kṛṣṇa during their tender years. For many parents, though, the challenge is how to engage them so completely that they don't waste time on frivolous things. In a morning walk conversation in Los Angeles (January 5, 1974), Prabhupāda described the tendency of materialists to waste children's time: "This is the difficulty. *Na te viduḥ svārtha-gatiṁ hi viṣṇum*. Because they are rascal, they do not know how to utilize time, what is the aim of life, where you have to go. These things they don't know. So they must waste time. Just like child. He wastes time in so many ways. It is the duty of the parents, guardians, to synchronize his activities so that he may not waste his time. It is the duty of the guardians. Similarly these rascals, they're wasting time. You have to engage them in Kṛṣṇa consciousness. Then their time will be utilized."

Of course, keeping young children engaged requires both patience and tolerance. Sometimes we run out of that. To make sure they were always engaged, I took my children with me everywhere I went – to home programs, *harināmas*, on book distribution, to festivals, Ratha-yātrā parades, other temples for vacation, and preaching programs in the schools and city parks. Even though they were too young to participate fully, exposure to these activities was beneficial because they developed an attraction for devotional service and gained positive association.

Should We Send Our Children to Preschool?

Parents are divided on the issue of whether or not to send their children to nondevotee preschools. In India especially there is a strong movement toward sending children as young as two to school.

It is not necessary to rush our children out the door and into school just because other parents send their children. In the first few years of life especially, children need as much attention as possible from their parents. We don't have to be too creative to keep them happy; we can simply let them imitate us in our day-to-day activities. Children at this age learn by playing, mostly by imitation. We can play make-believe Kṛṣṇa games and take turns with them where we are Mother Yaśodā or Kṛṣṇa or Balarāma.

But if we want to send our toddlers to preschool, it's important the school be Kṛṣṇa conscious. At this age children move from playing only with their parents to recognizing other children their age, and they will interact if given the opportunity. Toddlers are generally too young to be formally trained or reprimanded for misbehavior, but they do well if given an environment where they can imitate what others are doing. If they are with devotees, they will imitate devotional activities such as serving, cooking, or singing and dancing about Kṛṣṇa. If they are with kids who are unruly and misbehaved, they will also be unruly and misbehaved. Children are like sponges and will pick up whatever habits and language they observe.

Many of us have experience seeing toddlers imitate their mothers' cooking by rolling make-believe *capātīs* or stirring make-believe *dāl*. They will imitate *ārati* or build temples out of blocks or Play-Doh. If children at this age spend hours of their day in a materialistic environment, however, they will imitate the activities of materialists. Once they have been spoiled, it will be hard to change them. We can predict the future of children by the way they have been brought up during their first five years. Even those who received spiritual training may later follow a mundane path, but invariably they will return to their childhood spiritual training at some point. On the other hand, if they had only materialistic training during childhood, they will have a harder time adopting the principles of Kṛṣṇa consciousness quickly and effortlessly later in life. Śrīla Prabhupāda writes:

> Śrīla Jīva Gosvāmī remarks in this connection that every child, if given an impression of the Lord from his very childhood, certainly becomes a great devotee of the Lord like Mahārāja Parīkṣit. One may not be as fortunate as Mahārāja Parīkṣit to have the opportunity to see the Lord in the womb of his mother, but even if he is not so fortunate, he can be made so if the parents of the child desire him to be so. There is a practical example in my personal life in this connection. My father was a pure devotee of the Lord, and when I was only four or five years old, my father gave me a couple of forms of Rādhā and Kṛṣṇa. In a playful manner, I used to worship these Deities along with my sister, and I used to imitate the performances of a neighboring temple of Rādhā-Govinda. By constantly visiting this neighboring temple and copying the ceremonies in connection with my own Deities of play, I developed a natural affinity for the Lord. My father used to observe all the ceremonies befitting my position. Later on, these activities were suspended due to my association in the schools

> and colleges, and I became completely out of practice. But in my youthful days, when I met my spiritual master, Śrī Śrīmad Bhaktisiddhānta Sarasvatī Gosvāmī Mahārāja, again I revived my old habit, and the same playful Deities became my worshipful Deities in proper regulation. This was followed up until I left the family connection, and I am pleased that my generous father gave the first impression which was developed later into regulative devotional service by His Divine Grace. Mahārāja Prahlāda also advised that such impressions of a godly relation must be impregnated from the beginning of childhood, otherwise one may miss the opportunity of the human form of life, which is very valuable although it is temporary like others. (*Bhāgavatam* 1.12.30 purport)

Prayer is often the first way children learn to approach God, so it's good for parents to encourage the practice in their children. We can teach even very young children to recite simple prayers before eating and before going to bed. A three-year-old can memorize *ślokas* from *Bhagavad-gītā* just by hearing and repeating what they hear from older siblings. If we have more than one child, the siblings will be quite happy playing with each other.

So better if we can keep our children at home or in devotee-run childcare institutions, where they can hear about Kṛṣṇa consciousness from the beginning of their lives. If such childcare facilities are not available, we can try to cooperate with other devotee parents and see if we can find our children devotee playmates.

Deity Worship for Children

An important element in preparing the home for the homeschooled child is the introduction of Deity worship. Deity worship is essential in the education and training of our children because it trains them to be clean and punctual and to focus the mind on Kṛṣṇa. Bhaktivinoda Ṭhākura emphasizes the importance of Deity worship in chapter 11 of *Jaiva-dharma:* "The religions that have no provision for Deity worship face the danger that those children born into the religion and those just beginning spiritual life – both of whom may have little or no understanding of or deep faith in the Godhead – may become overtly materialistic and even develop aversion toward the Supreme Lord as a result of the absence of a Deity form on which to fix their minds. Therefore Deity worship is the foundation of religion for general humanity."

Prabhupāda also recommended Deity worship for all householders. Householders who worship Deities at home can bring up their children in a pristine atmosphere, in which they demonstrate practically how to love Kṛṣṇa. Parents can teach their children the importance of bowing down, chanting, dancing, and performing services such as cleaning the temple, making flower garlands, decorating the Deities, and observing festivals. Right from the beginning, children can be taught to offer everything to the Deities before using it themselves, including food, new clothing, and their talents. In this way a child can develop natural attraction for the Lord.

Children have a natural tendency to play, and instead of using this urge frivolously they can play with Kṛṣṇa, decorate Him, feed Him, and worship Him. When they are young they can worship and play with Kṛṣṇa dolls, and as they mature they can assist their parents in Deity worship. In a letter to his disciple Stokakṛṣṇa Dāsa (June 13, 1972) Prabhupāda wrote: "The children should always be instructed by taking advantage of their playful mood and teaching them to play Kṛṣṇa games like pretending to be cowherd boys, cows, peacocks, or demons, and in this way if they always think of Kṛṣṇa by playing just like they are actually present in association with Kṛṣṇa, then they will become Kṛṣṇa conscious very quickly. In addition, there should be a little ABC, then *prasāda,* then worshiping the Deity, then more playing Kṛṣṇa games, some *kīrtana,* a little more ABC, like that. In this way, always keep their minds and bodies engaged in different activities because children are restless by nature so they will want to change often."

Rādhā Priya (age 4) worships her Nimāi Nitāi Deities in Otaki, New Zealand.

Prabhupāda gives his own childhood as an example. "So children, they generally imitate the parents' habits or activities. So fortunately we had the opportunity of getting such a father. So we are imitating our father. In my childhood I imitated my father. He was worshiping Deity of Kṛṣṇa. So I asked him, 'My dear father, I shall worship. Give me the Deity of Kṛṣṇa.' So he gave me a little Deity of Kṛṣṇa and Rādhā and I was imitating. So beginning of life ... So these are actually facts. Mahārāja Parīkṣit also, he was playing with Kṛṣṇa, Kṛṣṇa dolls. Just like Mīrā Bāī. She was playing with Kṛṣṇa doll and later on she became a very high-grade devotee. So these chances are there." (Lecture, September 16, 1966, New York)

Prabhupāda writes of Uddhava's early Deity worship in his purport to *Śrīmad-Bhāgavatam* 3.2.2: "From his very birth, Uddhava was a natural devotee of Lord Kṛṣṇa, or a *nitya-siddha,* a liberated soul. From natural instinct he used to serve Lord Kṛṣṇa, even in his childhood. He used to play with dolls in the form of Kṛṣṇa, he would serve the dolls by dressing, feeding, and worshiping Them, and thus he was constantly absorbed in the play of transcendental realization. These are the signs of an eternally liberated soul."

We introduced Deity worship to our boys when they were three and five years old. They had their own four-inch Gaura-Nitāi Deities, to whom they became attached. I was with them when they did their worship. We would take several hours to dress, bathe, and decorate Them with ornaments. Then we would make an offering followed by *ārati* and *kīrtana*. Sometimes they would spill water or drop paraphernalia, but that is to be expected of small children. Overall, they took care of Gaura-Nitāi with love and respect. What was amazing was how they were absorbed for two to three hours without being distracted. They loved the worship. Anything they ate or drank they wanted to offer to their Deities, and they would remind us to do the same. It created a transcendental mood in the home, and it was easy for them to understand that everything should be done for Kṛṣṇa's pleasure. If they were disobedient it did not take them long to give it up because of their desire to please Gaura-Nitāi.

When children engage in Deity worship they understand that Kṛṣṇa is a person, a friend, and their worshipful object. He is approachable and can reciprocate with His worshipers. Deity worship is a natural way of evoking love of Godhead in children. No amount of explaining can do the same.

Another side benefit of Deity worship is that children learn the importance of cleanliness. They learn that they must bathe before they touch the Deities, and that even though Kṛṣṇa is their friend, He is not to be treated casually or like an ordinary person. It becomes easy to make Kṛṣṇa the most important family member, who needs to be kept satisfied and happy.

A Student's Perspective on Deity Worship

Rādhikā Ramaṇa shares his thoughts on what he learned by practicing Deity worship as a child

One of the nicest things about Deity worship is that it really solidifies the concept in the heart that God, Kṛṣṇa, is a person. When you start doing Deity worship at a young age, impersonalism is driven from the mind quite early; it becomes natural to relate to Kṛṣṇa in a personal way. A child sees the Deity and thinks, "Oh, what is the Deity feeling today? How is He doing? Is He happy? Upset? Did I decorate Him nicely or not? What does Kṛṣṇa want today? Is He hot or too cold? Maybe I should put a fan on Him."

So naturally, we start relating to Kṛṣṇa as a person, and the possibility of impersonalism becomes reduced. If we don't gain this concept when we're young, then later in life we have to train ourselves hard to constantly remember that Kṛṣṇa is a person and not to deal with Him impersonally. But children are naturally very personal, and just as they see a doll as a person, so they will see Kṛṣṇa as a person.

That becomes solidified very, very deeply, and then later, when they grow up, this quality extends to everyone else. The student, now grown, has the ability to relate in a personal way with every human being, and this becomes the foundation for good Vaiṣṇava relationships. Deity worship is important, and that's why Prabhupāda asked every *gṛhastha* to have Deities in the home – because it creates a personal relationship with Kṛṣṇa.

Some devotees question whether allowing small children to have this attitude toward Kṛṣṇa (and the Deity) might lead to some kind of improper *sahajīya* conception, in which God is considered to be cheap and too easy to interact with. Can the worshiper do whatever he wants to God?

There's always that possibility, I suppose, but we have to remember: "Books are the basis." There are two aspects to Kṛṣṇa consciousness: the practice or "working" relationship with Kṛṣṇa, and what we provide the intelligence. The intelligence has to be properly situated in order to balance the practice. Both have to be there.

Generally for a child, the intelligence develops only gradually, so in the beginning there's no fear of sahajīyaism. The distortions of sahajīyaism occur only if the intelligence is stunted and not developed properly. If that happens, and even as an adult a person doesn't see Kṛṣṇa in His proper role as the Supreme Lord and master, then there is a problem. But it's nearly impossible for a child to be a *sahajīya*.

The only thing a child needs is to be properly directed. The boundaries have to be set by the parents. "You can now offer this to Kṛṣṇa – but did you wash your hands?" So then children also understand, "Yes, Kṛṣṇa is my friend, but I am not on the level of the cowherd boys, who can take food from their mouths and offer it to Kṛṣṇa." Children understand, "No, I can't eat the food first. I have to wash my hands first. I have to be clean. Then I can go to Kṛṣṇa." So both things have to be there – the personal relationship with Kṛṣṇa and the boundaries.

Learning those boundaries is another big benefit of Deity worship, because children learn the difference between what's clean and what's unclean. They may not be able to practice this completely, but those principles are being set: "Okay, there are boundaries in life. There are times when you can't do something and times when you can. I really want to eat this, but oh, Kṛṣṇa's already gone to sleep. Now what will I do? I have to wait until tomorrow." Deity worship inculcates certain life boundaries also.

Deity worship is such a powerful practice because it accomplishes two seemingly contradictory goals. It breaks down the boundary of impersonalism, creating a personal relationship with Kṛṣṇa. But it also sets up the proper boundaries between the Lord and ourselves, because we're ultimately His servants and He's our master.

The Father's Role in Homeschooling

In most families, the mother assumes the primary role of homeschooling the children, but the father's role is crucial in the upbringing and spiritual welfare of the children. Śrīla Prabhupāda's own father, Gour Mohan De, set a good example:

> Many saintly persons used to visit my father's house. My father was Vaiṣṇava. He was Vaiṣṇava, and he wanted me to become a Vaiṣṇava. Whenever some saintly person would come, he would ask him, "Please bless my son that he can become a servant of Rādhārāṇī." That was his prayer. He never prayed for anything. And he gave me education how to play *mṛdaṅga*. My mother was against. There were two teachers – one for teaching me A-B-C-D and one for teaching me *mṛdaṅga*. So the one teacher was waiting and the other teacher was teaching me how to play on *mṛdaṅga*. So my mother would be angry that "What is this nonsense? You are teaching *mṛdaṅga*? What he will do with this *mṛdaṅga*?" But perhaps my father wanted that I should be a great *mṛdaṅga* player in the future. Therefore I am very much indebted to my father, and I have dedicated my book, *Kṛṣṇa*

> book, to him. He wanted this. He wanted me to be preacher of *Śrīmad-Bhāgavatam* and player of *mṛdaṅga,* and to become servant of Rādhārāṇī. So every parent should think like that; otherwise one should not become father and mother. That is the injunction in the *śāstra.* (Lecture, March 3, 1975, Dallas)

Because of his role in his spiritual education, Prabhupāda gave his father so much credit. When his father passed away, Prabhupāda missed him dearly. Satsvarūpa Dās Goswami relates in the *Śrīla Prabhupāda-līlāmṛta* (volume 1, p. 58):

> Abhay felt the loss of his father painfully. His father had given him everything he had ever wanted, had been careful to raise him as a pure Vaiṣṇava, and had always worshiped Rādhā and Kṛṣṇa. Although Abhay was a competent young man, he felt lost without his dearmost protector and friend. More than anyone else, Gour Mohan was the one who had always guided Abhay and treated him as the most special person. Without his father, Abhay now felt hopeless. He suddenly felt the same dependency he had felt as a small boy – but now without his father. The one who had always treated him as a pet son deserving all loving attention, the one who had given him whatever he had wanted and who had literally prayed to every holy man he met that his son become a great devotee of Śrīmatī Rādhārāṇī – that best well-wisher was now gone.

Fathers and Homeschooling

As far as homeschooling is concerned, the father's role varies according to the nature of the family, his job, and his inclination to teach. In some familes the father is actively involved in homeschooling – teaching his children particular subjects, for example – and in others he provides moral support and financial backup. Homeschooling works best when both parents are involved, so any help from the father is invaluable.

That said, it's obvious that many men have jobs that take them to work for eight or ten hours a day, so it's unusual for such fathers to be able to dedicate the same amount of time to homeschooling as the mother, who is at home with the children. The mother is with her children at all times, so she becomes the principal teacher; at a minimum, the father should be there to assist and support the mother.

My situation worked out like that. My husband, Ananta-rūpa Prabhu, gave us the financial stability we needed for me to homeschool our children. Sometimes he taught them math and science. We were running a temple while we were raising our boys, so even when he was home he had to oversee the needs of the temple, such as the Deity worship, festivals, preaching, and *prasāda* distribution. Even though these tasks filled his free time, those very things were key in educating our children because we were able to engage them in real-life tasks. Without his support in all the ways he provided it, it would not have been possible for me to homeschool my children. It is vital for children to see both parents working cooperatively to provide their children a home education, because then the children feel more enthused to perform better in all areas.

Not every family has the same situation we had, of course. Sometimes, due to financial considerations, both parents need to work outside the home. Homeschooling is still possible in such situations; I know of devotee families where both parents share the teaching responsibilities equally and adjust their work schedules so that one parent is always home with the children. Another possibility for working families is to set up a homeschooling cooperative, where several parents share the responsibility of teaching each other's children. (For more information, please see the chapter on "Staring a Homeschooling Co-op" and the FAQ on "Mothers who Work outside the Home.")

Fathers Encourage and Support

There are several important ways fathers can help with the home education of their children. Homeschooling can be stressful for the mother because the responsibility to succeed at it is immense. When children attend another form of school the mother may oversee what takes place but she isn't overly responsible for making sure her children learn. When she is homeschooling, however, she actually has to educate and train her children herself. She has to take time away from her cleaning and cooking to teach, but the cleaning and cooking must also get done. Often she can feel overwhelmed. So the first thing the father can do is offer her encouragement. This is difficult when one of the parents is not fully convinced about the benefits of Kṛṣṇa conscious homeschooling. A lack of conviction in either parent can make it difficult to homeschool successfully.

How can the father offer his encouragement? When he comes home after work, he can ask the children what they learned and applaud them and their mother for a good day's work. He can also help with chores around the house and look after the children so that the mother can take a much needed break at the end of the day. On his days off the father can spend time in devotional service with the children. This helps keep the bonds between father and children strong.

Fathers Assist in Teaching

No one is perfectly equipped in all areas. We may be strong in one area and weak in another. I am good with the humanities while my husband is good at math and science. So he would sometimes take our sons aside on the weekends and teach them math. Because of the pressures of his job and his temple presidency, he wasn't able to teach every weekend, so I used the Saxon Math series, which was easy for me to follow. Some fathers may be able to do what my husband did – teach on a part-time basis – and some may be able to teach their children a subject or two on a regular basis.

Fathers Chant With and Read to Their Children

Chanting with and reading to the children may last only fifteen minutes a day, but it can be a lot of fun. Our maxim is a family that chants and reads together, stays together. All families have to think of things to do together to keep their bond strong. As devotees it is natural that we

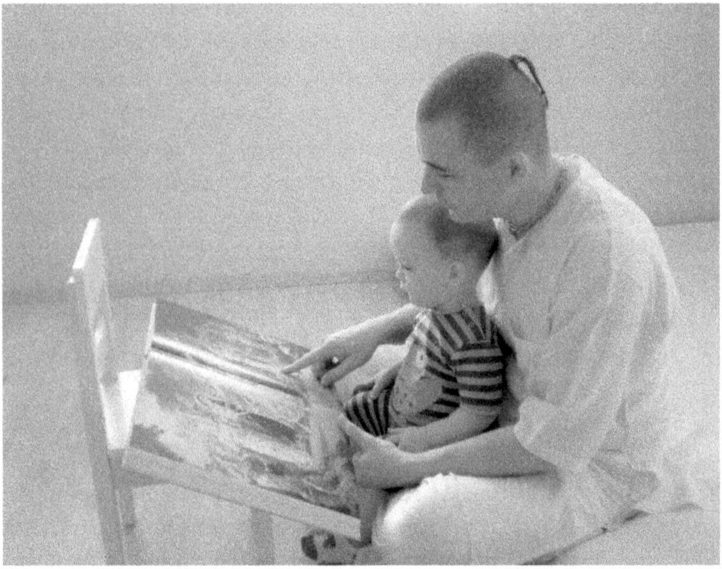

Yuvarāja Dāsa shows a picture of Lord Caitanya to his son Govinda (age 18 months) at their home in Oradea, Romania.

spend time together every day because the practices and goals of the parents are the same as those of the children. We parents have to chant and read every day, so we simply do these things as a family – with our children. It takes no extra effort or time, but the results are great. I personally read the entire *Śrīmad-Bhāgavatam* while reading with my children. The father may choose to read *Kṛṣṇa* book every day with them, perhaps in the evenings. This is good for him as well as his children.

Fathers Are Loving and Caring

Familiarity breeds contempt – or so the saying goes. But in devotional life this is not true because devotees learn to see each other as spirit souls, servants of Kṛṣṇa. The husband sees his wife as a servant of Kṛṣṇa, and the wife sees her husband in the same way. With this kind of vision it's easy for the father to be caring and understanding and the wife to serve her family selflessly.

Fathers Set Good Examples for Their Families

Setting a good example may be the father's most important role in homeschooling. For children, especially boys, the father is a hero and someone to emulate. Children observe every small detail of their father's habits and behavior, and if the father sets a good devotional example, his sons and daughters can grow up to become good devotees.

The intimacy between a father and his children shapes the children's character and habits and helps them overcome the *māyā* they will sooner or later be exposed to. My sons were always very close to my husband and marveled at the way he would stick to his principles in spite of hardships. For example, he was very particular about eating only *prasāda,* and my sons remember how he sometimes fasted or lived on dates and nuts on business trips because he had run out of home-cooked food. This principled behavior made a deep impression on my boys, and to this day they strictly follow the same principle about eating only *prasāda.*

Fathers Are Enthusiastic to Perform Devotional Service

Enthusiasm is a key ingredient in spiritual life, and when children see their parents are enthusiastic to perform devotional service they also become eager to help and sometimes even take leadership roles. My husband was always enthusiastic about celebrating festivals and engaging the family in cooking and decorating the temple for Kṛṣṇa. He also set a good example in Deity worship by always taking care that everything was clean and punctual. Overall, the children looked up to him and imitated his simple Vedic lifestyle.

Love in Homeschooling

Parents must give unconditional love to their children. Sometimes we see parents suppress their love toward their children for fear that the children will be spoiled. This is a grave mistake. Think of cows. Even though we might do everything needed to make them physically comfortable – keeping them clean, fed, and milked punctually – they will not give milk unrestrictedly unless they are given love. In the same way, unless children receive unconditional love, without suppression, they will not take to Kṛṣṇa consciousness happily and they will not be able to give the same love to Kṛṣṇa.

How can we learn to give this unconditional love to our children? The power of love is demonstrated by Lord Caitanya Mahāprabhu, whose mission it was to change peoples' hearts through love alone. There is no substitute for love, and when we love Kṛṣṇa this love for Him automatically translates into love for each other. Parents who see themselves and their children as servants of God do not hesitate to give that powerful and empowering love to their children.

Śrīla Prabhupāda said that even when parents and teachers discipline children, the children must also be given lots of love. Prabhupāda emphasized the element of love before punishment when dealing with disciplinary issues in the *gurukula*. He was against physical punishment: "Children should not be beaten at all, that I have told." (Letter to Bhānutanya Dāsī, November 18, 1972) The stick may be shown as a warning, but children should obey out of love, not fear.

So don't hold back. Love should flow easily between teacher and students or, in the case of homeschooling, between parents and children.

Love does not mean spoiling our children or failing to discipline them. Real love means giving our children Kṛṣṇa consciousness so they do not have to come back again to this material world. This is not only our duty but a test of our love for them. Misplaced love means that we take care of their bodily needs without giving them necessary spiritual training.

Therefore love is the key factor in training children in Kṛṣṇa consciousness. It was very natural for me to give all of myself to my sons. Like other mothers I showered them with *prasāda* and attention. I tried to encourage them and make their homeschooling a pleasant experience. My sons had plenty of surprises to look forward to because at times we would often skip our usual routine and substitute preaching or social activities. Sometimes we would read *Śrīmad-Bhāgavatam* for the entire morning (with short breaks) and discuss serious philosophical questions. When *sannyāsīs* came we tried to serve them nicely and so broke from our homeschooling routine while they were visiting. Kṛṣṇa conscious activities like these brought an element of sweetness to our relationship; because they were meant for Kṛṣṇa's service, they uplifted us. Activities on the bodily platform bring misery and frustration, but when we are filled with love for Kṛṣṇa and share that love with our children, our lives and theirs become perfect.

Academic Curriculum

The Scriptures as the Basis for Homeschooling

Śrīla Prabhupāda said that from the very beginning children "should be taught Sanskrit and English so in the future they can read our books. That will make them MA, PhD." (Letter to Jagadīśa Dāsa, April 6, 1977) The knowledge in Prabhupāda's books is advanced. Children can be well-educated, happy, satisfied, and even go back to Godhead by reading them.

As evident in many of his lectures, it is clear that Śrīla Prabhupāda desired the children in his *gurukulas* to read *Śrīmad-Bhāgavatam*. On July 12, 1974, speaking on *Śrīmad-Bhāgavatam* (1.16.22), Śrīla Prabhupāda confirmed that the *Bhāgavatam* would equip any child to know every subject. They would need nothing else. Please read the following quotation carefully:

> So in *Śrīmad-Bhāgavatam* you will find everything, whatever is necessity, for the advancement of human civilization, everything is there described. And knowledge also, all departments of knowledge, even astronomy, astrology, politics, sociology, atomic theory, everything is there. *Vidyā-bhāgavatāvadhi.* Therefore if you study *Śrīmad-Bhāgavatam* very carefully, then

> you get all knowledge completely. Because *Bhāgavatam* begins from the point of creation: *janmādy asya yataḥ.*

By giving them this foundation, children become confident of their spiritual identity and also do well academically. Prabhupāda's books inspire us to use logic and critical thinking, which are the main elements of academic education. Even a basic understanding of *Bhāgavatam* philosophy far exceeds the level of thinking found in most college courses.

Śrīmad-Bhāgavatam covers all subject matters. By teaching children through the *Bhāgavatam,* they have a head start on all other subjects. Later, when they have to study these other subjects through nondevotional books they will have the proper Vedic perspective and not be misled into atheistic or materialistic thinking.

It is easier to study the *Bhāgavatam* than the *Bhagavad-gītā* with children because the *Bhāgavatam* contains stories. It also contains all the philosophy of the *Bhagavad-gītā,* so there is no loss on focusing on the *Bhāgavatam.* We have seen that even a six-year-old can learn to read directly from Prabhupāda's books, and because of the books' potency the child's language skills quickly increase. Once children have a good command of language they can master any subject.

Prabhupāda wanted all subjects to be taught in a Kṛṣṇa conscious manner: "As soon as possible we should open our own school and teach children Kṛṣṇa consciousness through English medium, that is one of our programs. Our school will not be government recognized because we cannot follow the government syllabus. We want to teach only Kṛṣṇa consciousness.... try to introduce immediately Kṛṣṇa conscious instruction to the students through English medium ... Our girl disciples may be engaged for teaching them a little English grammar, reading and writing, geography, arithmetic, history, Sanskrit, but all of them should be Kṛṣṇa conscious – that is *bhāgavata* program." (Letter to Girirāja Dāsa, April 12, 1972)

How to Study Śrīmad-Bhāgavatam

I decided to try following this instruction in my homeschooling. I started teaching my sons through *Śrīmad-Bhāgavatam* when they were six and eight years old. At that age, neither of the boys could remain attentive through the long purports, so in the early years we mostly read only the verse translations. This was nice because the intriguing stories kept them reading with enthusiasm. We would stop frequently to discuss the stories and the spiritual lessons we could learn from them. Gradually, the discussions became deeper, and in order to answer their own questions the children would naturally be drawn to the purports.

Sometimes I would scan the purports in advance to pick out ones they might like to read. I would go as deeply into the subjects as I could with the boys, all the while establishing the power of the *Bhāgavatam's* viewpoint.

What was amazing was that just by reading *Śrīmad-Bhāgavatam* for two or three hours daily, the boys' language and comprehension skills became strong. I would give them occasional writing assignments, but we mostly just read and discussed. Not only were they reading at the college level within five years of me introducing this program, but their understanding of fine philosophical points was amazing. They had learned reasoning, logic, debating skills, and how to communicate effectively. Later, when they began to attend college, they had little problem learning American history, geography, science, English literature, anthropology, and sociology for the first time. I was surprised myself how well they did! They scored high in every subject, and the teachers said their understanding and maturity were better than those of their classmates. We have had the same experience with other children who have followed the *Bhāgavatam* method.

Is It Practical?

One may ask whether it is practical to teach only through Prabhupāda's books. Won't education through the scriptures do nothing but prepare them for a life of preaching and other devotional activities? Can the children gain enough knowledge and learn enough skills to live in the world, hold a job, get married, and carry the social and financial obligations that go with the *gṛhastha-āśrama*?

In our case we found that the scriptures equipped us to do all of the above because they teach not only the purpose of human life but the nature of the material world and how to live in it while one is preparing to go back to Godhead. The knowledge in the scriptures is complete – nothing is lacking materially or spiritually. For example, by reading *Śrīmad-Bhāgavatam* one can understand every psychological situation in the world.

A Student's Perspective on Bhāgavatam-Based Homeschooling

Rādhikā Ramaṇa shares his experience with Bhāgavatam-based homeschooling

When I was twelve someone mentioned to my parents that Boise State University allowed high school students to take classes at the university as part of their dual enrollment policy. This friend had noticed that I was good at writing and suggested that as a homeschooled student I could get permission to sign up for an English course. My parents thought it was a good idea, so we met with the Dean of Admissions to request special permission. I showed him some test scores and a few of the articles I had written for *Back to Godhead* magazine, and he granted me permission to register for a course in English composition.

As it happened, all the entry-level classes were full, and it was too late to register. But the English department chairman, Dr. Chaman Sahni, was an Indian gentleman who often visited the temple. He knew me and suggested I try for the second-level class – he thought it might still have an opening. When we checked, it was also full, but he said not to worry, I could try for the honors writing course, which always had fewer students. My parents and I didn't know what Kṛṣṇa had planned for me: Would I be able to handle an honor's class at the age of twelve?

Dr. Sahni encouraged me to try it. As it turned out, the first-level honors English writing course wasn't being offered that semester, so the chairman told me to sign up for the second-level honors course. I was accepted into that class. On the first day of class the professor handed out the reading list. It contained classical works like Shakespeare's *Hamlet* and Homer's *Odyssey* as well as some Mexican and American writers. I had never studied any of this material; our homeschooling was based only on Prabhupāda's books.

I was nervous! I still remember my first day, walking into the university classroom, a twelve-year-old boy surrounded by students six or eight years older, and this reading list – I couldn't understand it at all.

But then when the professor gave us the reading assignments and I read the books we were assigned it was surprising, because the *Iliad* and the *Odyssey* were stories of heroes and demigods of the Greek past. Not much different from reading the *Mahābhārata* and *Śrīmad-Bhāgavatam*. Shakespeare was full of philosophical ideas – I noticed references to reincarnation, the temporality of life, and Hamlet's existential predicament.

When we started writing our assignments and handing in papers, the professor was surprised that I was able to find these types of insights in the books. Most students were writing about the plot or storyline, but I was digging into the philosophy – what Shakespeare was trying to say, his view of the world, and so forth. The professor was surprised, and I ended up getting an A in that course. She was happy, but I was mostly just surprised – how did this happen?

The point we have to realize is that nowadays, the educational system is looking for people with critical thinking and reasoning skills, people who can be creative and innovative in finding solutions to problems. There may have been a time when education was just a matter of memorizing formulas and repeating them back on examinations, but those days are long gone. Both the job market and the educational system are looking for people who can take a problem, examine it critically, find a creative solution, and then implement that solution. Those critical thinking and reasoning skills are found so clearly and so powerfully in Śrīla Prabhupāda's books, especially in *Śrīmad-Bhāgavatam*.

Sometimes as devotees we get used to our Kṛṣṇa conscious philosophy and take for granted its depth and sophistication. For example, anyone growing up in Kṛṣṇa consciousness or with some experience of it can tell you that there are three manifestations of Godhead: Brahman, Paramātmā, and Bhagavān. Brahman is the impersonal absolute, Paramātmā is the Lord's localized form, present in the material world, and Bhagavān is the highest understanding of God – His personal form. Bhagavān has three types of energies, or *śaktis,* which are simultaneously nondifferent and different from the Lord.

Or again, one of the basic items in our philosophy is the difference between the body and the self. All of these ideas require a level of philosophical sophistication not present in the average person.

The vocabulary Prabhupāda uses in his books is also advanced. I remember when my parents were running Govinda's restaurant, as children, it was our job to introduce customers to the food, because in Boise people were not familiar with Indian cuisine. We would explain all the dishes to them and then at the end, if they were interested, we would walk them over to our book rack to see if they wanted to look at any of Prabhupāda's books.

We were talking to these customers – as normally as we knew how to at that age – and I remember they would look at each other in amazement at our vocabulary. My brother and I thought it was perfectly normal to use words like "ecstatic" and "transcendental," but the average English-educated person doesn't necessarily know the words we took for granted, or if they did, they were not part of their everyday vocabulary.

In other words, Prabhupāda's books are really at an advanced level. When he says that by reading his books you'll be "more than MA or PhD," it's because his books are at the MA and PhD level.

The most important thing to realize is that the concepts provided in the *Gītā* are not dogmatic – there is no "You do this, you do this, you do this, and now be silent and don't ask questions!" It's not like that. *Bhagavad-gītā* is a dialogue. Kṛṣṇa says something and Arjuna doesn't understand. He doesn't say, "Whatever you say, Kṛṣṇa, it's okay." He questions, "I don't understand. Your instructions are equivocal on this matter. You say one thing and then You say another." Arjuna asks the same question of Kṛṣṇa three times in three different chapters in three different ways: "I still don't understand the point. First You tell me to use my intelligence, then You say I should act. Which is it? Do You want me to take vows of *sannyāsa* or to act in this world?" Three different times Arjuna asks the same question. Why? Because he's thinking – he's using his intelligence. Kṛṣṇa says that if we study the *Bhagavad-gītā* properly we are worshiping Him with our intelligence.

We should, therefore, recognize the level of intelligence and sophistication present in the *Gītā*. Arjuna was far more intelligent than any of us. If the *Gītā* conversation was satisfying to him, it must be more than satisfying to us at our level of intelligence and understanding.

The *Bhāgavatam,* too, is full of questions, answers, and debates. Is God partial to His devotees or impartial to everyone? If God is all kind, why is there so much suffering in the world? Questions like these fill the history of philosophy both in the West and in India, and they're all addressed in the *Bhāgavatam*.

What's interesting is that if someone in the US wants to become a lawyer, one of the best preparations is a degree in philosophy. Law schools appreciate such students not because of the philosophical content but because of the understanding and critical thinking required to reach philosophical solutions. The process of thinking and asking questions sharpens the mind; if a student can deal with difficult problems and separate and distinguish and categorize and organize, then law schools know such a student will succeed.

None of us doubt the transcendental and pure devotional quality of the Vedic scriptures, but at the same time we have to realize that from an academic perspective, there is nothing lacking in *Śrīmad-Bhāgavatam.* It is the best of the very best. My younger brother and I have seen this many times in our own lives, and now there are so many devotee children in different parts of the world who have taken up studying all the language arts, all the philosophical subjects, history, geography, and so on through *Śrīmad-Bhāgavatam*.

And they're getting the same results we got. In Boise alone we already have three children who have started college at the age of twelve or thirteen, from families both Indian and American. There are also other children in other parts of the world who are focusing their studies on Śrīla Prabhupāda's books and achieving similar results.

In our devotee community in Boise, we have a family with two daughters aged six and seven years old. They come to *Bhāgavatam* class and we have them read the translation and purports aloud for the devotees there. At such an age they can already read Prabhupāda's English, which is written at least at a master's level, if not PhD. Just imagine how developed their language skills will be when they are older.

The ultimate goal of studying Prabhupāda's books is not that we gain some material qualifications but that we advance spiritually. But the point of my remarks is that we should have faith that when we pursue what Śrīla Prabhupāda wanted – when we pursue our spiritual direction in life – then the material will automatically be taken care of, with no lacking. It's impossible for anyone to be a devotee of Kṛṣṇa and remain ignorant, because the material aspect of life is a servant of the spiritual aspect. All material qualifications stand ready with folded hands, waiting for the devotee to accept them, if one can pursue with faith what Prabhupāda wanted. According to *Śrī Caitanya-caritāmṛta*, faith (*śraddhā*) is the firm conviction that if one performs devotional service, if one serves Kṛṣṇa, then everything else in life will be taken care of.

We can see this in a very practical way in Śrīla Prabhupāda's books – there is no literature in the world like *Śrīmad-Bhāgavatam*.

Teaching Śrīmad-Bhāgavatam to Children

Many parents ask whether I have a formal curriculum for teaching *Śrīmad-Bhāgavatam* to children. What I taught my children was less of a curriculum and more of a method. Once understood, this method can be applied to any section of *Śrīmad-Bhāgavatam's* 18,000 verses – a vast curriculum. The techniques of questions and answers, debates, and playing devil's advocate can be prepared by anyone simply taking a paragraph from *Śrīmad-Bhāgavatam*. Parents can write assignments, underline words, and use the dictionary to look up synonyms, pronunciations, and definitions.

A set curriculum would be too constraining because the parent would have to cover a specific topic. Rather, when we read dynamically with our children, a single point might lead to many other points, and we may find ourselves discussing geography, politics, history, or any other topics that arise. A fixed curriculum might be helpful, but since it can become constricting it is better to learn the methodology and create your own curriculum. The individualized, tutorial system of teaching has been used effectively for centuries in both India and the West, including at Oxford and Cambridge universities.

Educators at the primary level teach children concepts by presenting a number of related facts with the assumption that even if the facts are forgotten the concepts will remain. Our plan for Kṛṣṇa conscious homeschooling, then, is to teach important concepts, not through material means but through spiritual means using Śrīla Prabhupāda's books. Because of the nature of the modern economy, the set of facts children need changes constantly depending on the job they will have in the future and what status they will achieve in life. So why overburden a child with material facts that will soon be forgotten even by the outside world?

What's more important is that our children learn to prioritize, evaluate, and process facts. Being overburdened with temporary material facts doesn't make that job any easier. It's smarter all around to teach our children the concepts and skills they need, using a spiritual, unchanging, Kṛṣṇa conscious set of facts.

Our Method

This is what we did. We derived facts from Śrīla Prabhupāda's books, primarily *Śrīmad-Bhāgavatam,* and we used the skills and techniques that have been used in traditional cultures and which are still considered effective in today's teaching methodologies.

Many of us fail to realize the importance a good discussion has in education. At schools teachers speak and children listen – it's a monologue. Remember, though, that *Śrīmad-Bhāgavatam* is a grand discussion among sages. Such a discussion is an important part of teaching and learning, a part which is often lacking in today's schools. The success of homeschooling lies in the process of intensive discussion, which stimulates our children's minds to reason and at the same time teaches them to communicate and express themselves effectively.

The beauty of homeschooling is that if a discussion is fruitful there is no need to stop – there is no class bell telling students to move on to another subject. A good discussion can go on for three or four hours or, if it isn't productive, be cut short. If a young child is restless, we can read a few times a day rather than all at one time. There is no outside force limiting how much we study in this style of homeschooling.

Sample Sessions

Recently, I started a morning *Bhāgavatam* study group for five children (aged nine, seven, six, five, and four) in the Boise community. Of course the four- and five-year-olds cannot read fluently, so they read once in a while and the older children take regular turns reading the translations. When we stop for discussion, I generally start by asking questions. I make the questions easy for the four-year-old and harder for the seven- and nine-year-old. I move from child to child and ask questions based on each child's level of understanding.

I try to keep the children motivated and interested, making sure I don't lose their attention. Four-year-olds may not grasp all the philosophical points, but they are benefited just by sitting and listening. And it's amazing, actually, how much they *do* absorb. When older children speak, younger children tend to listen, and all the children learn a lot from each other's realizations and questions.

Discussion allows parents to teach two or more children of different ages simultaneously. Sometimes discussions go long, sometimes not, depending on the section of the *Bhāgavatam* under study. In my children's *Bhāgavatam* class we don't read the purports together – only the translations – but I pre-read the purports on my own so that I'm familiar with the points Śrīla Prabhupāda will make.

Reading the story of Prahlāda, Canto 7, chapter 4: We discussed the qualities of Hiraṇyakaśipu, how he controlled all the elements such as rain, fire, and air, and the lower, middle, and higher planets, because he wanted to become God. Nowadays, like Hiraṇyakaśipu, some scientists are also trying to control nature. Can they succeed? What happened to Hiraṇyakaśipu? Nature really controls *us*. Unless Kṛṣṇa sends rain there is no food. When blizzards, fires, storms, and hurricanes hit we are helpless. They have to subside by Kṛṣṇa's will. We cannot control them even with all of our material advancement. But, instead of controlling the will of God, if we simply control our senses and love Kṛṣṇa, then, like Prahlāda, we can be fearless and peaceful. Hiraṇyakaśipu could not control his senses – in a fit of anger he wanted to kill his own son. He was so greedy that he wanted to get more and more and was never satisfied.

After reading all the qualities of Hiraṇyakaśipu, I asked them what made Hiraṇyakaśipu proud. They took turns to tell me money, fame, power from his practice of mystic yoga, that he had a good wife – so devotees are careful not to hanker for these things because they know

Bhagavata-dharma Dāsa studies Śrīmad-Bhāgavatam with his children Nitāi (age 11, left) and Gopāl (age 13, right) in Ljubljana, Slovenia.

they could also become proud. But what if Kṛṣṇa awards us these things due to our past karma? Then we can use what we have been given by Kṛṣṇa in His service. In that way we will not become proud but will always remain humble.

Chapter 5: The next day we discussed Prahlāda's instruction to his teachers not to make distinctions between friends and enemies – to see everyone as servants of Kṛṣṇa. We talked about the equality of the soul in every body – in the bodies of men, women, animals, meat eaters, and devotees. After that I asked: "So does that mean we can embrace a tiger or a snake because we are all equal?" No, they all said. Prahlāda is telling us to respect others and show all living entities compassion because they are children of the same father, Kṛṣṇa. However, we must avoid the association of the envious and materialistic because they are attached to the wrong things. We should seek the association of devotees whose consciousness is drawn toward Kṛṣṇa.

We talked about real love. When Hiraṇyakaśipu placed Prahlāda on his lap, tears of affection glided down his face. Was his affection pure? We know Hiraṇyakaśipu was cruel and tried to kill his son. Real love has no selfish motive; that's the way Kṛṣṇa loves us. We can experience pure love for each other only if we love God, because He is the father and we are His children – just as when we love our father, we naturally also love our brothers and sisters. A father can also have real love for his children if he makes his family Kṛṣṇa conscious.

Dhruva Mahārāja Leaves Home (Canto 4, Chapter 8)

Dhruva Mahārāja, the five-year-old son of King Uttānapāda, left home to find the Supreme Personality of Godhead in order to take revenge for the insult he received at the hands of his stepmother, Suruci. She had told Dhruva he could neither sit on his father's lap nor inherit the throne because he had been born of a less-favored queen, Sunīti. Even though Dhruva was only five, the insult drove him to the forest to please Lord Viṣṇu so he could be blessed with a kingdom greater than that of his father, his grandfather Svāyambhuva Manu, and his great-grandfather Lord Brahmā.

After six months of devotional service under the guidance of his spiritual master, Nārada Muni, Dhruva saw Viṣṇu face to face. As soon as he saw the Lord, Dhruva became purified of his material contamination and felt ashamed for having asked Kṛṣṇa for something material. Now he simply wanted to serve the Lord's lotus feet under the guidance of his spiritual master.

Through this story we can discuss many deep issues. The parent would have to carefully study some of the purports ahead of time and perhaps note down key points. Let's go through chapter 8, "Dhruva Mahārāja Leaves Home for the Forest." Here are some of the questions parents can use to open the discussion, stopping at the appropriate verses as they come to them.

How can we see that Queen Suruci was arrogant toward Dhruva Mahārāja? Give some examples. What caused her arrogance, and how could she have avoided it, even if she wanted her son to be king? Can you think of examples in your life when you have been arrogant? How could you have avoided it?

How did Dhruva and his mother, Queen Sunīti, react to Suruci's harsh words? How can we tell that Dhruva's mother is a great Vaiṣṇavī, unlike his stepmother? What kind of advice did Sunīti give Dhruva?

Why did Queen Sunīti not stop her son from leaving home? Why did she encourage him to leave? Was she being a good mother by doing that?

How would you react if someone insulted you? Would you retaliate by harming the person, or would you take Nārada Muni's instructions to Dhruva?

Dhruva Mahārāja did not cause anyone pain when he worked to fulfill his desire. He did not retaliate against his stepmother but took shelter of the Lord as his mother had advised him. Why does Sunīti say we should approach only the Supreme Personality of Godhead, even for material benedictions, and not the demigods?

Why are the different features of the Lord likened to a lotus flower?

What is the only solution to material problems, as exemplified by Dhruva Mahārāja?

Who is Nārada, and why did he come to help Dhruva in the forest?

What arguments does Nārada use to encourage Dhruva to go home?

Initially, Dhruva Mahārāja could not accept his spiritual master's advice because he did not have brahminical qualities. Is it okay for a disciple to ask his spiritual master to give him different instructions just because the first instructions are too difficult to follow? Why is it important to be honest with your spiritual master and reveal your heart?

Why was Dhruva Mahārāja successful in both his material and spiritual endeavors? Can you think of the key actions that made him successful? What are some of your own realizations about this story?

Gajendra and the Crocodile (Canto 8, Chapters 2–4)

What is the most important lesson to be learned from the story of the elephant and the crocodile? What in the story touches you most?

Gajendra realized that his family members could not protect him from the danger of being attacked by the crocodile, so he surrendered to the Lord and asked Him for protection. Next time you are alone and in danger, would you cry out to Kṛṣṇa for protection?

Crying out to Kṛṣṇa needs practice since we are more used to asking each other for help. What steps can you take so the next time you are in danger, you can do what Gajendra did?

Śrīla Prabhupāda says that the reason the crocodile was stronger than the elephant during the fight, even though the elephant is a much stronger animal, was because the crocodile was in its natural setting – the water – whereas for Gajendra, water was a foreign place. Prabhupāda advises us to stay in a normal position in life so we can practice Kṛṣṇa consciousness peacefully. What would be a normal condition for you as a child, and what would be abnormal?

Both Gajendra and the crocodile were great souls in their previous lives, but because of accidental misconduct on their part they were cursed to take animal bodies. Do you believe in reincarnation? How would you convince someone about reincarnation?

Why is devotional service never a waste of time even though not completed in a single lifetime? In the lives of both Gajendra and the crocodile, how was this true?

Why was Gajendra a more elevated personality than the crocodile?

Why is Kṛṣṇa considered the kindest, most merciful personality – more than our own mothers and fathers? How can you convince someone of this, especially when externally it appears that other people or situations in the material world are the cause of our happiness?

It is said one should not ask the Lord for material benedictions. How is it that both Dhruva Mahārāja and Gajendra asked the Lord for such things?

Indra, Bṛhaspati, and Vṛtrāsura (Canto 6)

Was Indra's offense to his spiritual master Bṛhaspati accidental or on purpose? What do you learn from this story? Why is such an offense so much graver than other offenses?

Why did Lord Kṛṣṇa agree to help the demigods against the demon Vṛtrāsura even though Indra was at fault when he killed a *brāhmaṇa* (Viśvarūpa)?

Who is a devotee and who is a demon? In this story we see that a demon is a great devotee of Kṛṣṇa – better than Lord Indra.

It appears externally that a great devotee like Vṛtrāsura was not protected by Kṛṣṇa whereas Indra was. Why is it that Vṛtrāsura was more favored by the Lord than Indra, even though the latter was physically protected by the Lord and regained his kingdom?

Vṛtrāsura was fearless even after knowing that Indra would kill him with his invincible thunderbolt. Most of us are afraid of dying. How can we become fearless like Vṛtrāsura?

Why does the Lord not bestow material benedictions on a devotee who wants to advance spiritually? What if we have material desires but also want to be good devotees? Why does the Lord force us to give up our material desires when he sees a sincere desire in us to be near Him?

Writing and Grammar

For writing assignments I gave my children questions from what they had just read – simple questions when they were younger and more thought-provoking questions as they grew older, trying as often as possible to relate the questions to practical life. I also selected vocabulary words from the text – again, according to the boys' ability to understand. We discussed the meanings of words, sometimes looking them up in the dictionary, and then, the boys made up their own sentences using the words. As they read the *Bhāgavatam* they picked up meanings of even difficult words through the context.

I taught a little formal grammar from a grammar book, but my boys learned how to write and speak well principally by reading, writing, and discussing. During discussion times I would encourage my children to read, participate, inquire, and speak their realizations. Parents who want to be more formal can find a good grammar workbook and spend fifteen minutes a day on grammar. Writing included answering questions and composing short essays and scripts for dramas. More suggestions can be found in the chapter "The Five R's: wRiting."

Learning English through Śrīmad-Bhāgavatam

Parents and teachers who have taught their children *Śrīmad-Bhāgavatam* from early on have experienced how easily their children pick up language skills, especially reading and comprehension. Even a seven-year-old can understand difficult concepts, because the subject matter of *Śrīmad-Bhāgavatam* encourages good thinking skills. The *Bhāgavatam* is full of analogies, allegories, figurative speech, and metaphors – all of which encourage reasoning and help the child learn to think analytically and critically. The simple analogies Prabhupāda uses to explain different spiritual topics – the existence of the soul, for example – are easily understood by children.

Analogies

Why use analogies? In chapter 15 of his book *Jaiva-dharma,* Śrīla Bhaktivinoda Ṭhākura explains, "This material world is a reflection and transformation of the spiritual world. Yet because there are certain characteristics in material nature still similar to those of the spiritual world, spiritual subjects are discussed using appropriate explanatory analogies, which take advantage of these similarities."

Prabhupāda is renowned for clarifying profound philosophical truths with down-to-earth analogies. By tying together elementary logic, simple scientific observations and deductions, and the truths stated in bona fide scripture, he teaches us the most difficult concepts from the *Vedas,* establishing faith that the Vedic scriptures are the source of perfect knowledge. Prabhupāda's straightforward analogies expel the illusion of the soul's false material identity.

It is impossible for a person in material consciousness, thinking he is just his body, to understand the soul and Supersoul – unless he hears the analogies Kṛṣṇa and his devotees give in the scriptures. Śrīla Prabhupāda uses several analogies to explain the difference between the soul and the body: the wearer of garments and the garments themselves, the tiller and the field, and the operator and the machine.

Let us examine how Prabhupāda uses analogies to effectively explain the concept of the soul. Prabhupāda once encouraged a religious editor from the Associated Press to stick with the analogy of the car and the driver until he fully understood the difference between the body and the soul (Room Conversation, July 16, 1976, New York). Prabhupāda explained that the body is like a car, and we, the soul, are its driver. The car cannot function until the driver sets the car in motion, just as the body is dead until the spirit soul enters it. However, the car and driver have different identities. The driver is not the car and the car is not the driver. The car cannot drive without the driver. Both are working, but of the two, the driver is more important regardless of whether or not he is in the car.

In the same interview Prabhupāda explains that the purpose of ISKCON is to understand who the driver of the car is and why he is more important than the car. Because people do not understand the difference between the car and the driver, the body and soul, they work only for the body and cannot understand the value of the Kṛṣṇa consciousness movement. We are working on the driver of the body, on the spirit soul, and that is our greater contribution.

Prabhupāda then takes the analogy further: the car requires fuel as the driver requires food. "So people in general, when they see that we are not giving petrol to the driver, they are surprised.... They think that petrol is the food of the driver!"

In other words, satisfying the body does not satisfy the person within the body. The driver's food is different from the food meant for the car. The car requires petrol, but the driver needs fruits, vegetables, and grains. Materialistic people do not realize that the food for the driver is different from the fuel for the car.

On July 27, 1976, Mike Robinson of the London Broadcasting Company visited Śrīla Prabhupāda at Bhaktivedanta Manor and asked him where the Vedic scriptures come from. Prabhupāda used the analogy of a microphone. "Whenever there is some new material creation – like this microphone, for instance – there is also some literature explaining how to deal with it. That literature comes along with the creation of the microphone. Similarly, the Vedic literature comes with the cosmic creation to explain how to deal with it.... The literature issued by the manufacturer of this microphone is bona fide. So if anyone follows that bona fide literature, he can deal with it. Otherwise, it is not authorized."

Prabhupāda often explained the transmigration of the soul from one body to another like this: by changing one's shirt from a white one to a red one does not mean the person wearing the shirt has changed. The shirt changes but the person remains the same. Similarly, the body changes and the soul does not.

Prabhupāda used many humorous and simple analogies to defeat scientists and their atheistic views. A scientist may claim there is no God, but Prabhupāda points out that in a big city things are being run with so much orderliness – traffic moves in a certain way, for example – that behind it all the government must be working to control it. Similarly, the orderliness in the creation is due to the government of God and His laws." (Lecture, January 28, 1975, Tokyo)

Other common analogies Prabhupāda uses to expose the limited perspective of many modern scientists: the "frog in the well" and the "nipples on the neck of a goat." A frog in a well that has never seen the ocean speculates as to what the ocean must be like, and scientists who have never seen the kingdom of God still profess to be very learned.

Prabhupāda uses analogies profusely to help his audience understand spiritual concepts through material examples. To prove that animals have souls: "The animal is eating; you are eating. The animal is sleeping; you are sleeping. The animal is defending; you are defending. The animal is having sex; you have sex. The animals have children; you have got children. You have got a living place; they have got a living place.... If your body's cut, there is blood. If the animal body's cut, there is blood. So all the similarities are there. So why you deny one similarity? Analogy. Analogy means points of similarity. So this is logic. You have read logic? There is a chapter, analogy. Analogy means points of similarity. If the points of similarity are so many things, why one similarity should be avoided? That is not logic. That is not science." (Lecture, July 27, 1976, London)

When a gentleman objected to Prabhupāda's use of analogies, he stood by his method adamantly: "When there is a truth spoken by God that living entities are My part and parcel, *mamaiva,* why shall I not give the analogy? How do part and parcel act? I must give an analogy. Otherwise, how can anyone understand?" (Lecture, September 5, 1971, London)

Prabhupāda's analogies range from the simple to the difficult, so we can use them to teach our children according to their level of understanding. In the their early years children may not fully understand analogies, but by repeating or memorizing them they will later understand many difficult philosophical concepts with their help.

Children who grow up learning Kṛṣṇa conscious philosophy through these analogies learn language skills effectively. They will have no problem with university studies, and even Shakespeare and other classical writers will seem easy to them.

Metaphors

Along with analogies, *Śrīmad-Bhāgavatam* abounds with metaphors, allegories, and figurative speech. All of these help us understand what would otherwise be impossible to understand. Analogies are comparisons or similarities between two things; metaphors, allegories, and figurative speech are comparisons with a more descriptive or poetic flavor.

For example, *Śrīmad-Bhāgavatam* (10.58.2) explains that when the Pāṇḍavas saw Lord Kṛṣṇa after a long separation, they "all stood up at once, like the senses responding to the return of the life air." Prabhupāda comments in his purport: "The metaphor used here is quite poetic. When a person is unconscious, the senses do not function. But when consciousness returns to the body, all the senses spring to life at once and begin functioning. Similarly, the Pāṇḍavas all stood up at once, enlivened to receive their Lord, Śrī Kṛṣṇa."

Among the popular metaphors Prabhupāda uses frequently is one comparing *bhakti* to a devotional seed. Only after we water this seed with chanting and hearing does it grow into a creeper that ultimately finds its way past the material world to the shelter of the lotus feet of Kṛṣṇa.

An easy metaphor for small children: Prabhupāda compares himself to a mailman who delivers the mail without opening it, meaning he delivers Kṛṣṇa's message in the *Bhagavad-gītā* without changing it. Prabhupāda also uses the sun as metaphor, like when he compares the different aspects of God's nature with the difference between the sun's rays and the sun itself.

For older children: King Kulaśekhara's prayers in the *Mukunda-mālā-stotra* are full of metaphors. In the eighth *sūtra,* the king prays to the Lord, "The desert of material existence has exhausted me. But today I will cast aside all troubles by diving into the lake of Lord Hari and drink freely of the abundant waters of His splendor. The lotuses in that lake are His hands and feet, and the fish are His brilliant shining eyes. That lake's water relieves all fatigue and is agitated by the waves His arms create. Its current flows deep beyond fathoming."

A common simile in the *Mukunda-mālā-stotra* compares the material world to the sea, and the Lord (or His lotus feet) to a boat that can rescue us. No matter how expert we are as swimmers, we cannot survive on our own in the rough expanse of the ocean. Even if our friends and family encourage us otherwise, trying to swim the ocean of material life on our own strength will lead only to failure. We must turn to the Lord to be saved.

Allegories

One of the most popular allegories given in *Śrīmad-Bhāgavatam* is the story of King Purañjana in Canto Four, explaining what transmigration of the soul really is and how one can find relief from the bodily conception of life. The great sage Nārada Muni compares King Prācīnabarhi's condition to that of King Purañjana, warning him of the perils of material life.

In the same chapter, Nārada Muni also uses the allegory of the deer to describe the conditioned soul's turmoil. Śrīla Prabhupāda elaborates in his purports (*Bhāgavatam* 4.29.53–54):

> Here is an allegory in which the King is advised to find a deer that is always in a dangerous position. Although threatened from all sides, the deer simply eats grass in a nice flower garden, unaware of the danger all around him. All living entities, especially human beings, think themselves very happy in the midst of families. As if living in a flower garden and hearing the sweet humming of bumblebees, everyone is centered around his wife, who is the beauty of family life. The bumblebees' humming may be compared to the talk of children. The human being, just like the deer, enjoys his family without knowing that before him is the factor of time, which is represented by the tiger ... Vedic literatures therefore advise that we should understand our constitutional position and take to devotional service before death comes.
>
> The deer in the flower garden is an allegory used by the great sage Nārada to point out to the King that the King himself is similarly entrapped by such surroundings. Actually everyone is surrounded by such a family life, which misleads one. The living

entity thus forgets that he has to return home, back to Godhead. He simply becomes entangled in family life.

The above allegories may be difficult for a small child to completely understand, but explaining their messages in a simple form helps, and as the child grows older his or her ability to appreciate allegories will grow.

Figurative Speech

There are many examples of figurative speech used in the *Bhagavad-gītā, Śrīmad-Bhāgavatam,* and *Śrī Caitanya-caritāmṛta,* providing us with great spiritual lessons. One popular example is the comparison of the body to a city with nine gates: "When the embodied living being controls his nature and mentally renounces all actions, he resides happily in the city of nine gates [the material body], neither working nor causing work to be done." (*Gītā* 5.13)

In his introduction to the ninth chapter of *Śrī Caitanya-caritāmṛta, Ādi-līlā,* Prabhupāda summarizes the figurative example of "the desire tree of *bhakti*":

> A summary of Chapter Nine has been given as follows by Śrīla Bhaktivinoda Ṭhākura in his *Amṛta-pravāha-bhāṣya.* In this chapter the author of *Śrī Caitanya-caritāmṛta* has devised a figurative example by describing "the desire tree of *bhakti.*" He considers Lord Caitanya Mahāprabhu, who is known as Viśvambhara, to be the gardener of this tree because He is the main personality who has taken charge of it. As the supreme enjoyer, He enjoyed the fruits Himself and distributed them as well. The seed of the tree was first sown in Navadvīpa, the birth site of Lord Caitanya Mahāprabhu, and then the tree was brought to Puruṣottama-kṣetra (Jagannātha Purī), and then to Vṛndāvana. The seed fructified first in Śrīla Mādhavendra Purī, and then in his disciple Śrī Īśvara Purī. It is figuratively

described that both the tree itself and the trunk of the tree are Śrī Caitanya Mahāprabhu. Paramānanda Purī and eight other great *sannyāsīs* are like the spreading roots of the tree. From the main trunk there extend two special branches, Advaita Prabhu and Śrī Nityānanda Prabhu, and from those branches grow other branches and twigs. The tree surrounds the entire world, and the fruits of the tree are to be distributed to everyone. In this way the tree of Lord Caitanya Mahāprabhu intoxicates the entire world. It should be noted that this is a figurative example meant to explain the mission of Lord Caitanya Mahāprabhu.

Teaching children through figurative stories is a lot of fun. We can even explain stories by drawing pictures and coloring different elements of the story for clearer understanding. Difficult concepts are made easy through creative renditions, which increase reasoning and analytical skills.

Studying History through Śrīmad-Bhāgavatam

While homeschooling my children through the scriptures I did not realize the effect such schooling would have on them until after they grew up and I saw them present the Kṛṣṇa conscious philosophy to others and practice it themselves. Needless to say, the study of *Śrīmad-Bhāgavatam* had a powerfully positive effect on them. Besides giving them spiritual benefit, character development, and strong faith, it also educated them in a variety of subject areas. In this chapter I will try to explain why it is good to study key subjects through the *Bhāgavatam* before "regular" books are introduced to children. Here, I will focus on history.

What Is Real Education?

Acquiring information is not the main challenge of our times. Far more important and difficult is to be able to ascertain the source of information, evaluate it critically, decide what is useful, and then present it with one's own realizations. A student who can do this is considered intelligent and educated. The study of *Śrīmad-Bhāgavatam* gives one such an education.

Śrīla Prabhupāda encouraged the study of history through the

Bhāgavatam. He said modern history can give details up to three thousand years ago, but the *Bhāgavatam* can give the history and culture of the entire planet for millions of years. How? Prabhupāda explains that the Vedic culture was once spread throughout the world. The ancient name of India was Bhārata, which referred to the entire planet. "India, the king or the emperor of Hastināpura, he was the emperor. Now, seven seas, seven islands, they are mentioned in the Vedic literature. Seven islands. So the emperor would be emperor of the whole earth, and there was everywhere the Vedic culture. Everywhere the Vedic culture was, more or less, principally in that part which is known as India. But in other parts also, the Vedic culture was there. And the Europeans, they belonged to the *kṣatriya* family, and the Americans also coming from them." (Lecture, December 16, 1973, Los Angeles)

Vedic culture is called *sanātana,* or eternal, and even today we can find ancient remnants of this culture. For example, Naimiṣāraṇya in northern India is at least five thousand years old. We know that because it was there that the *Bhāgavatam* discussion between Śaunaka Ṛṣi and thousands of sages took place. Thousands of pilgrims still visit Naimiṣāraṇya every year, and there are many other such ancient places in India.

Śrīla Prabhupāda says, "*Itihāsa* means history, and *purāṇāni, purāṇāni* means old *itihāsa*. All the statements or narrations described in *Śrīmad-Bhāgavatam,* they're all historical evidence, they're not imagination. Sometimes the so-called scholars and research students, they say it is fancy or something imagination. No. They're all history. It is said here, *itihāsam. Itihāsa* means history." (Lecture, August 23, 1971, London)

"*Śrīmad-Bhāgavatam amalaṁ purāṇam. Amalam:* spotless. This *purāṇam,* this old history of the world, this is also history. Just like this incident, Parīkṣit Mahārāja was cursed by a *brāhmaṇa,* he was the king, emperor of the world, and how he met his death – these things are described in this history, is it not? So this is also history. But it is not ordinary history, not history, chronological history, as we generally mean, but it is a history of the most important men in the world.

Just like Parīkṣit Mahārāja. He is the most important, at least one of the most important kings in the world. His history of death and life is historical fact." (Lecture, December 22, 1969, Boston)

The *Bhāgavatam* not only gives historical facts but also provides a thorough analysis of the lives of these great souls. Children develop good reasoning and critical thinking skills by studying these stories, which have deep spiritual values – unlike stories of leaders in recent history who were after power and worldly adoration. Materialistic leaders and soldiers are forgotten in the course of time; they make way for another era in history.

Understanding Parīkṣit Mahārāja's behavior and motives requires intelligence and analytical skill. His life raises deep questions that require deep answers. For example, was it proper for Parīkṣit Mahārāja to throw a snake around the sage's neck? And why did the king not reverse the curse even though he had the power to do so?

The *Bhāgavatam* contains historical narrations of the many saintly kings who ruled the planet in bygone ages. One such king is Yudhiṣṭhira Mahārāja. He had a flawless character, he never spoke lies, and he upheld religious principles. The people under his rule were satisfied, happy, and prosperous, and Mother Earth, out of gratitude for his pure rule, supplied his kingdom with abundant natural resources. The *Bhāgavatam* also describes the lives of Pṛthu Mahārāja, Kapila Muni, and Ṛṣabhadeva, all expansions of the Supreme Lord, whose teachings are the ultimate in spiritual knowledge. There are the stories of child saints such as Prahlāda Mahārāja, who never lost faith in Kṛṣṇa's protection despite all trials, and Dhruva Mahārāja, who saw the Lord face to face in only six months because of his unparalleled determination.

There is the history of Gajendra the elephant, who achieved the favor of Lord Viṣṇu because of his sincere prayers. These prayers came after an intense realization that his many family members and friends could not save him from the attack of the crocodile – he could only be saved by Kṛṣṇa. There is the story of Kapila Muni, who taught his mother *sāṅkhya* philosophy and thereby liberated her from the material world. In the pages of *Śrīmad-Bhāgavatam* we see that all these righteous kings and devotees, while they performed their duty as responsible leaders, had only one goal: to establish religious principles and promote God consciousness. That is the duty of every head of state and responsible person. On the other hand, *Śrīmad-Bhāgavatam* also gives us examples of kings who, because of greed and excessive power, failed to establish religious principles and were ultimately vanquished by Kṛṣṇa or His agents. In this way, we can learn from both the good and bad sides of history.

All these accounts are true histories of great personalities who lived in prior *yugas*. They are not fiction, mythology, or recent creations, as some modern scholars say, but the transcendental activities of Kṛṣṇa and His devotees meant to liberate the conditioned souls and take them back to the spiritual world. The author of the *Bhāgavatam,* Śrīla Vyāsadeva, is perfect, so the material is presented in a perfect way. Once our children have understood *Bhāgavatam* history they can go on to study secular history with the right perspective.

The study of history means finding the source of everything animate and inanimate. Even something inanimate like a microphone has a source, a history. Someone collected all the necessary ingredients and put them together in order to fulfill the object's purpose, namely, to magnify sound for large audiences. Similarly, the whole creation has a history – who created it, how it was created, and what purpose it serves. After understanding this, the most important thing is to use the creation for its intended purpose. That is real knowledge. For example, if we spend all our time trying to figure out how the microphone was created – tear it apart and study it – but never use it for its intended purpose, the endeavor is pointless.

Śrīla Prabhupāda says that modern historians are not interested in finding the ultimate source of everything; they are more interested in physical laws and how they act, and they see wonders in physical phenomena around them. They become so bewildered by this physical glamor that they usually forget it was created by the Lord.

Śrīmad-Bhāgavatam, on the other hand, teaches us that Kṛṣṇa is the source of the creation and the supreme controller of it. The purpose of this temporary material creation is to bring us to the point of surrender to God so we can go back to Godhead. *Śrīmad-Bhāgavatam* is the transcendental science by which we can know the origin of everything, our relationship with God, and our duty toward the betterment of human society.

We read in the purport to *Śrīmad-Bhāgavatam* 11.2.14, "This is the extraordinary power of *bhāgavata* history, as contrasted with useless, mundane historical accounts, which ultimately serve no purpose. Although mundane historians justify their work on the plea that we have to learn from history, we can practically see that the world situation is now rapidly deteriorating into unbearable conflict and chaos while so-called historians stand helplessly by. But the *bhāgavata* historians who have faithfully heard *Śrīmad-Bhāgavatam* can give perfect and potent instructions for the restoration of a peaceful and blissful world. Therefore those who are inclined to enrich their intellectual life through the study of history should educate themselves in the historical narrations of *Śrīmad-Bhāgavatam*. This will bring them the perfection of intellectual and spiritual life."

Teaching Children Philosophy

The philosophy of Kṛṣṇa consciousness is profound and wide-ranging, so parents sometimes wonder whether its tenets are too sophisticated for children to learn. Can we teach children about the soul, karma, and reincarnation in a way they can actually understand?

There are many examples in our scriptures of children who became pure devotees just by hearing transcendental knowledge. A good example is Prahlāda Mahārāja, who received transcendental knowledge while still in his mother's womb. Similarly, Dhruva Mahārāja saw Lord Nārāyaṇa face to face after receiving instructions from Nārada Muni. Knowledge about the soul is not dependent on material factors like intelligence, age, race, or gender. Very young children may not yet be able to understand the more complex aspects of the Kṛṣṇa conscious philosophy, but they can understand simple concepts, such as that a soul is present in every living body.

The Existence of the Soul

In one of our recent *Bhāgavatam* classes for children we discussed the difference between living and nonliving beings. Little Sarah said the difference between living beings and matter is that living beings move and nonliving matter does not, so I asked what makes a living entity move around. Five-year-old Mukunda said excitedly, "Bones!"

"Well," I said, "earthworms don't have bones."

Five-year-old Vrinda chimed in, "Legs!"

"Well, snakes don't have legs."

So we went through some other possible causes for life, with me playing devil's advocate. We went through other parts of the body – hair, eyes, hands, legs, stomach – and I asked them whether we were any one of these things. If we cut our hair and put it on the table, is that us? Of course not. Gradually the children began to grasp that there is something else that gives the body life: the energy from the soul.

The Vedic scriptures say that this cosmic manifestation is made up of twenty-four material elements. Using simplified Upaniṣadic reasoning with children, we can rule out the twenty-four material elements as the cause of life, starting with the five gross elements (earth, water, fire, air, and ether), the five working senses, the five knowledge-acquiring senses, and the three subtle elements (mind, intelligence, and ego). The soul is hiding within these wrappers, and one by one we can unravel them with a penetrating and intelligent mind.

Once we have rejected all other possible causes of life, we can understand that the twenty-fifth element, the soul, is the cause of life. This spiritual spark is subtler than an atom, proton, neutron, electron, or anything else we may discover now or in the future. Beyond the soul is the Supersoul, Kṛṣṇa, who is directing the soul's activities. Not a blade of grass moves without His permission. We are the sparks, and Kṛṣṇa is the great fire.

Only the spiritual touch can bring dead matter to life. To prove this to our children, we can take them into the kitchen and show them how a machine (such as a blender) cannot work unless someone presses the "on" button. We can also show them how unlikely it is that a blender can assemble itself or reproduce. Only a living being can do those things. So how can we say that life comes from matter? A skyscraper cannot give birth to other skyscrapers. Only the superior energy (Kṛṣṇa) can manipulate the inferior energy (matter). Within the mother's womb, the spirit soul assembles all the materials necessary to build its body, and that body then continues to grow throughout life because the soul is present.

After discussing the origin of life like this during our children's *Bhāgavatam* class, we all went outside, where we saw a little squirrel frolicking. How was that squirrel moving so enthusiastically? Yes, the soul is the symptom of life, they all agreed. There is a duck in the bushes that has been sitting on her eggs for the last couple of weeks. She hardly eats or sleeps; she seems to be meditating on her ducklings, yet to hatch. Every day the children watch her after class. I point to a rock lying nearby. Can rocks have babies? No. So what's the difference between the duck and the rock? The duck is spirit and the rock is dead matter. Life only comes from life.

Vegetarianism and Karma

After discussing the concept of the soul, I led the children naturally into a discussion on vegetarianism. It's easy to understand why we should not eat meat if we understand that each body is home to a soul. The children understood why they should not eat animals like the duck outside, which is so cute and will soon be followed around by even cuter hatchlings. Children are kind and gentle by nature and, if given knowledge and a choice, most would rather be vegetarians. Animals feel pain – children understand that. By teaching them about the soul, karma, and reincarnation, their natural softness develops into compassion for other living entities, especially animals.

The children and I discuss how the cow is our mother because she sacrifices her blood for us in the form of milk. After taking the last drop of milk from her body we should not kill and eat her. Kṛṣṇa gave Pūtanā the position of a mother in the spiritual world simply because she fed Him her breast milk (even as she tried to kill Him). We can explain to the children how from milk we make sweets like rasagullas, sandesh, gulab jamuns, rasmalai, sweet rice, and other things like butter and ghee. We can also explain how milk nourishes the brain and gives the body strength. The cow is a vegetarian animal in the mode of goodness and loved by Kṛṣṇa.

We also talk about karma – how we get a sinful reaction when we kill – which means one day we too will have to be killed. But plants and vegetables also have souls, they notice, so how can we eat anything? Kṛṣṇa says He likes to eat fruits and vegetables, so if we offer them to Him, He will take our sinful reactions for killing them away.

Reincarnation

After discussing the soul and karma, reincarnation is not a difficult concept to understand. I explained to the children that when we die the soul leaves the dead body and moves into a new body – the body of a baby – and life starts again. We can see how the four seasons come and go in cycles – spring, summer, autumn, winter – and then it is spring again. In the same way we are born, grow to adulthood, get old, die, and then are born again in a different womb.

After participating in the class, a four-year-old girl consoled her mother after the recent death of her grandfather, assuring her mother that he had simply moved to another body.

Teaching Science from the Vedic Perspective

Often older students, especially those who have not been home-schooled, have been exposed to the theories of atheistic science – the Big Bang or the idea that the chemical composition of the body's cells is the actual cause of life. Here is how I have discussed these theories with my sons and other homeschooled children.

The Big Bang Theory

If we look up in the night sky, full as it is of stars and planets, it's natural to wonder where the universe came from. One explanation from modern scientists is the Big Bang theory, which says that in the beginning, all matter was concentrated at a single point, which then exploded. The explosion transformed tiny particles into atoms, and then into stars, galaxies, planets, and finally, life. This explanation is now openly propounded in children's textbooks, on television shows, and in science magazines. It is a story that grabs the imagination of and seems more reasonable to many people than religious accounts of creation. But what is this theory trying to accomplish? It is propounded by people who are trying to explain the origin of the universe in a mechanistic way, without the presence of a personal God, a controller, an intelligent designer.

According to the Vedic scriptures the *mahat-tattva* (total material energy) comes alive with living entities (an explosion you may say) when Mahā-viṣṇu glances at it. Where is the evidence that matter acts without a catalyst? Śrīla Prabhupāda gives an example that's easy for children to understand: We can plant many vegetables in the earth, but unless the sunshine glances at them, they will not grow. It is not that the earth will automatically explode with vegetables. Another example he gives is that today, people blow up mountains by putting dynamite into them. The dynamite is placed and ignited by a person; it's not that the mountains explode on their own. Similiarly, when Mahā-viṣṇu glances at the material energy, the *mahat-tattva* explodes with living beings, and all the material elements come into existence.

Another way to explain this to a child is by pointing to the orderliness of creation. Everything in the world is ordered and systematic – the sun rises and sets exactly on schedule, the seasons come and go with regularity, the birds lay eggs during the right season, and so on. But if everything came about by an explosion, how could things be so orderly? Have we ever heard of things becoming orderly on their own? In fact, they are more prone to become disordered over time when left on their own – and then someone has to put them back in order. When firecrackers go off, or bombs detonate during war, the people scatter in fear and, in the case of bombs, buildings may collapse. Things that had been orderly become haphazard. Only a human being can bring order back by cleaning up the mess. Similarly, houses become messy and dusty over time, but do they clean themselves automatically? Can files organize themselves in a filing cabinet?

Prabhupāda asks where an explosion like the Big Bang really came from: "Explosion is going on, but behind all these explosions, all these transformations, is the Supreme Lord. That is here. And it is confirmed in the *Bhagavad-gītā* (9.10): *mayādhyakṣeṇa prakṛtiḥ sūyate sa-carācaram/ hetunānena kaunteya jagad viparivartate.* They do not see who is behind this explosion. That is their ignorance or poor fund of knowledge. We have got practical experience that no explosion takes place without the touch of a human being. Similarly, even there was explosion going on, but there is a touch of the Supreme Being." (Lecture, April 2, 1975, Māyāpur)

Prabhupāda gives another example of how sometimes there is an explosion when acids and alkalines mix. But this explosion does not take place spontaneously. That is, it only happens when a chemist mixes the acid and the alkaline in the laboratory. In terms of the universe, the chemist is the superior energy of Kṛṣṇa and the chemicals are His inferior energy, or matter. Thus the inferior energy can be produced by the superior energy but not vice versa. Similarly, only when Mahā-viṣṇu impregnates Mother Nature through His glance do all the living entities become active in the *mahat-tattva*.

The scriptures say that the spiritual and material worlds cannot be understood by a person who is not a devotee of the Lord. A nondevotee cannot understand the limits of his own planet, what to speak of the size of the universe, even if he were to travel for millions of years at the speed of mind: "But if there is question of mental speed, it is more speedier than the *vāyu* speed. We have got experience. Many thousand miles, by your mind, you can reach within a second. So with the mental speed, airplane, if you start today and go for many millions of years, still it will be not possible to find out wherefrom the explosion is coming. That's it." (Lecture, April 2, 1975, Māyāpur)

The Origin of the Earth

Modern scientists say that the earth was formed by gaseous substances like hydrogen condensing over time. But Kṛṣṇa explains that these gases (*vāyu*) come from a living source, Kṛṣṇa, and not from matter. Prabhupāda gives the example of a tree. The tree comes from a small seed, "but who gives the seed? That is answered in the *Bhagavad-gītā* (7.10): *bījaṁ māṁ sarva-bhūtānām* ... [Kṛṣṇa] gives the seeds, and He is life.... *Vāyu* is gas, is it not? ... And finer than the *vāyu* is the ether, the sky. Finer than the sky is the mind. Finer than the mind is the intelligence, and finer than the intelligence is the soul. So they do not know this. They capture only middle thing, *vāyu*. Wherefrom the *vāyu* came? Wherefrom the gas came?" (Lecture, December 3, 1973, Los Angeles)

Chemical Evolution

Modern scientists say life came from the chemical reactions in cells, so they plan to create life by themselves creating chemical reactions. But chemicals don't produce living beings; living beings produce chemicals.

Śrīla Prabhupāda consistently argued against any theory that based itself on chemical evolution: "Yes, that chemical evolution is part of life demonstration. That I have already explained. Just like the chemical, citric acid, coming from lemon tree, a life. It is coming. So all chemicals are being produced ... Just like in your body, in my body, there are so many chemicals. Because the body is there, the chemicals are coming. In my urine you will find so much, so many chemicals. In my stool you will find so many chemicals. Wherefrom the chemicals coming? Daily, enzymes, so many other chemicals are coming. Simply the medical man analyzes the urine, and so many chemicals are there. Wherefrom it came? Because I am living entity, the chemicals are coming in my urine, in my stool, in my cough, in my secretion. It is coming. Therefore it is concluded that chemicals are produced by life, not life is produced by chemicals." (Morning walk, December 3, 1973, Los Angeles)

Frankly, scientists cannot even create an ant, what to speak of a human being. By not giving credit to God, the scientists mislead the innocent public and uselessly spend billions of dollars trying to create things that aren't even beneficial to society.

Biological Evolution (Darwin's Theory)

Evolutionists say that life began with a few simple life forms like amoebas. The huge variety of species we see today came about because those early, one-celled creatures mutated and over time became new creatures. Sometimes the genes are not perfectly copied during reproduction, and the next generation can differ from its parents. Over long periods of time, Darwinians say, these small differences become big differences, and whole new species can develop. But in fact, the minute differences from one generation to the next never lead to a new species. There is a strict limit to how much a plant or animal can mutate. A pink rose bush may "accidentally" produce white roses because of a recessive gene or a mutation, but it will never produce lotus flowers no matter how long we wait. A man may accidentally be born with six fingers, but he will never be born with hooves. God's creation is perfect, Śrīla Prabhupāda says, and the laws of nature are inviolable. The different species all exist simultaneously, and the living entities take birth in one or another species according to their different desires and mentalities.

The Vedic view is the inverse of Darwin's evolution. According to *Śrīmad-Bhāgavatam* the great sages and demigods produce all the lower species of life. In other words, lower intelligence comes from higher intelligence. This is because the cause must always have within it the properties of the effect; otherwise, where does the effect get its qualities? Thus all the species are created in descending order, and the living beings accept the body most suited to their consciousness. As the consciousness of the living beings evolves, they move into higher and higher species of life. So the evolution of consciousness goes on according to our interactions with the modes of nature, which are under the Supreme Lord's control.

Śrīla Prabhupāda: "So they are thinking the rice is producing the scorpion. It is called *taṇḍula-vṛścika-nyāya*. But rice cannot produce a life. The real fact is a scorpion lays down the egg within the rice, and by the fermentation it comes out. Just eggs. And the small creature comes out. And foolish creatures, they think it that the rice is producing scorpion. That is not possible. So they are putting forward this evolution theory that man is coming from monkey, but no monkey is producing a man. Nobody has seen. There are so many things. They put forward some theory, but it is not fact." (Lecture, January 3, 1974, Los Angeles)

When the children are older and ready for more detailed explanations, we can teach them from books like *Forbidden Archeology: The Hidden History of the Human Race*, by Michael A. Cremo and Dr. Richard L. Thompson, *Mechanistic and Nonmechanistic Science: An Investigation into the Nature of Consciousness and Form*, by Dr. Richard L. Thompson, *Nature's IQ*, by Balazs Hornyanszky and Istvan Tasi, *Origins: Higher Dimensions in Science* (a BBT magazine containing articles by ISKCON science writers), as well as from Śrīla Prabhupāda's enlightening purports and conversations. All these sources provide arguments against modern atheistic theories and offer the Vaisnava conclusion.

Teaching children the science of the soul and how material creation takes place can be both challenging and rewarding. We can train our children to counter arguments from materialists who want to explain our origin without giving credit to God. In a language suitable to our children's understanding, we can play devil's advocate with them and establish the supremacy of Vedic philosophy. Prabhupāda's morning walk conversations are especially revealing, and as parents we can hear or read them so we can carefully guide our children in the right direction. Our own faith and understanding will increase tremendously during the process, and thus we can help our children understand that they are not products of matter but spiritual beings, servants of Kṛṣṇa.

How to Deal with Adult Topics in Śrīmad-Bhāgavatam

If children watch television or attend a school run by nondevotees, they will be frequently exposed to sex and violence. And we all know what such exposure can do to young, impressionable minds. But what about the sex and violence that appears in the pages of *śāstra*? Are these elements as detrimental as their materialistic counterparts? Actually, no. Whether or not we read the *Bhāgavatam* to them, all children will be exposed at one point to sex and violence. Most will ask questions about them. But through the *Bhāgavatam* they have an opportunity to learn a perspective different from the one they would learn elsewhere: that sex and violence, like all activity, is meant for a higher purpose.

Relations between Men and Women

Numerous verses and purports in the *Bhāgavatam* contain references to sex, but all of them aim at underlining the importance of engaging in sex only according to religious principles – to procreate God conscious children. There are many examples of people who produced exalted children through the proper use of sex. For example, progenitors like Dakṣa (*Bhāgavatam* 4.1.11) and Kaśyapa Muni (*Bhāgavatam* 6.6.24–26) produced thousands of children in order to populate the earth. The

Bhāgavatam does not view sex negatively; rather, it shows how to use it in Kṛṣṇa's service.

We also learn, in the *Bhāgavatam,* what happens when sex is used improperly, for sense gratification. The results are always detrimental, as we see in the story of Diti and the birth of her son, Hiraṇyakaśipu (*Bhāgavatam* 3.14). The story of Purañjana (*Bhāgavatam* 4.25–29) offers another good example of the warning the *Bhāgavatam* provides. Although the story describes lusty relations between a man and a woman, we also see the results of such behavior as we read the story. Purañjana and his beloved wife are both attacked by the soldiers of time (old age and death), and thus they encounter much material suffering. Nārada Muni narrates this story to King Prācīnabarhi in order to teach him the importance of living according to religious principles as a *gṛhastha.*

So the *Bhāgavatam* gives both: the glories of producing good progeny through proper sex as well as the perils of engaging in sex simply for sense enjoyment. With their parents' help, children will understand this message clearly. I read the entire *Bhāgavatam* with my children, including the Purañjana and Diti stories, and through this they learned important lessons about the nature of the world. Children will eventually pick up information about sex just by being in the world. Isn't it better that they learn of it first from the *Bhāgavatam* rather than through television or friends? Naturally, we as parents must set clear boundaries on such discussions based on what we feel is age appropriate for our children. My own children understood that *brahmacārīs* and *brahmacāriṇīs* do not discuss the details of sex, and thus they knew certain questions were off limits for them.

When children are young they need to understand one basic principle: even though everyone in the material world is bound by attraction to the opposite sex, if we can use this desire in Kṛṣṇa's service to raise a devotee family, this same attraction will help us make spiritual advancement.

When the *Bhāgavatam* describes the beautiful body of a woman, we can explain how a woman's body is naturally made to nurture a child.

Every woman should be seen as a mother, and thus her body should not be seen as an object of lust. With such education, children will learn to respect all women as mothers.

Although the *Bhāgavatam's* references to sense enjoyment can sometimes be a little awkward for parents, we should remember that the *Bhāgavatam* is transcendental and will always benefit our children. One day when our children are older we will be thankful they learned the proper place of sex in Kṛṣṇa's service. We are giving them a solid foundation to live a Kṛṣṇa conscious life, whether as *gṛhasthas* or *brahmacārīs.*

Violence in Śrīmad-Bhāgavatam

In the Seventh Canto of *Śrīmad-Bhāgavatam* we hear the story of Lord Nṛsiṁha killing Hiraṇyakaśipu by pulling out his intestines with His nails. The *Mahābhārata* contains scenes of intensive fighting between the Pāṇḍavas and the Kauravas, such as the ruthless killing of Abhimanyu, who fought alone against many experienced warriors. In the *Kṛṣṇa* book, Kṛṣṇa kills a number of demons and kills them in creative ways: He tears Bakāsura apart by the beak, He and Balarāma throw Dhenuka and his demon friends into palm trees, and He suffocates Aghāsura. Are such violent stories appropriate for our children to hear and read?

First, we should understand the difference between good and bad violence. Kṛṣṇa Himself declares in the *Bhagavad-gītā* (4.8) that He descends to protect the pious and annihilate the miscreants. When Kṛṣṇa or His devotees kill, they are using violence to root out a worse violence, just as one uses a thorn to remove another thorn. Śrīla Prabhupāda explains in his purport to *Śrīmad-Bhāgavatam* 3.21.50 that the potency to protect the pious and annihilate the miscreants is given by the Lord to the king for the purpose of protecting the citizens and punishing criminals.

Of course, the king or government must understand proper and improper uses of violence as well. Prabhupāda gives the example of Arjuna, who mistakenly believed at the beginning of the *Bhagavad-gītā* that all violence was adharmic and refused to fight. After Kṛṣṇa urged him, however, Arjuna followed Kṛṣṇa's orders and became a true follower of religious principles. Prabhupāda writes that we cannot manufacture our own religious principles through mental speculation. "The members of modern civilization manufacture defective religious principles through speculative concoction. This is not *dharma* ... *bhāgavata-dharma* comprises only that which is given by the Supreme Personality of Godhead. *Bhāgavata-dharma* is *sarva-dharmān parityajya/ mām ekaṁ śaraṇaṁ vraja*: one must accept the authority of the Supreme Personality of Godhead and surrender to Him and whatever He says. That is *dharma*." (*Bhāgavatam* 6.1.40, purport)

Thus in the *Mahābhārata* the Pāṇḍavas uphold religious principles and are empowered by the Lord to fight on the battlefield after all peace attempts fail. They aspire to follow proper codes of conduct during the battle, such as not attacking anyone who is unarmed, not hitting below the belt, and a number of other warrior ethics. Children who read stories from *Śrīmad-Bhāgavatam* with descriptions of violent scenes will understand that the Lord and His great devotees sometimes use violence to kill demons and protect the innocent.

By seeing the Lord act in this way, our children will understand the reality of material life, where it is impossible not to be a victim or perpetrator of violence in one form or another. In the material world, people commit violence toward others because their senses have not been satisfied and they feel frustrated or vengeful. Our children will understand that there are always negative consequences to such violence, and Kṛṣṇa Himself often appears to stop it and protect His devotees. In this way, our children feel safe and confident in the Lord's protection.

Śrīla Prabhupāda explains in a conversation, "The fighting here takes place because everyone wants to lord it over material nature. So there is a difference of interest. I want to be lord, you want to be lord: now we must fight. But in Vaikuṇṭha, the spiritual world, there is only one Lord and all others are servitors. Therefore there is peace." (Lecture, August 25, 1968, Montreal)

In many television shows, graphic video games, and movies there is no end to the gratuitous violence. On the other hand, whatever violence is described in the scriptures is taking place for a purpose, and once that purpose is fulfilled, the violence ends. Children who in the scriptures see violence being carefully and properly used will generally not express violence in their own lives. *Śrīmad-Bhāgavatam* is transcendental, so it can never have a negative effect.

When choosing devotional movies, however, parents should judge them on an individual basis to make sure they are well written and that the content is appropriate for their children.

Why Does the Lord Fight?

In the Seventh Canto of *Śrīmad-Bhāgavatam* we read how the Lord took the awesome form of a half-man, half-lion just to protect his child-devotee Prahlāda. This shows the great sacrifice the Lord is willing to make for His devotees. Śrīla Prabhupāda said, "Nonviolence and violence – everything is there in the Absolute Truth. Here we have got bad effects of violence, but when violence is performed by the Absolute, it has no bad effect, it has only good effect." (Lecture, August 25, 1968, Montreal) When Kṛṣṇa kills, He not only protects the devotee but liberates the demon as well. Hiraṇyakaśipu and all the demons Kṛṣṇa killed during his Vṛṇḍāvana pastimes achieved His mercy.

Furthermore, sometimes Kṛṣṇa has His devotees play the role of demons so He can enjoy chivalrous pastimes. Śrīla Prabhupāda explains: "Just like we sometimes see mock fighting, because that fighting spirit is there. The father and son, the little son is fighting with the father. That is not fighting, but only a mock fight. But the fighting spirit is there. You cannot deny it. Similarly, the fighting spirit is sometimes exhibited by the Supreme Personality of Godhead. If He wants to exhibit such fighting spirit, who will fight with Him? Ordinary living beings cannot fight with the Supreme Lord. Therefore some of His devotees, some of His associates, must fight with Him." (Lecture, August 25, 1968, Montreal) Of course, while fulfilling His desire to fight Kṛṣṇa is also establishing *dharma* on earth and giving pleasure to His devotees, who appreciate His chivalrous qualities.

A Student's Perspective on Adult Topics in Śrīmad-Bhāgavatam

Rādhikā Ramaṇa shares his thoughts

Recently I was at the Radhadesh temple in Belgium, where I was asked to give the morning *Bhāgavatam* class. The devotees were reading the story of Mahārāja Purañjana, and the particular purport I was assigned was a description of women's breasts. Prabhupāda explains in great detail the kind of attraction breasts have for men. I could see the devotees were a little uncomfortable, as is natural given the topic, so I started off by telling my own experience of how, when I was about ten years old, I studied this same section of the *Bhāgavatam* with my mother. It was a little uncomfortable, a little odd, but I remember the conviction my mother had that if it's in *Śrīmad-Bhāgavatam,* it's pure and good for everyone.

No one grows up innocent today. If we don't hear about sex from *Śrīmad-Bhāgavatam* we'll hear it somewhere else; and if we hear it somewhere else we can be sure it will be from the perspective of sense gratification – how to enjoy the body of a man, how to enjoy the body of a woman, and how to exploit the other for sense gratification. You can find this in any media you encounter today. It's the nature of the world, the nature of Kali-yuga. It was so much nicer that I was exposed to these topics through *Śrīmad-Bhāgavatam* rather than anywhere else.

The same goes for violence. Sometimes parents are worried that there is too much violence described in the scriptures – killing and fighting – and that their children reenact the scenes. Some parents may feel that this is just as much a problem as the violence children are exposed to in movies and video games. But there's a big difference between the two, because there are different kinds of violence. Śrīla Prabhupāda says violence itself is never good, but sometimes violence is necessary when all good argument and reason fail. Everyone admits there are times when violence is necessary – Kṛṣṇa showed this at the Battle of Kurukṣetra, described in the *Mahābhārata,* when He asks Arjuna to fight.

What children learn from studying *Śrīmad-Bhāgavatam,* though, is that when a situation calls for violence, we don't have to take the lead and commit it ourselves. Rather, Kṛṣṇa will take care of things. Kṛṣṇa is the supreme controller, and He's always there to protect His devotees. This becomes a point that settles in deeply: I don't have to worry, Kṛṣṇa is my protector. In Vṛndāvana, only Kṛṣṇa and Balarāma kill demons – no one else does it. Nanda Mahārāja, Mother Yaśodā, the cowherd boys – they never have to do anything. Kṛṣṇa is always there to protect them.

There's plenty of violence in *Śrīmad-Bhāgavatam* – sometimes gruesome violence. Sections of the Paraśurāma story describe rivers of blood, with heads and hands floating in that river. This somehow satisfies the side of human psychology that wants to have some battle and warfare and something "heavy." But everything in the *Bhāgavatam* is put into perspective. Kṛṣṇa is the protector. Kṛṣṇa does these things so we don't have to do them. Kṛṣṇa will take care of everything.

In this way violence is placed in its proper perspective, rather than the gratuitous violence we find in films. Movies are filled with unlimited amounts of killing. Why? It's just killing for the sake of killing. "Boom, boom, boom" – bombs and guns and who's dying and why no one even knows or cares. The killing just goes on and on, whereas in the *Mahābhārata* or *Rāmāyaṇa* there's a purpose behind the violence. Devotees of the Lord serve the Lord in a particular way, with the goal of reestablishing *dharma*.

These subjects can sometimes be difficult, but we should have faith that *Śrīmad-Bhāgavatam* will always be of benefit, because it will always put things in the right way. It's so much nicer to learn about the world through the eyes of *śāstra* than to encounter it elsewhere – but we can be sure that we *will* encounter it at some point or another.

The Five Rs: Reading

Children usually begin their formal education when they are five years old. For most of us, until we came under Śrīla Prabhupāda's shelter, educating our children meant finding reputable schools with good academics. Good academic study meant good jobs, sufficient money, and a comfortable family life. Prabhupāda changed our way of thinking about education. Instead, he has challenged us to think deeply about what real education is. He writes, "Education means *bhāgavata* education: to understand God. That is wanted: *athāto brahma-jijñāsā*. Education should be given in such a way that the student should be very, very inquisitive. Inquisitive about what? Inquisitive about Brahman, not about this body." (Lecture, September 15, 1976, Vṛndāvana)

Therefore the education the *Vedas* glorify and recommend evokes a child's natural curiosity about the Supreme Absolute Truth. Why is such education better than what most of us received? Just as children need to learn reading and math to get along in the world, they also need to learn of their spiritual identity, the purpose of life, and how to get out of this material world. Children who understand they are spirit souls, meant to serve the Supreme Lord, will not waste their human life but will instead help others find life's real meaning.

Keeping Prabhupāda's instructions close to heart, we can educate our children in a way that incorporates both academic and spiritual training. This is what I tried to do in my homeschooling. During the early years, we focused on what I called "the five Rs":

Reading
w**R**iting
a**R**ithmetic
Raga (music)
Rote (memorization)

If children master these five Rs in their early years they will be prepared to study any subject in the future. In this chapter we discuss the first R, reading.

Learning to Read

Children between the ages of three and five can learn to read. In our Boise community we have several families who are homeschooling their children, who are between the ages of three and seven. Once a week they get together as a group to teach their children to read.

The two oldest, Sarah (seven) and Angela (five), can read Prabhupāda's books fluently, so they come with their mother to help the younger children learn to read. Collectively the children review the sounds for each letter of the alphabet. Then they break up into pairs, depending on their age and proficiency level, and a mother is assigned to work with each pair. She guides, corrects, reviews, and teaches new sounds. The atmosphere is joyful and the children enthusiastic to learn. Engaging the older children in teaching the younger ones is beneficial for both. The subject is reinforced for the older children, and the younger children are inspired to learn better.

There are many Kṛṣṇa conscious books available at www.krishna.com, www.krishnaculture.com, blservices.com, and other such sites that are good beginning readers. Starting from the age of six, children can try to read books like Śrīla Prabhupāda's *Kṛṣṇa* book, *Bhagavad-gītā As It Is, Śrīmad-Bhāgavatam,* and *Śrī Caitanya-caritāmṛta*. They may not understand the finer points and will likely stumble over a number of the words and phrases, but with a parent's help they will gradually overcome these hurdles and be blessed both spiritually and academically. There are other books written by senior devotees that also provide good reading resources – *Śrīla Prabhupāda-līlāmṛta,* by Satsvarūpa dāsa Goswami, for example, or *The Six Goswamis of Vrindavan* and *Vaishnava Saints,* by Satyarāja Dāsa, *Diary of a Traveling Preacher,* by Indradyumna Swami, and others. These are also valuable for reading during festivals and special study units.

Aside from teaching children to read, it's important to read *to* children, because it increases their comprehension and vocabulary. I read regularly to my sons before they went to bed. Our favorite book was *Śrīla Prabhupāda-līlāmṛta,* and they would be so absorbed in hearing it that they did not want me to stop reading. We loved this time together discussing Śrīla Prabhupāda's transcendental pastimes – his staunch faith, his struggles in India and the West, and his ultimate success in spreading the mission of Lord Caitanya to all corners of the world. An eleven-year-old homeschooled boy named Govinda from Maryland regularly listens to lectures by His Holiness Radhanātha Swami. As a result, his understanding of Kṛṣṇa conscious philosophy is so deep that he can give classes on the *Bhagavad-gītā* and has won several philosophy essay contests.

Prabhupāda wanted children in the *gurukulas* to study his books deeply. With the knowledge they gain, he said, they would be able to find solutions to all kinds of problems and become good citizens, even leaders, of society. One who does not know the purpose of life cannot help anyone, not even him or herself. Therefore in Vedic society all the great leaders were also great devotees and holy sages and able to properly guide others in life's mission.

Prabhupāda was confident that his books were complete and could award all material and spiritual benedictions, but he warned that unless his books were taught to children in an atmosphere of love and trust they would have little effect: "Let them be able to read our books very nicely, and that will be their higher education. Keep them always happy in Kṛṣṇa consciousness, and do not try to force or punish or they will get the wrong idea. By and by, if they are satisfied in this way, they will all grow up to be first-class preachers and devotees." (Letter to Satsvarūpa Dāsa, February 16, 1972)

Discussion is an important part of reading. It breaks up the monotony of reading for children, and can add both interest and challenge. By using Śrīla Prabhupāda's books as our basic texts, children learn all aspects of the language arts: composition, comprehension, and vocabulary as well as critical and analytical thinking and reasoning. Parents can present their own realizations to instill finer philosophical points in a way their children can understand.

By giving children an opportunity to express themselves and clear any doubts or questions they may have about what they're reading, they will also gain self-confidence and learn communication skills. Parents can establish the supremacy of the Vedic literature by playing devil's advocate or bringing the issues being discussed into the practical sphere. Reading and discussion lead to good speaking, debate, and logical thinking.

And Prabhupāda said that reading his books is a pure devotional activity: one can become a pure devotee simply by reading the scriptures. The heroes in the scriptures have impeccable character and qualities, and these virtues will rub off on readers – and that's especially true of young readers.

The Five Rs: wRiting

Śrīla Prabhupāda encouraged all his followers to write. He said that writing is like chanting (*kīrtanam*) because it allows us to repeat what we have had learned from scripture. Writing is also preaching, because it encourages others to take to Kṛṣṇa consciousness. "And our men, all our men should write. Otherwise how we shall know that he has understood the philosophy? Writing means *śravaṇaṁ kīrtanam. Śravaṇam* means hearing from the authority and again repeat it." (Lecture, June 20, 1975, Los Angeles)

Śrīla Prabhupāda said that anyone who has heard attentively about Kṛṣṇa will be able to write. A person may not have a scholarly background, but his books will be accepted because they are based on authoritative sources. In contrast, he said, writing by scholarly nondevotees is of no value but is only a jugglery of words. "Just like these children. We have got so many children, devotees here. It is not possible that they are understanding the subtle philosophical statements of *Bhagavad-gītā*, but because they are sitting and hearing, they are writing. You see? But whatever he writes, it is right." (Lecture, March 12, 1970, Los Angeles)

These statements by Śrīla Prabhupāda should give us an incentive to teach our children to write well. Writing follows reading naturally because it's normal to want to express what we've read in our own words. Writing helps children develop in all areas of the language arts, especially in vocabulary, comprehension, spelling, and logical thinking. When children are about nine or ten we can teach them to write by using Śrīla Prabhupāda's books. They can compose essays on what they have read, comment on current events through the eyes of *śāstra,* or give answers to thought-provoking questions we assign them. Through these exercises they learn the different stages of writing, such as planning, drafting, revising, and editing. A few years later they are able to do research and understand the meaning of allegories, figurative language, and contradictions. They should be able to think critically, form their own understandings, and then express them coherently.

We can try different ways to encourage our children to write on Kṛṣṇa conscious subjects. Here are some of the things I did with my children.

Writing on Bhagavad-gītā

During my homeschooling, I heard that Sureśvara Prabhu was teaching a Bhakti Śāstrī correspondence course for adults, so I wrote to him and asked if he would kindly teach Rādhikā Ramaṇa. He agreed, and we signed up for the class. Sureśvara sent questions written for an eleven-year-old, and after my son answered them Sureśvara Prabhu would correct them and send them back with comments, grades, and lots of encouragement. Besides the usual questions, he would also send challenging ones that required application of Kṛṣṇa's teachings to real-life situations. I remember one in particular that was based on chapter 2, verses 62–63: "Complete this scenario: A teetotaler enters a bar with his friends ..." Rādhikā Ramaṇa wrote a two-page story about a man who was trying to practice spiritual life but who succumbed to temptation with his old friends. The man went through the stages of falldown Krsna describes in *Bhagavad-gītā,* but then picked himself up again through good association.

Writing for Back to Godhead or a Local Newspaper

My son was inspired to write and gained a lot of confidence through the

Gītā course. Eventually, Sureśvara Prabhu suggested Rādhikā Ramaṇa write for *Back to Godhead* magazine. Of course, this was a challenge in the beginning – the editors would send back his articles asking for substantial revisions. Writing for BTG was a big step and brought out a new dimension to our homeschooling, and it made me begin looking for additional opportunities for him to publish. The local newspaper in Boise had a weekly religion column in which proponents of different faiths could present their philosophy and their views on current topics. They accepted Rādhikā Ramaṇa to represent "the Hare Kṛṣṇa faith." He wrote that column bimonthly for four years – until he left Boise for graduate school. This was a wonderful opportunity to reach people who would otherwise not be interested. The articles were well liked; he would get appreciative letters from readers and encouragement from his professors at the university.

Writing Plays

While my older son was busy with assignments for BTG and the local newspaper, my younger son, Gopal, was writing in other ways. His writing style is direct, upbeat, and engaging, and he liked to write scripts for the plays we hosted at the temple. We focused on children's plays because we discovered that they provided an easy way to preach Kṛṣṇa consciousness to parents. Seeing their own children joyful at play practice often rekindled the adults' desire to serve in the temple and participate more in temple programs. Writing plays is hard work for a child, but it's also an effective way to learn language. For Gopal, it involved reading a story from the scriptures, summarizing and writing it out as a dialogue, and editing for grammar and flow. He did not mind the hard work because he loved acting and directing plays with his friends. It was a lot of fun for everyone.

My children also wrote essays about upcoming festivals, the appearance or disappearance days of our *ācāryas,* and visits to the holy *dhāma* or national parks for vacation. In the early years I encouraged them to write a few sentences on birthday and invitation cards to friends. The children of a homeschooled family in Boise write letters daily to Lord

Jagannātha, Lord Baladeva, and Lady Subhadrā after *snāna-yātrā,* while they are sick, asking them to get well soon and bestow their mercy.

An important point to remember is that writing is not something most children do spontaneously or even willingly, so we have to make it fun for them. The trick is to ask them to write about things they want to write about! Writing plays was fun for my son because he would actually see his work performed.

Publishing a Newsletter

Another task that belonged primarily to Gopal was publishing a temple newsletter. Every month he had to write a couple of articles for the newsletter, giving the latest temple news and a list of upcoming events. He also wrote a children's corner, for which he created crossword puzzles and other Kṛṣṇa conscious games. He learned responsibility, how to meet deadlines, and received hands-on experience with editing, publishing, copying, and mailing.

Writing for Kṛṣṇa can be a wonderful and satisfying service, and we should help our children see it that way.

The Five Rs: aRithmetic

Needless to say, arithmetic or mathematics is essential for children at all levels of schooling. Mathematics is a basic life skill, and it's key to all the sciences, including physics, chemistry, engineering, and computer science.

There are a number of excellent math textbooks that work well in a homeschool setting. I used the Saxon Math series, which covers everything from basic arithmetic to calculus. The Saxon textbooks provide detailed explanations of math concepts, formulas, and techniques, and they are easy for children to read and understand on their own. There are also several other good math series available, such as Bob Jones and Abeka.

Parents often worry they will not have the necessary skill to teach their children mathematics past the elementary or middle school level. We can all teach math at an elementary level, which is the stage at which children need the most explanation and guidance. Once they grow older, they will be able to largely teach themselves by reading the explanations and doing the practice exercises. Also, if one of the parents is better at mathematics than the other, he or she can always help with math and science while the other parent takes care of the other Rs.

The Five Rs: Rāga (Music)

Children have a natural desire to sing and play musical instruments. If we don't direct them toward Kṛṣṇa conscious music, then later in life they will experiment with other kinds of music, meant for sense gratification. Śrīla Prabhupāda taught us that art, music, dance, and all other human talents should glorify the Supreme Lord. In one lecture he said, "Now, here, the *bhakti-yoga* system is that if you stick to the hearing of Hare Krsna and the music, melodious music of *khol, karatāla,* then naturally you become detestful for hearing other songs. So this is practically *indriya-saṁyama,* control of the mind and senses." (Lecture, August 24, 1968, Montreal)

Music provides a wonderful way for children to express their creativity, and it is something they will value throughout their lives. Right from the beginning of a child's life we can introduce the chanting of the Hare Kṛṣṇa mantra and have devotional music playing in the house. This will not only create a wonderful atmosphere but will also make the child musically inclined. In the early years, we can hand our children simple instruments like clackers, tambourines, triangles, cymbals, and small drums – instruments that don't require complex training to sound good. We can encourage them to gradually play on beat by taking their hands in ours and showing them how others are playing. Prabhupāda encouraged his disciples to use these simple instruments

Rādhikā Priya (age 7) plays the harmonium at her home in Knoxville, Tennessee, USA.

in the early days before they knew how to play *mṛdaṅga* and harmonium. He taught them the "1-2-3" beat, and the "swami step."

With my children, for the first five years we clapped and used these simple instruments. I have little musical ability, so after they turned six I took them to a piano teacher, since we had no harmonium teacher in Boise. They learned piano for about three years. Then Gaṇapati Swami, who visits Boise regularly, suggested the children learn to play the harmonium by ear by putting on a chanting tape and finding the notes on the harmonium. It actually worked, and gradually they improved and were able to play more complicated tunes by ear. Because he was two years younger, Gopal did not have much piano training, but he did well playing the harmonium. Parents can try either way or both. Some amount of training in piano is beneficial, because students learn to read music and some musical theory like chords, scales, and rhythm, which are common to all instruments. Children need a lot of encouragement when they practice, and we should try to make music lessons both fun and challenging enough that our children feel they want to progress.

I remember that some of the most enjoyable times in our homeschooling were when we played music together – chanting and playing musical instruments. My boys learned to play *karatālas* by practicing during *kīrtanas,* and *mṛdaṅga* from a *mṛdaṅga* guidebook available from the BBT. When traveling devotees came through Boise, the boys would learn new beats from them and practice them during *kīrtana.*

A Student's Perspective on Music

Rādhikā Ramaṇa shares his thoughts on the importance of music in a balanced life

A few years ago I visited a young devotee family in Europe. Both husband and wife are well educated and learned in Sanskrit. They have two young children, and of course they were trying their best to incline their children toward the *śāstras* and teach them what they needed to know to excel academically. But that was it – there was no musical or other creative side of life in the family. So when I visited I encouraged them to teach their children harmonium or *mṛdaṅga* or some other form of artistic expression so they could grow up well rounded.

Too often nowadays we get so busy in academic studies that we feel any distraction is a waste of time. If I spend an hour singing or playing *kīrtana,* that's an hour lost from studying. The pressure for us to accomplish can be intense, but we should keep in mind that the creative side of life is as important as the academic side.

My remarks encouraged this father, so he taught himself to play the harmonium just so he could teach his children. The next time I visited, he said his house – his whole family – had changed. They felt completely transformed, because the children loved their evening time together for *kīrtana*. One of the children had found a special calling in playing harmonium, and the father was learning to play *mṛdaṅga* so he could add it to the children's repertoire. He had discovered a completely different side of his personality, what to speak of trying to share it with his children.

Having a creative outlet like music is especially important in the twenty-first century, because no matter how good our lives are, there are always times when we become overwhelmed by the pressure of daily living, whether we are out in the workforce or still in school. At those times, if we have some means of tapping into this other aspect of the brain and expressing ourselves creatively, it can be a great relief. Our minds are always spinning with plans and ideas, but sometimes we need to turn off the head and work from the heart. We all need to have a space where we can go, an area of life where we say, "This is not about what I think; this is just my expression of devotion to the Lord." People do this in different ways – some by painting, some by sitting and practicing *mṛdaṅga*, some by picking out a new melody on the harmonium, and some just by sitting and singing *kīrtana*. We all need some of that in our lives.

Part of the reason why the whole world is dying of stress nowadays is because we've made everything so one-sided. If an activity doesn't have quantifiable results it's considered useless. What did you accomplish in the last hour? If you can't quantify your productivity, then whatever you did was a waste of time! Number of textbook pages read, marks scored on an examination, research completed, lines of code written – once everything in life becomes quantifiable we have a surefire recipe for stress.

Seventy-five or eighty percent of workers in the United States say that at some point in life they'll seek professional help to deal with their stress, and in India those statistics can't be far behind. The more educated and affluent we become, the worse the problem gets. Students at the top universities are practically dying of stress – even children who are ten years too young for university are dying of stress because of the academic coaching and hard work and the pushing, pushing, pushing in their lives – especially when their parents know that just a minor improvement in marks might mean the difference between admission and being left out.

In stressful situations like these, music or another creative outlet becomes all the more essential for a well-rounded person.

The Five Rs: Rote Memorization

Rote learning means memorizing material by repeating it. In the West especially, rote memorization has a bad reputation among educators because it doesn't guarantee that a child has comprehended the material. Obviously, we want our homeschooled children to actually understand what they learn. We don't want parrots. But there are a number of things that need to be memorized because it is useful and beneficial to have immediate access to them. Rote memorization can be an effective technique for such facts.

Examples include multiplication tables, phonics rules, basic formulas in physics, and the periodic table in chemistry. Notice that several of these subjects are considered "advanced," but even advanced topics include facts that have to somehow be memorized.

Another important area for memorization is verses from the *Bhagavad-gītā* and *Śrīmad-Bhāgavatam*. By learning these verses early, our children will have lifelong access to them, both for preaching Kṛṣṇa consciousness and for personal application. Reciting verses is a wonderful way to remember Kṛṣṇa as we go about our daily work, and Śrīla Prabhupāda would do it often. We can help our children repeat, memorize, and understand the *ślokas* and their word meanings. They can also write the verse for the day on flashcards so that reviewing it later is fun and easy. They can make a project to learn one verse a week (or day!) until they learn an entire chapter of *Bhagavad-gītā*. One homeschooled boy in Boise did this as a summer project and then recited 108 *Bhagavad-gītā* verses at a special event in the temple.

Rote learning is an important part of homeschooling. There were no books in ancient Vedic education. Children were educated by hearing from the guru. Therefore the Vedic literature is known as *śruti*, "that which is heard." Memorization makes the mind strong and sharp. Children can quickly memorize practically anything, and even as adults they will never forget the verses or other facts they learned when they were small. Learning verses especially is a lot of fun for children, especially if we give them opportunities to use and recite them.

A Student's Perspective on Rote Memorization

Rādhikā Rāmaṇa shares his thoughts on the most important things to memorize and the best way to learn them

Rote memorization is not unfamiliar to those who are educated in India, even though it is more or less absent from Western education. It used to be that rote memorization was an important part of any curriculum – students had to memorize their multiplication tables up to twelve times twelve, and then the schools reduced it to ten times ten, and now some American schools are only teaching up to eight times eight. Why do kids need to memorize multiplication tables, anyway? Isn't that what pocket calculators are for? Besides, the teachers don't want the kids to just be able to multiply. The new educational paradigm demands that students actually understand mathematics, and everyone knows that understanding doesn't come from memorization of a bunch of unrelated facts.

Brain Exercise

Rote learning as a technique has been devalued because of the emphasis on critical thinking, creativity, and problem solving (all of which are important), but memorization is still valuable. I had a professor of medieval music who was particularly upset whenever anyone called his time period "the Dark Ages." He insisted that people living during the medieval times had four hundred times the memory of the average person today – not because they had bigger brains or any physical advantage but because they used their memories a lot more. Most people were illiterate, and everything they knew had to be carried in their heads. Even if a person knew how to read and write, paper was expensive and hard to find, so no one would waste a folio writing down anything that didn't need to be recorded.

The printing press hadn't been invented yet, so people didn't have vast libraries of reference books they could look things up in – the ordinary way to know a fact was to memorize it, and because of this the memory would seem to expand. There's no known limit to the size of the human memory. Sometimes we say our brains are full – we need to empty something out before we can put something else in. But the brain isn't like an attic. Our brains might grow tired, but they're never full.

Nowadays, of course, our brains are tired because we don't use them much. Don't even mention writing and paper – today we all have computers and Blackberries and G3 connections to the Internet, and none of us need to remember anything.

Neglecting to exercise the brain creates a weak mind, because memory is regarded as the primary characteristic of a sharp intelligence. If we don't use it, we'll lose it.

Developing the memory is particularly important for children, because when they are older the brain will tend to retain whatever power it has developed in young childhood. We have the advantage here, because we can exercise our memories by learning verses from scripture. Śrīla Prabhupāda was especially happy when children (or adults, for that matter) memorized Sanskrit verses from the *Bhagavad-gītā* or *Śrīmad-Bhāgavatam*. And as much as we adults might have to struggle with such things, it's easy for children to memorize verses. At a certain age it seems as though children need only focus on a particular verse for a few minutes, maybe read it through three times, and they memorize it just like that. That's how good the memory is when you're young.

Memories That Never Leave Us

Besides, whatever a person learns in childhood is never forgotten. I've been learning verses throughout my education, but the verses I learned in the first few years, when I was about six, I've never forgotten. At that age I had this elaborate project of wanting to memorize all seven hundred verses of the *Bhagavad-gītā* – I never completed it, but we started on it. My brother and I memorized verses from the first and second chapters, and I cannot forget them. There might be a verse from chapter 9 or chapter 12 that I have to think about to recall, but those verses I memorized from the second chapter are so deeply imprinted that I never have any difficulty reciting them.

The hope is that once we have things like those imprinted on our memories at an early age, they'll be so deeply ingrained that when we really need them they'll come back immediately. It doesn't matter whether we're preaching in a class or facing danger and wanting to remember Kṛṣṇa – those early memories will pop up without significant effort on our part.

This is true even of ordinary memories. All of us have had the experience of going about our daily lives and suddenly flashing back to a movie scene or suddenly remembering the words of a film song. If we were asked to write down everything we knew, we wouldn't include these things on the list, but something triggers the memory and there they are. We may not even remember the name of the film, but the scene is as vivid as the first time we saw it. What happens, then, if at the time of death, we're desperately trying to meditate on Kṛṣṇa's lotus feet and suddenly we're staring at Amitabh Bachchan or some famous Hollywood star in our mind's eye?

Instead, suppose that we fill our children's memories with Kṛṣṇa conscious images. No matter what happens – even if they grow up and become nondevotees, giving up their Kṛṣṇa conscious lifestyle – those memories are still there. Just as you can never lose a film song, so you can never lose Kṛṣṇa once He's in your mind. He's even deeper than any film song.

There are so many stories proving this point. I once heard of a

Westerner who happened to see one of our big city Ratha-yātrā parades. This fellow was in a car accident and had a near-death experience. Immediately after getting out of the hospital he went to his local Hare Kṛṣṇa temple and told the devotees that when his life flashed before his eyes the only thing he could see was the face of Lord Jagannātha – especially His big, beautiful eyes. He was not a devotee, and it had been years since he had attended the Ratha-yātrā, but he had been there and had looked at Lord Jagannātha, wondering who He was. He didn't know it at the time but his brain and heart had formed an impression, and when he was near death he again saw Lord Jagannātha's face.

Rote memorization can be a complete waste of time, just as so many Western educators claim, but it can also be most valuable if it is applied properly. Our *śāstras* are not ordinary sound vibration; they are spiritual sound vibration. We know the impression that film songs leave on our minds – just imagine how much deeper the impression of spiritual sound vibration must go, penetrating to the soul. Once these spiritual sounds are embedded in the soul, in the mind, in the heart, they never leave us, and they become one of the hooks that Kṛṣṇa uses to pull us back.

Techniques for Memorizing Sanskrit Verses

Learning verses by heart can be a lot of fun. My mother used to make a game out of memorizing verses. We would set goals for ourselves: "I want to memorize this many verses in this many days." We were children, of course, ambitious and excited, so most of the time we fell short, but the goals were motivating and helpful.

A group of children can work together on a "memorization marathon," perhaps over the summer or when they have extra time, and at the end of the learning they can hold a little event where everyone comes together and listens to them recite their verses. A devotee child in Boise memorized 108 verses from the *Bhagavad-gītā* over a summer, and his parents put on a program at the temple. They made photocopies of all the verses with the translations so the congregation could follow along as he recited, and everyone enjoyed the event. He felt happy and confident, and had a small opportunity to demonstrate his accomplishments. The event even garnered newspaper coverage in the US and India for his feat at such a young age.

One time I decided that I wanted to memorize the verses of the *Mukunda-mālā-stotra,* those beautiful prayers of King Kulaśekhara. Prabhupāda was fond of this book, so I decided I would memorize one verse every other day. My system was to write the verse on a flashcard and tape it to my bedroom door. The rule I set for myself was that I couldn't enter the room without reciting the verse, so every time I went into my room I had to stop for a minute and practice the verse from memory. However many times I had to go into my room, that many times I reviewed the verse. I learned many wonderful verses as a result.

Rote memorization doesn't deserve its negative reputation so long as it's used appropriately. There are many creative ways to make memorization fun – perhaps adding in a little transcendental competition or otherwise making it into a game. In this way, learning verses – the same task that for adults can be boring and difficult – is easy and fun for children, because for them memorization is the easiest thing in the world. It doesn't take much work at all.

Sanskrit

Śrīla Prabhupāda wanted devotee children to learn both English and Sanskrit so they could study his books deeply: "Our students specifically, they should take care of reading *Śrīmad-Bhāgavatam*. We have therefore prescribed in our school that let them simply learn Sanskrit and English, because English translation they will be able to read, and the Sanskrit verses are there. And from the very beginning, if they begin education with the *Bhagavad-gītā* and then come to *Śrīmad-Bhāgavatam* and read the whole literature, then they will be more than MA, PhD. More than. The knowledge will be so advanced." (Lecture, July 12, 1974, Los Angeles)

Śrīla Prabhupāda did not want the children to study Sanskrit simply to become grammarians or scholars. Rather, he wanted them to learn Sanskrit and English so they could read his books and teach them to others. "Our aim is not how to make the students a big grammarian. No. That is not our purpose. How to make him fully Krsna conscious. That is the aim of this *gurukula*." (Lecture, March 31, 1976, Vṛndāvana) He asked that every Sanskrit class begin and end with *kīrtana*.

Often when adult devotees approached Śrīla Prabhupāda with a desire to learn Sanskrit, he engaged them instead in preaching. He cautioned them that a little knowledge is a dangerous thing – we can become proud and lose our focus on devotional service. To learn

Sanskrit properly, one has to study grammar diligently for at least twelve years.

But Śrīla Prabhupāda encouraged Sanskrit as a subject in the *gurukula* since children can be properly trained in the language from an early age. In this way they can understand the meaning of the scriptures more deeply and use that knowledge to practice and preach Kṛṣṇa consciousness. Prabhupāda said when we study the Sanskrit verses, we'll find a treasure house of meaning in each word.

Lord Caitanya set a good example of how to study Sanskrit when He opened His grammar school in Navadvīpa at the age of sixteen. In this school He simply explained Krsna. Later, Śrīla Jīva Gosvāmī, in order to please the Lord, composed a Sanskrit grammar book called *Hari-nāmāmṛta-vyākaraṇa* in which all the rules of grammar were composed of the Lord's holy names. Thus anyone who learned the rules would be reciting the names of Kṛṣṇa and receiving immense spiritual benefit.

Śrīla Prabhupāda emphasized that children should attend the morning *Bhāgavatam* class every day along with their elders and recite the Sanskrit verse, word meanings, translation, and purport. Then they should discuss all the points in the verse. "So read *Bhāgavatam*, pronounce the verses very nicely. Therefore we're repeating. You hear the records and try to repeat. Simply by chanting the mantra you'll be purified.... One who is chanting this verse, and one who is hearing this verse, he is becoming pious automatically. Pious. To become pious one has to endeavor so much, do this, do that, but if you simply hear these verses of *Śrīmad-Bhāgavatam, Bhagavad-gītā*." (Lecture, April 14, 1973, Los Angeles)

Śrīla Prabhupāda said the Sanskrit verses in his books are meant for our understanding and memorization. We repeat the verses again and again so we can memorize and recall them when we need them. "In Sanskrit literature every word has got particular meaning, particular thought. Therefore it is called *saṁskṛta* ... purified literature." (Lecture, May 14, 1976, Honolulu)

How to Teach Sanskrit

If you don't know Sanskrit, then the best way for your children to learn the language is to find a local devotee who can teach them on a regular basis. In Boise we were fortunate to have a Sanskrit teacher, Gary Thomas, who is a self-taught Sanskritist. In fact, he is an expert linguist and knows more than ten languages. He diligently taught my sons once a week for several years. He always made it fun and challenging, and sometimes they would remain absorbed in their lessons for two or three hours at a time. At that time he used Kuśakratha Prabhu's three-volume primer and Śrīla Prabhupāda's *Bhagavad-gītā* as his main textbooks. Gary is now preparing his own home-study correspondence course for children, and is already field-testing it with a few students in different parts of the country.

A Student's Perspective on Learning Sanskrit

Rādhikā Ramaṇa explains why he thinks learning Sanskrit is important, along with memories of his own study

In his letters to parents and to disciples in charge of the *gurukula,* Śrīla Prabhupāda again and again emphasized two subjects as most important: English and Sanskrit. The reason, he said, is that by learning these two subjects students would be able to study his books. All knowledge is present in those books, so he said these two subjects are the most important tools for studying them.

Besides being invaluable for studying Śrīla Prabhupāda's books, knowing English and Sanskrit well are useful from an academic and cultural perspective. English is now key to both jobs and businesses anywhere in the world, and Sanskrit is the key to our wonderful heritage as the mother language of Vedic culture.

Prabhupāda didn't expect all his disciples to learn Sanskrit. Many times, when adult devotees told him they wanted to learn Sanskrit to better study the *śāstras* Prabhupāda told them there was no point. He said, in effect, I've already translated all of these books for you. You don't have to study Sanskrit. It takes so much time and effort to learn it. But when he spoke about children he always said they must study

Sanskrit. Our children should be learning Sanskrit. The point is that when young, students have enough time to learn the language properly, and what they build in childhood they can use for the rest of their lives.

Studying Sanskrit with a Teacher

Ideally, parents can find the right kind of Sanskrit teacher. In India, Sanskrit is still part of the curriculum, and in North India it's typically required up to the seventh or eighth standard. But it's often regarded as a boring and tiresome subject. My friends in India used to complain about it all the time – all the forms they have to repeat, *phalam, phale, phalāni,* and so on. It's frustrating for them, and why wouldn't it be? They have no interest in learning Sanskrit. What's the point? Their attitude is that they're learning a dead language they'll never use.

But as devotees we have a lot of motivation. That's why finding a devotee Sanskrit teacher is the best. We were fortunate in Boise to have an American named Gary Thomas, a friend of devotees for many years. He used to come and eat at Govinda's restaurant, which my parents were running. He had studied Sanskrit on his own for years, and we realized he was a linguistic genius. But he always said his language abilities came to him honestly, and that anyone could learn as much as he had. Anyway, Sanskrit was his love, the favorite of all the languages he had learned, so he was happy to teach us.

He taught us the grammar gradually, taking into account our youth and inexperience, so we were never overwhelmed with hundreds of grammatical forms to memorize all at once, even though we did eventually learn hundreds of forms. But what made it so exciting for us, so enthusing, was that as a devotee he was able to connect what we were studying to things of practical importance to us. Every time he taught us a new verb form or noun case ending, we would see it immediately in the *Bhagavad-gītā*. For example, he would teach us that the object or accusative case (*dvitīya*) ends in *-am,* like *phalam,* and then he would say, "See, in the *Bhagavad-gītā* verse, '*patraṁ puṣpaṁ phalaṁ toyam*' – four words all in the accusative case, all as the direct objects of '*yo me* *bhaktyā prayacchati.*" In that way he would demonstrate new forms we were learning from sources we knew – songs from the morning program, commonly memorized verses from the *Gītā* and *Bhāgavatam*. Everything felt relevant. All of a sudden we were seeing things in our day-to-day *pūjā* that we had never noticed before, and it was making sense to us. So if parents can find a devotee teacher who can teach Sanskrit in connection with Kṛṣṇa, that's the best way. It's very, very nice, and actually can become very enthusing.

Gary would teach us at the restaurant. The official class was supposed to last for about an hour and a half or so, but I loved it so much that sometimes we'd go for three or four hours. He'd keep teaching and we'd keep learning, back and forth. And at that point I realized that this was what I wanted to do with my life – when I realized how much I loved the Sanskrit language and that I wanted someday to go into a field that involved it.

Children are different, so some will be more inclined toward language study and some less so. That's natural. Not everyone is into languages. But as Gary says, thousands of years ago even little babies learned Sanskrit, and any child can still do it and find it interesting, if it's taught in the proper way.

Studying Sanskrit without a Teacher

In India it's not so difficult to find a good Sanskrit teacher, and even in the West they are more and more available. But if it is difficult, for some reason, then it's possible to learn at least some Sanskrit by using Prabhupāda's books. Prabhupāda himself said in many places that if anyone studied his books carefully they could learn Sanskrit. This is why he gave the word-for-word meanings in all his books – he wanted his disciples to know by heart not just the translation of *dehino 'smin yathā dehe* but what every word of the verse means. Knowing the Sanskrit behind the verse translations is a powerful tool for preaching. If you listen to Prabhupāda's lectures, rarely will he quote an entire verse. Usually he quotes one word, or one line, maybe *kaumāraṁ yauvanaṁ jarā,* because he knows exactly what each word means. So he'll quote only the line relevant to the point he's making. It's not parrot memorization. He knows every word and how it applies to what he's speaking about.

Further, in one place Prabhupāda says that every word in the *śāstras* is a treasure house of meaning – every word. Sometimes you hear Prabhupāda giving a lecture on a verse from the *Bhāgavatam*. He'll choose one word from the verse, and the entire lecture will be based on that one word. He'll take that word and explain it this way, then in another way, then in a third way, and so on.

This is why Prabhupāda wanted children to learn Sanskrit – because knowing Sanskrit creates so many opportunities for preaching and relishing our *śāstras* and appreciating Prabhupāda's purports. If you don't have a Sanskrit teacher, you can still memorize verses, learn the word-for-word meanings, and it's not so difficult. You'll notice how *sandhi* works – you take *īśa* plus *upaniṣad* and get *īśopaniṣad*. These are basic things any devotee can get, and I know Western devotees who've picked up a lot of Sanskrit just because they have studied Prabhupāda's books closely with dedication.

Practical Benefits of Studying Sanskrit

One of the side benefits of learning Sanskrit is that learning one's mother tongue becomes easier, and this is true even if you don't speak a north Indian language but any language in the world. My own grasp of English grammar, for example, became so much better after learning Sanskrit, because there's no grammar as precise and detailed as Sanskrit grammar. All the different cases and forms, different types of verbs, different types of nouns, the way the language is set up – everything is so precise in Sanskrit that if you learn all the different cases and the *vibhaktis* and so forth, you can use that knowledge in any language. In our homeschooling, we studied some English grammar, but most of my understanding of English grammar came from studying Sanskrit. I could see that what was happening in Sanskrit also happens in English. So learning one's mother tongue becomes easier. Of course, if you speak a language derived from Sanskrit, then there's no limit to the advantage and you can become a proficient speaker. You'll find yourself using advanced vocabulary in your native language. There are so many advantages gained from studying a little Sanskrit.

Books for Primary and Older Children

Devotee parents should give their children suitable books to read in order to nurture their Kṛṣṇa consciousness. Fortunately, there are now many instructive and devotional children's books written by ISKCON devotees, so children have a wide variety to choose from. These books are composed with the idea of enhancing the devotional attitude of the reader and to remind one that Kṛṣṇa is the Supreme Personality of Godhead. Like Śrīla Prabhupāda's books these additional books create love and compassion in the hearts of their readers and resist the materialistic thinking of mainstream society.

Even though not all nondevotional books have degraded material in them and it may be necessary at times to teach from them, we should try our best to avoid using them in the early stages of our children's lives. Children are susceptible to influences around them, and if we teach through devotional books they will be protected from the contaminating influence of the material world. Children can and will read other books when they are older, in college. By then they will be fixed in their devotional lives and will know right from wrong.

Nondevotional books tend to reinforce the ideas that we are the body and that gratification of the body is the chief aim of life. Science books usually promote the atheistic ideas that life came from chemicals and that there is no difference between body and soul.

Books for Primary-age Children

Many children's books are now available at krishna.com, krishnaculture.com, and blservices.com. These books provide variety for children. In homeschooling we can save a lot of money we would generally spend sending our children to public schools and instead spend it on devotional books.

Most of the children's books now available are adaptations from *Śrīmad-Bhāgavatam*, *Kṛṣṇa* book, and *Śrī Caitanya-caritāmṛta*. Now Ūrmilā Devī Dāsī has pioneered a series of Kṛṣṇa conscious "Learning to Read" books for primary school children. Ūrmilā has a doctorate in education and three decades of teaching experience. Her books are designed to help children learn to read, understand, and speak English as well as about traditional culture, values, and ecological living. The complete series consists of three sets (Beginner, Intermediate, and Advanced). Each set comes with a Talking/Recorder pen, which allows children to touch the pages and hear the stories in one of twenty-five languages. The program is systematic, which makes learning easy and ensures good comprehension and thinking skills. Instructions are so detailed and clear that even inexperienced teachers can get great results.

Ūrmilā eventually plans to have complete educational materials for ages 2–18 – all subjects and levels – with topnotch educational content and Kṛṣṇa as the center, the goal, and all the points in between.

Books for Older Children

When my children were growing up there were fewer children's storybooks than there are now, so I would read them *Kṛṣṇa* book and explain the stories in a simplified way. We also looked at pictures in the thirty-volume *Bhāgavatam* set (they have more pictures than the eighteen-volume set), and I would retell the stories from the pictures. What was amazing is that my children never grew tired of seeing those pictures or hearing the same stories told over and over again.

Later, as they grew older, they read *Śrīmad-Bhāgavatam* and the *Bhagavad-gītā*. We supplemented these two main books with books by *sannyāsīs* and other devotees.

We read books by Satyarāja Dāsa (Steven Rosen) like *The Six Goswamis of Vrindavan, Śrī Pañca Tattva: The Five Features of God,* and *Narasimha Avatar: The Half-Man/Half-Lion Incarnation.* We also read books by Satsvarūpa Dāsa Goswami like *Nimāi and the Mouse, A Handbook for Kṛṣṇa Consciousness, Śrīla Prabhupāda-līlāmṛta,* and *Readings from Vedic Literature: The Tradition Speaks for Itself.* Books by Mahānidhi Swami included *Samādhi, The Art of Chanting Hare Krishna,* and *Prabhupada at Radha Damodara.* By Tamāl Krishna Goswami we read *Jagannātha-Priya Nātakam: The Drama of Lord Jagannātha, Yoga for the New Millennium,* and *Servant of the Servant.* Nowadays there are many other books published by *sannyāsīs* and other devotees – books by Indradyumna Swami, Radhanātha Swami, and Śacīnandana Swami, for example. Two books we especially enjoyed reading were the *The Hare Krishna Explosion: The Birth of Krishna Consciousness In America (1966–1969)* and *Vrindaban Days: Memories of an Indian Holy Town,* both by Hayagrīva Dāsa.

High School and College for Homeschooled Children

Devotee parents sometimes have pressing issues in their lives and have to send their children to school. Perhaps they have to work, as happens in the case of single parents. Even to them I suggest they not send their children to public school during the four years of high school. Their children can take high school exams privately or enter college early, taking one or two beginning level classes every semester. The introductory classes in any college are not much more difficult than high school, so children are able to handle them quite easily.

Why should we avoid public high school for our children? Many adults and young people have told me that the high school years are the toughest emotionally for teenagers because of the intense peer pressure to give in to drugs and illicit sex. Most teenagers have their own lifestyle – what they eat, how they live, the coolest way to think and dress, and how they relate with each other. In order to be accepted by their friends, our children will be pressured to do the same.

Our Experience

My boys skipped public high school and went to college early. Colleges are a safer environment because there is much less pressure to conform. In fact, students and teachers generally value cultural and philosophical differences, which is one reason there are so many cultural and religious student clubs at any university.

How did my sons start college early? During our homeschooling years we ran Govinda's restaurant in downtown Boise. I did the cooking and the boys waited on the customers. When the restaurant was slow my children did homework or had their Sanskrit lesson with Gary.

One day, Dr. Chaman Sahni, a temple patron who was also an English professor at Boise State University, came into the restaurant and talked to my boys. He noticed how well Rādhikā Ramaṇa read, so he suggested he take an English class at the university. Dr. Sahni said that even though my son was only twelve, his English was at the master's level, and he suggested we talk to the dean and ask permission. To gather proof of Rādhikā Ramaṇa's capability, we took some *Back to Godhead* articles Rādhikā Ramaṇa had written over the last two years and letters of recommendation from different high schools where he had spoken on Kṛṣṇa conscious philosophy. The dean was convinced and allowed him provisional admittance based on his grade results at the end of the semester.

All the beginning English classes were full. We could either wait for the next semester or let him try an English honors class. Waiting probably meant going through the admissions process again, so we decided to let him try. There were a number of classics on his syllabus, but he had never read any of them before. He had read only Prabhupāda's *Śrīmad-Bhāgavatam, Bhagavad-gītā As It Is,* and a few other spiritual books. We were nervous, but after Rādhikā Ramaṇa turned in a few homework assignments without our help and wrote an in-class essay, we were relieved to see he was doing well. The teacher was also surprised. How was it that our son, now only thirteen, had the knowledge and maturity to understand the literary classics she was teaching? We informed Rādhikā Ramaṇa's professor that he had read many books from the *Vedas,* ancient books of knowledge, that gave him the ability to think and reason critically. She was impressed. She knew my son was different. He was a Hare Kṛṣṇa and believed in karma and reincarnation, besides being a serious vegetarian.

Prabhupāda's books, especially *Śrīmad-Bhāgavatam,* contain all the material and spiritual knowledge needed to live a happy life. After reading them my boys had no problem reading any other books, even as young teenagers.

Thanks to the daily study of Śrīla Prabhupāda's books, philosophy was another of Rādhikā Ramaṇa's strengths, so during the first semester he also took an Introduction to Philosophy class. Again he surprised the teacher with well-written papers and good comments during in-class discussions. The following summer he took twelve credits (a full academic load) and covered some of his basic core requirements in history, psychology, government, and mathematics. By fall he had accumulated enough credits to be admitted as a full-time student.

The teachers and students loved Rādhikā Ramaṇa not for his well-written papers but because he was a kind, humble boy who was always willing to help others. A professor noticed how Rādhikā Ramaṇa would help other students in their studies, and once commented, "He does not build his success on others' failure." He won BSU's Top Ten Scholars award and received the silver medallion from the university, the highest honor any student had ever received. He was chosen as class valedictorian, and his speech at the graduation ceremony moved many in the audience to tears. As part of his speech he also sang a *śloka* from the *Bhagavad-gītā.* At his graduation party, many professors came to our house and chanted with us.

My younger son, Gopal, followed Rādhikā Ramaṇa to college when he was thirteen. Gopal also got good grades and was the youngest student (at seventeen) to graduate from the College of Engineering. His teachers noticed he was able to study independently and solve problems far better than other students. Gopal attracted some of his friends to the Kṛṣṇa conscious philosophy and frequently gave out books and *prasāda.* Everyone knew he was a Hare Kṛṣṇa devotee, and they sometimes spotted him in downtown Boise conducting *harināma* on Wednesday nights. Some of them would stop by his bookstall and buy Prabhupāda's books.

My sons were proud and happy to be devotees. Both of them

sometimes wore *tilaka* and *dhotīs* to the university. They started a Vedic student club and received permission to distribute Prabhupāda's books once a week in the Student Union Building. We organized many chanting programs at the university, where all four of our family members played musical instruments and chanted the *mahā-mantra* together. Even though we were far from professional musicians, students and teachers enjoyed our chanting. For several years we put on a "Festival of India," an indoor event at the university, with an hour-long drama on the advent of Lord Kṛṣṇa and performances by ISKCON devotee dancers. We also arranged programs for visiting *sannyāsīs*, and my children were able to see firsthand how to preach at the university level. Both of them had advanced association and good role models throughout their childhood and adolescent years. Later, they had opportunities to speak in classes in the Sociology, Communications, Philosophy, and History departments.

While planning for our children's academic future we should remember not to push them into careers they may not be suited for. For example, in India it is common for parents to encourage their children to choose medical or elite government careers without taking the trouble to find out their children's aptitudes.

Of course, it is ideal if our children can choose careers that can also incorporate Kṛṣṇa consciousness to some degree in their daily work, but it's often not possible. Still, by daily *sādhana* and engagement in Kṛṣṇa conscious activities, they will be able to understand the higher purpose of whatever occupations they are in and will be able to dovetail their earnings as well as their time and energy in Kṛṣṇa's service. My sons' interest in learning and teaching naturally led them into areas of writing and preaching, where they could use their studies to spread Kṛṣṇa consciousness.

Even though Prabhupāda many times said university education is too materialistic, he always appreciated the academic achievements of his disciples and engaged them in his preaching. For example, he encouraged Dr. Bhakti Svarūpa Dāmodara Mahārāja, Drutakarmā Dāsa, and Sadāpūta Dāsa to write and preach, and he was always willing to give them time to discuss their fields with him. As parents we can carefully discern the natural inclinations of our children and guide them to enter professions according to their nature. Also, we should train our children to offer the results of their work to Kṛṣṇa – both their talents and their earnings.

Prabhupāda wanted to establish a *varṇāśrama* college to train devotee children in their particular occupations after they graduated from primary *gurukula* education. The *brāhmaṇas,* he said, should be trained to develop godly qualities and become expert at teaching or preaching. The *kṣatriyas* should be trained to manage and protect, the *vaiśyas* to grow food, till the land, and protect cows, and the *śūdras* to work under the direction of others. Prabhupāda said a *brāhmaṇa's* teaching aptitude does not mean teaching simply in the area of schools or colleges – a *brāhmaṇa* can teach martial arts, food production, and cow protection. But the key requirement is that the *brāhmaṇa* must have the natural inclination to be a teacher and leader and should also develop godly qualities and good character.

"Some of the children in our Indian school have a scholastic bent of mind, so they're educated in Sanskrit and higher studies. Some of them have a *vaiśya* bent of mind, and they work in the *gośāla* helping to develop and milk the cows. Some have parents working at the handloom, and if the children also have that desire, they're trained to be handloomers. In this way we will be able to develop a city of fifty thousand devotees." (Room Conversation, November 2, 1977, Vṛndāvana)

How to Skip High School

The typical way to skip public high school is to take the GED, the high school equivalency exam. Unfortunately, the minimum age requirement to take the GED is seventeen. Because of their superior academic skills many homeschooled children are ready for this exam earlier – between fourteen and sixteen or even younger. There are several ways around this problem. One approach that has worked for many devotee homeschooled children with strong, high school–level language and math skills is to take the SAT or ACT test, one or both of which are usually required for admission into American universities. The SAT has no minimum age requirement, so any homeschooled student can take it once he or she has paid the fee. Decent scores on the SAT or ACT allow students to enter a university or local community college directly, without a high school diploma.

Devotee children who have followed this method have ventured to apply for community colleges and universities when they are as young as fifteen or sixteen – in some cases, even younger. For students under eighteen, many institutions of higher education have an early admissions procedure. Typically these procedures require placement tests, a good grade point average for course work, and an interview with a school representative. Preethy Menon, a devotee from Naperville, Illinois tried this route with two of her daughters, Shruti and Swathi, and plans to follow the same course with her youngest daughter, Swetha:

> Four years ago, I attended Aruddhā Mātājī's homeschooling seminar in Chicago and was very inspired to homeschool my daughters, who were attending public schools at that time. My first daughter, Shruti, was still a sophomore in high school, my second daughter, Swathi, was finishing her middle school, and my youngest, Swetha, was in third grade. Based on her ACT scores, Shruti was able to go to DuPage Community College, where she completed her first two years of college education at a fraction of what we might have paid at any college for tuition. At DuPage she successfully completed an honors program and was awarded a complete tuition waiver for up to eighteen credits for a score of at least 25 on the ACT. When Shruthi completed about fifty credit hours at DuPage, she transferred to the undergraduate program at the University of Illinois at Chicago (UIC).
>
> My middle daughter, Swathi, skipped public high school completely and did all her high school–level work at home. Like her older sister Shruthi, Swathi also started community college at sixteen years of age, gaining admission on the basis of her ACT scores.

> Swathi scored very well in the English component of the ACT simply by studying Śrīla Prabhupāda's books, hearing devotional lectures, and writing essays as assignments. Some of her assignments were evaluated by a devotee friend. Her English teacher at DuPage was impressed with her writing and comprehension abilities. Following her sister, Swathi is planning to transfer to UIC from DuPage Community College within the next year. Generally, a student is eligible to transfer to a four-year college after completing twenty-four credit hours at a community college, with some specific courses completed, such as English composition and math. One needs to find out ahead of time whether the four-year college the student is planning to attend will accept the courses offered by the community college. Swetha is homeschooled as well and is now in the seventh grade. She envisions taking the same path as her two sisters.

For those who do want to earn a high school diploma privately without attending a public high school, there are many homeschooling groups that award high school diplomas if you follow their curriculums or work with them to create something both you and they accept. For those who want to create their own curriculum from outside books, Saxon (and many other companies) provide homeschoolers with a range of textbooks, answer keys, homework sheets, tests, and online help. Parents and students can even avail themselves of online tests and evaluations as potential resources. They can write and print their own transcripts by following the instructions in homeschooling books that show sample transcripts; these books are available in libraries and online, although these transcripts are not accepted everywhere.

Each state has its own homeschooling laws, which provide different options to homeschoolers who want to skip high school. Parents should check the laws and opportunities available in their home state. For example, Kaiśorī Devī Dāsī, who homeschooled her daughter and a number of other children, writes about her experience in Florida:

In Florida, homeschooling parents are allowed to create a document for their children stating when their high school classes are complete. The university and community colleges accept that as a diploma, so to speak.

My daughter was sixteen when she applied to universities. She attended one year of a private high school (at her request – they were teaching something specific related to her career interests), so she did end up graduating with a high school diploma, but on the diploma it was written than she had only attended one year of high school, so she had no real GPA. But we found that universities around the country accepted a portfolio and syllabus we put together to prove her skills and show what she had studied over the years. She was actually accepted into the honors programs of every university she applied to, partly based on that portfolio and partly based on her high SAT score.

Most of my other students did high school with me for the first two or sometimes three years, but then went into the dual enrollment program at Santa Fe Community College. Placement tests for 99% of them set them in college level courses, and all those courses were transferable to the University of Florida. So in effect they started attending university when they were fifteen or sixteen and skipped high school altogether. In Florida, homeschool students must register with a public high school to attend the dual enrollment if they don't want to pay for textbooks. It also gives them an actual high school diploma when they complete the high school part of their requirements at the dual enrollment program. These are basically the same foundation classes they would have to take during their first two years of university anyway, and they are given both high school and college credit for them. When they have completed their high school requirements at the college, they receive a high school diploma and officially start university, but they are now in their third year.

So there are different ways around the high school diploma problem, and parents should research their options and find something that works for them.

The Learning Community International

There is a wonderful umbrella organization run by Nandapatnī Devī Dāsī that provides different homeschooling opportunities for parents anywhere in the US and throughout the world. Called The Learning Community International (TLCI), her group is an accredited school designed to provide support in two main ways.

First, personal consultations help families design curriculum plans each year. TLCI has a ready-made curriculum available, but parents are free to use it however they wish. For example, parents can teach English using *Śrīmad-Bhāgavatam* and the TLCI would still give their children academic credit for it. Extracurricular activities such as preaching, drama, and cooking can also be counted toward the annual grade review.

Second, TLCI keeps academic records, and at the end of each school year awards accredited diplomas recognized in the US and several other countries. TLCI has curricula from kindergarten through high school. For more details, please contact Nandapatnī (Nancy Stempel), Associate Director of TLCI, at nstempel@tlci.us.

Things to Look for When Choosing a University

When choosing a university for your children, it's best to try to find a university for undergraduate work where there is the possibility of devotee association either on campus or in the city nearby. If your children are leaving home for the first time, it can be really difficult for them to have to make serious decisions on their own without any support system. Having devotee association is valuable not only for practical things like *prasāda*, but deeper things like staying strongly faithful.

Having that association may mean our children cannot attend a more prestigious school, but the value of having Kṛṣṇa conscious continuity nearby both spiritually and to help our children feel comfortable cannot be underestimated. Sometimes people want to send their children to super prestigious schools like Harvard or Yale for their undergraduate degrees, but this isn't of much actual benefit when the children are planning to do graduate work, because once they finish their graduate degrees, few people ask where they did their bachelor's work. The first degree becomes almost irrelevant, even though you might have spent $100,000 on it. It's much better to stay close to home (even if it means attending a state school or a smaller university), remain in good association, get used to college life, and then go elsewhere for graduate work. By the time the student is ready for his or her master's, he or she will be older, have developed a good academic record, and probably be able to get scholarships for the graduate work. Financially, then, it's better for the parents, and the child will be mature enough to handle things by that time.

One US school I can recommend is the University of Florida. The Alachua community, full of wonderful association and a large group of Kṛṣṇa conscious youth, is nearby. The devotees serve *prasāda* on campus every weekday – typically six hundred plates a day go out, although recently they've been setting a new record of over one thousand plates a day. The school itself is proud of the program and promotes it. A recently published list of top ten things every freshman should experience at the University of Florida included "Eat a Krishna lunch." Devotees operate a preaching center two minutes' walk from campus, so it's easy to attend morning and evening programs.

I can also recommend Boise State University. Our temple is a two-minute walk from campus, with really nice association and the beautiful Deities of Śrī Śrī Rādhā-Baṅkebihārī. Several other devotees besides my sons have studied there. This is the ideal college situation, where the student can get a good material education while maintaining association with devotees.

For graduate work, there's Oxford University in England, where both of my sons have worked through their graduate programs. Devotees are also studying there in the undergraduate program. Together, these devotee students form a strong, supportive community, with many of the devotees living together in one big house, taking turns cooking *prasāda* for the Deities. As our communities grow there will be more and more devotee children going to school, so every year there seem to be more and more good choices. If we keep Kṛṣṇa as our primary goal, then materially everything will work out. That's just a fact.

Starting a Homeschooling Co-op

Homeschooling is popular in America, with about 1.5 million children homeschooled in 2007 – that's 2.9 percent of all American students. Parents shoulder a burden when they choose to homeschool their children, but we see more and more that families who homeschool come together and share their talents and resources with each other to broaden the scope of their children's education. Homeschooling really works well in groups, because parents can tap into resources provided by other families.

Families who live in the same area can pool their talents. For example, a mother who is good at math could teach a math class for local homeschoolers, specifying what age group she's interested in or taking any age at all. A family into science might set up a laboratory at home so local homeschoolers can go once or twice a week for science lessons. Other parents might be interested in leading field trips or in arts and crafts. They too can open their interest to other children. This type of cooperation can create both a nice exchange and a mood of community.

A mother who is good at understanding *Śrīmad-Bhāgavatam* or *Bhagavad-gītā* could teach a daily, weekly, or monthly class on the scriptures. As children reach high school and some subjects become more difficult to teach, parents could even hire outside teachers for specialized courses such as science, art, or music. This is more affordable when done by a group rather than by individual families, so if there is a devotee community, even just three or four families, coming together makes homeschooling easier and more practical. The possibilities for cooperative homeschooling are vast. Kaiśorī Devī Dāsī describes her experience:

> One other source of cooperative involvement can come from volunteering. My daughter and I became "Environmental Educators" – she was nine or ten at the time – working with the University of Pennsylvania's Environmental Education center. We mainly took school groups out to teach environmentalism and nature studies, but the place had a garden plot they let my daughter design and develop and was home to injured birds of prey, which were part of the demonstrations, so required that she learn to handle them. Other devotee families, seeing us do that, also joined in, and aside from the value of carpooling, they were probably the best science classes any of these children got.

One thing that discourages some parents from homeschooling is the shortage of social contact, so a big advantage of homeschooling co-ops is that they give children opportunities to interact with other children and improve their social skills. Children can learn in a more traditional setting while still associating with like-minded devotee parents and children. When children see other children being homeschooled on a daily basis in a Kṛṣṇa conscious manner, their faith in Kṛṣṇa is solidified. They make strong friendships with other devotee children, which provides relief for parents, especially during their children's teenage years.

Another major advantage to forming co-ops is that families can plan events together and receive a great deal of help from each other. Members can, on a rotating basis, plan festivals in their homes, or events like preaching programs, *harināmas,* book distribution days, and birthday parties for their children or members of the devotee community. If families are geographically far apart, then parents might get together only for festivals or once-a-month events.

Going It Alone

Even though homeschooling works best within a community, it can still be successful even if one is isolated from other devotees. We discuss ways of creating the right social atmosphere for Vaiṣṇava homeschoolers in a later chapter, "Social Life for Homeschooled Children."

When my family started to homeschool, we were by ourselves in Boise, Idaho – practically the only devotees around, and one of a handful of Indian families in a city of 200,000 people. We started a temple, which became the center of activity for many Indians in the area, and through the temple my children had plenty of opportunity to interact with other children and adults, and to preach.

Now other devotee homeschooling families in Boise live near the temple and come together for fun events like dramas, musical events, *Bhāgavatam* classes, and morning and evening *āratis*. We don't yet exchange subject teaching, but the temple is a resource and the hub of many activities where homeschooling parents and their children can do things together.

Homeschooling in India

Homeschooling is increasingly popular in countries like the US, Canada, the UK, and New Zealand, but is still relatively unknown in India. Slowly but surely, though, more and more Indian parents are finding that homeschooling is a practical alternative to conventional schooling, especially in larger cities like Bangalore, Pune, and Delhi.

There are several reasons why Indian families choose to homeschool. First, many parents are dissatisfied with the conventional system of education – too often it focuses on exam-oriented academic achievement without regard for a child's psychological condition or overall development. Second, by its nature secular schooling ignores the spiritual growth and character development of its students. Third, parents want to protect their children from undesirable influences in nondevotee association.

A few ISKCON communities in India have created their own schools, such as Gopal's Garden, a Kṛṣṇa conscious day school in Mumbai, but where these organized alternatives are not available, many parents see homeschooling as their best option.

National Institute of Open Schooling

Last year the Indian government enacted the Right to Education Law, which provides free and compulsory education to all children between six and fourteen years of age. Many parents are confused by this law and mistakenly believe it prohibits them from homeschooling. In fact, the central government established the National Institute of Open Schooling in 1989 as an autonomous organization to help achieve educational policy goals in India. The NIOS offers a variety of courses at a number of study centers, but what is important for homeschoolers is that the NIOS has been vested with the authority to examine and certify pre-degree students who have registered – almost eighteen million students have been certified at the secondary, senior secondary, and vocational levels. Public examinations are held twice a year.

Children taught at home can be registered with NIOS's Open Basic Education program starting at the age of six, and they can then appear for examinations for standards III, V, and VIII. These examinations are optional, but registration is valid proof that a child is being schooled (although the law does not intend to enforce registration or recognition from any government or other agency for homeschooling).

Children who have reached the age of fourteen can register with the NIOS and take the Standard X or XII examination, and thus become eligible to apply for admission to any private or public university regardless of whether they have ever attended a government or private school. They need not present a portfolio nor show any documents other than a birth certificate. Students are tested in English and four other subjects of the student's choosing. The NIOS also makes provisions for children studying science, allowing them to go to a neighborhood school to complete laboratory work.

The NIOS has a website: www.nios.ac.in

Other Options and Resources

Another option for qualification is the International General Certificate of Secondary Education (IGCSE), offered by University of Cambridge International Examinations (CIE). More information about the IGCSE is available on the Internet.

For parents in India thinking of homeschooling, it may be useful to join a support group to determine the program best suited to their children's needs. Although such groups' philosophical viewpoints may not match ours, they can offer useful curricular and legal resources. An Internet search will reveal homeschooling support groups in a number of cities.

Anantshesh Dāsa in Pune homeschools his children and is willing to answer questions from other devotee families in India. Contact him by email at anant.vaknalli@rediffmail.com

In a book this size, it's not possible to include information on the legalities of homeschooling in each country of the world. When planning how to school your children, please research your local laws before beginning to homeschool. You can also do an Internet search for homeschooling groups in your country.

Extracurricular Activities

Preaching Is the Essence

Śrīla Prabhupāda said a tree is known by its fruit. Similarly, whatever a student learns while homeschooling can be seen in how well he or she can explain Kṛṣṇa consciousness to others.

Many of us think childhood is a time only to learn and that children can't teach before they're finished learning, but we must remember that teaching (and preaching) itself is a type of learning. People learn things best when they teach them to others. Here is what my younger son Gopal wrote about his own experience teaching.

> When I was thirteen, I took the Bhakti Śāstrī course, for which I had to study the *Bhagavad-gītā, The Nectar of Devotion, Nectar of Instruction,* and *Īśopaniṣad.* A year later, the devotees in the Boise temple asked me to give a two-week seminar on the first nineteen chapters of *The Nectar of Devotion*. I distinctly remember, when the time for the seminar came, I was preparing my notes all day long, studying *The Nectar of Devotion,* and reading its chapters over and over again. Then in the evening I was explaining it to the devotees and answering their questions. In this way, by the time the seminar came to an end, I had a far deeper understanding of *The Nectar of Devotion* than when I

had studied it for the Bhakti Śāstrī course. I realized that of all the people in the seminar, I had benefited the most.

Through preaching children gain a greater understanding of our philosophy and strengthen their faith in Kṛṣṇa as they articulate their own experience of Kṛṣṇa consciousness in a way that makes sense to others. They have to answer questions, respond to arguments, and sometimes deal with challenges. Public speaking, marketing, debate, interpersonal communications, and conflict management are taught in many schools and colleges, yet by preaching, devotee children automatically learn all these skills. Conducting preaching programs at schools – initially at elementary and secondary schools, and later at universities – was a significant and effective part of our homeschooling. Here is how we went about it.

Programs for Children Under Five

We contacted preschools, childcare centers, and Montessori schools to see if they would be interested in hosting programs on the Vedic culture from India. People in Boise know us as the Hare Kṛṣṇas, and many like and respect our philosophy. Some of the schools invited us over.

We planned for each event in detail. We practiced different tunes for the *mahā-mantra,* decided on the content of the talk, cooked *prasāda* sweets, and gathered the paraphernalia to take with us. We took along a few of Prabhupāda's books to give to the teacher, musical instruments, a peacock fan, and a conch shell. We dressed in our devotional attire with *tilaka* and neck beads.

We divided our presentation into different topics about India: geography, music, food, dress, and dance. This covered several aspects of Kṛṣṇa consciousness – chanting, vegetarianism, why the cow is sacred, and the Kṛṣṇa conscious lifestyle. Our children made small presentations on the music and dance of India. At the end we told stories of Kṛṣṇa with the help of the *Kṛṣṇa Art* book. The school children were completely fascinated by these stories and always wanted to hear more. Kṛṣṇa captured their hearts.

With children this age we parents conducted the programs and our children assisted us. Even though we did the majority of the talking, our children would sometimes explain their traditional dress, eating habits, and musical instruments. They would chant with us and distribute *prasāda*. The idea was that by observing and participating in the programs our children would eventually be able to conduct them without our help. The programs were always a success, and each time, the boys came home more convinced of the philosophy and more confident of their identity as devotees of Kṛṣṇa.

I also went to public libraries and asked if we could arrange programs there. The libraries were almost always willing, and sometimes they even advertised our programs for us.

Programs for Children Between Five and Ten

After we had gained enough courage and experience with programs at preschools and libraries, we decided to visit public and private elementary schools. These are tougher to get into, so I tried a different tack. I contacted friends, acquaintances, and members of the temple congregation whose children were attending local elementary schools and asked them to consider holding programs in their children's schools. Some of them agreed and asked the school authorities for permission.

Teachers generally allotted us thirty to forty-five minutes of classroom time. We would usually begin by explaining the geography and ancient culture of India and its connection with religion and spirituality, since the temple is the center of all activities. That would bring us to vegetarianism and the *Bhagavad-gītā*. Every few minutes we would invite questions from the students and teacher, and they often raised topics like why the cow is sacred, reincarnation, our dress, the meaning of *tilaka*, yogis, the Ganges, and festivals. Then we would chant the *mahā-mantra* with *mṛdaṅga* and *karatālas*. We would write the words to the mantra on the blackboard, and all the students would repeat it and try to sing with us. For larger events we would invite a Bharat Natyam dancer, who would dance and explain the meaning of her gestures.

As we became ever bolder in our preaching, I contacted schools directly whenever I heard they were teaching a unit on cultural diversity or comparative religion. At one public school, a sixth-grade teacher was teaching a special unit called "Discover Idaho," a diversity program to educate children about different cultures in our state. Another time, a private school wanted to devote a week to India in all their classes, kindergarten through sixth grade. We went from one classroom to another, talking about Kṛṣṇa consciousness and answering many questions. On another occasion, a public school invited us to put on an India Day for their four hundred students. We invited women from our temple congregation to help us with classical Indian dancing, mehndi, and face painting, while we talked about Kṛṣṇa conscious culture and philosophy. We also distributed *prasāda* at these programs, of course, and at our India Day we distributed about four hundred pieces of papadum.

Sugopī (age 6, center) dances with other children during a school program in Boise, Idaho.

Our biggest program came when the school district invited us to share our culture in fourteen public schools. They had received funds from the state government to hold diversity programs in their schools. We put on presentations for two weeks, a performance every day, and they paid us $1,000 for it.

We tailored our programs according to where they were held. If we expected a conservative audience, we made the program more cultural;

if we expected a more liberal attitude, we made a more directly Kṛṣṇa conscious presentation. Nevertheless, we always had chanting and *prasāda,* some talk on our lifestyle and food habits, and some basic philosophy of the soul, karma, and reincarnation. There were always questions at the end from both children and parents. It was amazing – most of the questions were about Kṛṣṇa consciousness, which allowed us to preach quite openly. After all, they had invited us! At the end we always served *prasāda* snacks, which would remove any misgivings, if any lingered. We found our expectations about the teachers and students were often wrong. Where we expected to encounter difficulty, people turned out to be quite friendly and wanted more Kṛṣṇa consciousness, and vice versa, so over time we learned not to guess and developed a fairly standard program as far as we were able.

Our children enjoyed these programs very much. A program day would be different from the normal study routine, but the boys were learning invaluable skills that would be impossible to teach in a classroom. Not only were they learning communication and oratory skills, but their hearts were becoming fixed in Kṛṣṇa consciousness.

Programs for Children Ten and Older

As my boys matured we got in touch with area high schools to find out if they would be interested in having a class on Vedic religion, philosophy, and culture. Some high schools offered comparative religion courses and readily agreed.

When we were first invited by Bishop Kelly High School, a private Catholic school, my older son was twelve years old and seemed ready to speak. My younger son, ten, was a good harmonium player and singer. Together they made a wonderful team. We were enthusiastic but nervous, because this was to be their first program for a high school class. We decided carefully on the content of the talk and practiced our *saṅkīrtana,* timing and refining it. The program went very well, and there were a large number of sincere questions from the students. My son told me later that he had been so nervous his legs were shaking, but no one had noticed. The early years of training, observing, and participating had borne fruit. He spoke on *sanātana-dharma,* karma, reincarnation, and mantra meditation. And of course there was a *kīrtana,* which brought the whole class together. The students immediately relaxed and even started clapping and singing with only a little encouragement.

The teacher was so impressed with the boys that she invited us every semester. She also placed many of Śrīla Prabhupāda's books in the school's library. The high school students enjoyed the program so much that on days when we visited, word would spread through the school, and many students would skip their own classes and come to ours. One time a senior devotee was visiting Boise, and we suggested to the teacher that he could give the class instead of my sons. But the teacher was adamant that the boys speak. "The beauty of your religion is that the youth of your faith can explain it so nicely and convincingly," she said.

After several years of our visiting the high school, the teacher now brings her students to the temple for the Sunday program as part of the requirements for her comparative religion course. The visiting students participate in the entire program – *kīrtana,* class, *ārati,* and *prasāda.* The teacher likes the chanting especially, and encourages every student to sing the *mahā-mantra* by doing so herself. During the *ārati* the students often join in the dancing. It is really quite amazing and fun!

Whenever traveling *sannyāsīs* visited Boise, we would arrange guest lectures for them at local universities. We chose classes that could relate to Kṛṣṇa consciousness and then called the teachers to find out if they would be interested in a Vedic perspective on the subject. Often the professors agreed. Eventually, the boys were also able to speak to the classes during the school year. At the universities we focused more on philosophy and less on chanting and dancing. These classes were longer and more challenging, and covered various subjects, including philosophy, sociology, education, literature, art, music, and theater. We always took free books for the teacher and invited the students to visit the temple.

Churches and Interfaith Dialogue

Another wonderful way to reach out to the local community is by participating in interfaith services held at local churches. These interfaith programs are often held for public holidays like Thanksgiving and New Year's Eve. Usually, we would be given five minutes to chant the *mahā-mantra* and read a prayer or verse from the *Bhagavad-gītā*.

We would also participate in panel discussions put on by local interfaith groups. Here, the boys learned how to present their own philosophy in relation to other religious views, and to appreciate the commonality of all religions.

Social Life for Homeschooled Children

By Kṛṣṇa's arrangement, twenty-five years ago we found ourselves in Boise, Idaho with no temple or devotee association. We decided to start a center so we could gradually develop good association. Initially it was hard to find good friends for our children, but as our temple expanded and more people embraced Kṛṣṇa consciousness, the children had plenty of friends to play with. They played games and sometimes practiced dramas for festivals together.

Children are playful by nature and need friends to play with. They can be creative and imaginative while playing, thereby helping in their overall growth and development. They also learn important social skills. Kṛṣṇa would be so absorbed in play with His friends that He would forget to eat, and Mother Yaśodā would have to call Him in. While we understand that playing is a crucial activity for children, we must also be careful that children play with friends who are Kṛṣṇa conscious so they develop good habits.

Sleepovers

Association is important in devotional life and every other activity. Gang members hang out together, and so do devotees, musicians, and mathematicians. Sending our children to sleepovers or slumber parties was a difficult decision for us. Initially, we allowed the boys to stay overnight at the homes of congregation members and other devotee families, but we were mortified to discover that while they were there they watched television all day or played video games because their friends didn't know what else to do. We also noticed subtle changes in their consciousness, such as a sudden need for toys and games they previously had no interest in. We would spend several days undoing what they picked up in only a few hours at someone else's house.

Eventually we decided to have sleepovers only at our home so that we could look after our sons and the children who attended. We saw that one or two good devotee friends was better than a lot of friends who were not necessarily devotees. As parents we have to keep a watchful eye on our children and teach them the difference between good and bad association. If we teach them to make intelligent choices while remaining respectful toward everyone, they will be happy and grateful to us later in life.

Parties

We rarely went to nondevotee parties because invariably there would be meat, cakes with eggs, onions and garlic, and other noneatables served, whereas we preferred only to eat *prasāda*. If we did have to go, we would eat before we went and discuss the importance of eating only *prasāda* with our children. Children need repeated, gentle reminders. My younger son Gopal remembers his experiences avoiding unoffered food at parties:

> It was almost like we had a secret pact with Kṛṣṇa and we were not going to let Him down. This was actually quite exciting for us. I remember we had so much variety of fresh *prasāda* at home that we felt satisfied. My mother would often make pizza, and cookies without eggs. My mother was teaching us the importance of eating only *prasāda* and some of the austerities that may go with this principle. However, to us it didn't feel like we were

missing anything, because there was always so much *prasāda* around. These austerities actually felt like fun, and we had a real sense of accomplishment.

Also what made a big impression on me was that our parents never went anywhere without us. Wherever they went, we went. There was no such thing as adult parties or kids' parties. Their life was an open book. In other words, we never thought that when we would become adults we would be able to do things that as children we were denied. Their fun was the kind of fun we also liked. We helped them cook, clean, sew, dress the Deities, garden, do laundry, go for walks, play, sing, and so on. In our early years we did not have many devotees for association. We mainly had each other and discussed a lot of things together. Not only were they our parents but good friends as well.

The Importance of Adult Association

During their formative years children are quick to pick up habits from their environment. If they are around devotees and good role models, they will emulate them.

Therefore Śrīla Prabhupāda stressed the importance of exemplary adult association for devotee children. Of course, our children can play, wrestle, and frolic with other devotee children, but good adult association should be given precedence over peer association. Prabhupāda said, "If the children simply do as their elders are doing, that is, regularly attending *maṅgala-ārati*, rising early, chanting, eating *prasāda,* looking at books, worshiping the Deities, then automatically they will become trained up in the right way and there is no need for special program for education. Children will always do as they see others doing, so if by the good association of their parents and the other older persons, they will come out nicely fixed in Kṛṣṇa consciousness." (Letter to Satyabhāmā Dāsī, February 28, 1972)

In today's society, because of the overemphasis on peer association, we see that children and young people lack a sense of responsibility and have difficulty finding their place in life. For example, instead of helping adults, teenagers see themselves almost as a different species. Young people and children today don't like to mix with adults. They have their own subcultures with their own music, language, and clothing styles. Kṛṣṇa conscious children, however, do the same kinds of activities as their elders – chanting, dancing, studying the scriptures, attending feasts, and participating in plays and festivals.

Attend Temple Functions Regularly

An effective way to develop social skills in children is to take them regularly to the temple and encourage them to participate in programs. They can volunteer at the temple or take part in plays and *kīrtana*. The children will make long-lasting friends. We can also involve them in Sunday schools, Bhakti Vṛkṣa, and Nāma Haṭṭa gatherings by encouraging them to do *kīrtana,* skits, or small, occasional individual performances. Children should feel like active participants at every event; otherwise, they lose interest.

Preaching Helps Children Develop Socially

Besides practicing Kṛṣṇa consciousness ourselves it is important to give Kṛṣṇa to others. Sharing Kṛṣṇa consciousness gave my children ample opportunity to develop their social skills. Through the preaching programs we organized the children learned to make presentations on Kṛṣṇa consciousness. We watched with surprise as they explained the philosophy with ease and answered questions that were sometimes challenging. In the temple, they often took part in festivals and plays, talked with guests, and eventually gave classes. We spoke and chanted at outdoor city events and went on book distribution and *harināma,* where they interacted with others. They participated in Sunday school and Nāma Haṭṭa events, where they could recite *ślokas* and perform in stage plays.

Another important venue for social interaction came when we started the restaurant. The children would run the cash register and make small talk with the customers.

Playing for Kṛṣṇa

Śrīla Prabhupāda wanted our children to play in ways that enhanced their Kṛṣṇa consciousness. He was not in favor of toys or games that led to forgetfulness of Kṛṣṇa. Rather, he wanted us to engage our children's playful tendencies by encouraging them to reenact Kṛṣṇa's pastimes – by playing as Mother Yaśodā or Nanda Bābā, cowherd boys in the forest, or demons like Aghāsura attacking Kṛṣṇa. For indoor play, Prabhupāda preferred that children improvise with household items like bowls and spoons, as children have done for centuries in natural cultures. He disliked games that supercharge a child's brain and put him or her in an anxious state. Śrīla Prabhupāda writes, "Not that we shall give them many games for playing, these so-called scientific methods of learning are artificial, unnecessary, and on the whole I do not have much trust in this Montessori system or any other such system of teaching. Your idea for having altars to train the children in Deity worship is very nice." (Letter to Satyabhāmā Dāsī, February 28, 1972)

Great Souls at Play

We should encourage children to imitate a Kṛṣṇa conscious lifestyle, following the example of great souls like Parīkṣit Mahārāja, Uddhava, and Mīrā Bāī. *Śrīmad-Bhāgavatam* (2.3.15) tells us, "Mahārāja Parīkṣit, the grandson of the Pāṇḍavas, was from his very childhood a great devotee of the Lord. Even while playing with dolls, he used to worship Lord Kṛṣṇa by imitating the worship of the family Deity." If children play Kṛṣṇa-centered games, we will soon find that they remember Kṛṣṇa all the time. Śrīla Prabhupāda writes about his own childhood, "Śrīla Jīva Gosvāmī remarks in this connection that every child, if given an impression of the Lord from his very childhood, certainly becomes a great devotee of the Lord like Mahārāja Parīkṣit. One may not be as fortunate as Mahārāja Parīkṣit to have the opportunity to see the Lord

Jivakeśa Devī Dāsī guides her children and their friends in making garlands for Kṛṣṇa in Almviks Gård, Sweden.

in the womb of his mother, but even if he is not so fortunate, he can be made so if the parents of the child desire him to be so. There is a practical example in my personal life in this connection. My father was a pure devotee of the Lord, and when I was only four or five years old, my father gave me a couple of forms of Rādhā and Kṛṣṇa. In a playful manner, I used to worship these Deities along with my sister, and I used to imitate the performances of a neighboring temple of Rādhā-Govinda. By constantly visiting this neighboring temple and copying the ceremonies in connection with my own Deities of play, I developed a natural affinity for the Lord." (*Bhāgavatam* 1.12.30, purport)

Śrīla Prabhupāda's father also helped him refinish an old cart, and he had great fun celebrating Ratha-yātrā with his friends. Prahlāda Mahārāja was not interested in play unrelated to Kṛṣṇa. During his own childhood Śrī Uddhava also played with Kṛṣṇa dolls and imitated the family's Deity worship (*Bhāgavatam* 3.2.2).

Prabhupāda said the best way for children to play is to do whatever the elders in the home, temple, or *gurukula* are doing. In other words, when we chant, dance, cook, or worship the Deity, the children should imitate these activities. Children can imitate cooking while playing outside by making *purīs, capātīs,* sweets, and rice with Play-Doh or mud. Inside they can use balls made of wheat dough in the corner of the kitchen.

Śrīla Prabhupāda explains, "They should be taught just to do like the elders, that is, rise early, cleanse, attend *maṅgala-ārati,* read our literatures, chant, go for *saṅkīrtana*, like that, and besides that, a little ABC, mathematics, geography, history, that's all. And teach the small children to play Kṛṣṇa games: one child is a cow, another is cowherd boy, they go to the forest, there are demons there, Kṛṣṇa kills the demons, like that; in this way, let the children play Kṛṣṇa games, then attend *ārati,* then learn some ABC, then play some more, have *kīrtana,* little ABC, and by keeping them always diversified they shall not lose interest and will keep their attention always focused around Kṛṣṇa." (Letter to Girirāja Dāsa, July 30, 1972)

So if we surround ourselves with devotional service, our children will also play by imitating all kinds of devotional service. When they are under five, we can purchase soft toys that are peaceful and devotional – Kṛṣṇa puppets and dolls, for example – rather than electronic toys that increase their identification with the body and disturb the mind. As they get older, their need for toys decreases and we can dovetail their playing tendency in some practical service, such as doing chores, worshiping the Deity, and acting out roles in devotional dramas. Helping their parents with household and preaching activities can also be lots of fun for children.

Participation in Organized Sports

As for organized sports, Prabhupāda did not allow heavily competitive games but mentioned sports like running, swimming, wrestling, and flying kites.

Many parents have asked me whether children should join organized team sports like soccer or baseball. Physical activity is an important part of a child's life, but we have to choose what activities they perform carefully to ensure that the environment and association are beneficial for them. Some parents sign their children up for so many sports that the children have no time or energy for spiritual activities. Prabhupāda called this "overendeavor," which leads to forgetfulness of Kṛṣṇa.

I know a homeschooled boy whose mother is a devotee but whose father is not. The parents disagree over which sports their son should participate in. In the end, the father insisted that his son join the (American) football team and attend football practice two or three times a week. After some time on the team, though, the boy's grades dropped, as did his spiritual enthusiasm. Furthermore, he picked up bad language and culture on the football field, and was exposed to all kinds of conversations between the children regarding their relationships with the opposite sex.

A girl I know was pushed by her parents to excel at swimming. She was always exhausted and fell asleep at devotional programs. Her coach and friends kept pushing her to eat meat so she could develop more stamina.

Children do need plenty of exercise to develop a healthy body and mind, but this can be accomplished in a Kṛṣṇa conscious manner. When I was homeschooling my children, I was also worried that I wasn't giving them enough exercise, so I had them join the city soccer team. We dropped it within a couple of months, however, because of the filthy language being used on the soccer field and in the changing rooms. My children didn't seem to mind leaving the team. Instead they took swimming lessons at the YMCA once a week. Besides this, they were physically active in all kinds of service at our preaching center. We needed help cleaning, cooking, worshiping the Deity, taking care of devotees, distributing books, and in many other areas. All these activities were just like play for them. They enjoyed doing them and felt a sense of accomplishment and pride. And they learned many skills that could be used in Kṛṣṇa's service.

Expensive Toys, Again

What about computer and video games? If our children are absorbed in computer and video games it means they are not properly engaged. Video games are harmful physically, mentally, and spiritually – as we have already discussed in other chapters.

How to Have Real Fun

Kṛṣṇa conscious fun is different from ordinary, mundane fun. There is so much joy in the simple act of attending evening *ārati* every day. Have you noticed how children at *ārati* are always jumping and dancing while the adults try to keep them under control? Such simple, clean fun. When the children do plays, they get a chance to act out their parts with energy, expressing themselves loudly as demons or as Lord Kṛṣṇa or one of His incarnations. During a recent play for Lord Nṛsiṁhadeva's appearance day in Boise, the children had the opportunity to act out a number of roles. One teenage boy played Lord Nṛsiṁhadeva, and he happily pulled Hiraṇyakaśipu onto his lap and pretended to tear him apart. A ten-year-old girl played the part of Prahlāda's mother, where she could act out her version of a worried mother. A six-year-old boy felt protected by the Lord in the role of Prahlāda. Play practices often go on for weeks, during which time the children can dovetail their playing tendency in wonderful ways. Children engaged like this do not hanker for the artificiality of toys or the mundane enjoyment of video game parlors and playing in an unreal environment. At our center we have had countless plays over the last twenty years, and the parents say the children think of nothing else in the periods when practice is going on.

We can also engage our children in festivals and Deity worship. As a child, Śrīla Prabhupāda organized a Ratha-yātrā festival with his neighborhood friends. During *snāna-yātrā* in Boise, we get the children to string dried fruit garlands for Jagannātha and sew His bathing clothes. We have a cleaning day when everyone comes with gloves to dust and mop. Leading up to Ratha-yātrā, a couple of children get involved for weeks in building the chariot – handing items to their parents or helping with the painting. Other children are involved in packing peanuts, raisins, and sunflower seeds for distribution, and decorating. This year, a little four-year-old boy kept asking everyone for service and imitating the other devotees. His older sister makes Kṛṣṇa conscious quizzes by taking facts from the *Kṛṣṇa* book. This kind of play can absorb a child's mind completely. Engagement in Kṛṣṇa's service is so uplifting that it satisfies all a child's senses.

Festivals

As a child Śrīla Prabhupāda showed great eagerness to celebrate festivals. He once spoke of his efforts to celebrate Ratha-yātrā. "When I was five or six years old, any carpenter I saw, I would ask him why don't you make a Ratha-yātrā cart for me. 'Yes, why not,' they would say. I would have my father take me to the carpenter shop, but none of them would make it. One old lady saw me crying on the street because I could not have the Ratha-yātrā cart built. She asked my father why he is crying and my father explained because he wants a Ratha-yātrā cart but no carpenter is making it. I have got one, said the old lady, and my father purchased it from her. He bought oil paint for me and I painted. I was also preparing fireworks for the occasion. I saw little books how to do it." (Lecture, September 6, 1977, Bhaktivedanta Manor)

There are many examples in the scriptures of the Lord and His devotees celebrating festivals. Kṛṣṇa and the residents of Vṛndāvana were always in a joyous mood, and they celebrated by dressing up and decorating themselves, singing, dancing, and feasting. In Vṛndāvana Kṛṣṇa celebrated many festivals with His friends – Govardhana-pūjā, Holī, Gopāṣṭamī, His own birthday, Candana-yātrā during the hottest month of the summer, the advent of the spring season, and full-moon days like Śārad-Pūrṇimā. In Gaura-līlā Lord Nityānanda and His childhood friends regularly enacted plays that were so real the residents of Ekacakra were amazed. Prabhupāda also reminisces that in his youth he and his friends produced a play on the life of Lord Caitanya so effectively that the audience was moved to tears.

Śrīla Prabhupāda said that ideal householder life is one in which every single family member has the opportunity to hear and chant. Together, they should worship the Deity, observe festivals, and invite friends over and serve them *prasāda*.

In his purport to *Śrī Caitanya-caritāmṛta* (*Madhya-līlā* 3.203) Śrīla Prabhupāda gives the example of Advaita Ācārya to illustrate this point for all of us. "Advaita Ācārya set an ideal example for all householder devotees in His reception of Lord Caitanya Mahāprabhu and His devotees and in His execution of a daily festival at His home. If one has the proper means and wealth, he should occasionally invite the devotees of Lord Caitanya who are engaged in preaching all over the world and hold a festival at home simply by distributing *prasāda* and talking about Kṛṣṇa during the day and holding congregational chanting for at least three hours in the evening."

Prabhupāda wanted major celebrations like Janmāṣṭamī and Gaura-Pūrṇimā to attract many people to the temple so they could chant, dance, and eat *prasāda*. He himself never missed a festival, and oftentimes managed and organized them even when it meant great physical austerity. One time when a devotee attending the 1976 Māyāpur festival asked him whether he was tired after so many busy days of conducting the festival, he said, "What 'tired'? So many people are coming and hearing about Kṛṣṇa. When you're preaching, you feel refreshed." (*Śrīla Prabhupāda-līlāmṛta*, volume 6, p. 183)

Learning through Festivals

Children love festivals. They provide a break from the normal routine of homeschooling and are a chance to show their love and appreciation for Kṛṣṇa consciousness in a practical way. Children can assist in festival preparation in many ways such as cleaning, organizing, decorating, and participating in plays and Kṛṣṇa conscious games – the atmosphere can become surcharged with spiritual energy. They can have their friends over and sing and dance with them.

When parents open their homes to friends and family, the children easily learn the concept of sharing and service. They understand that everything belongs to Kṛṣṇa and should be used in His service. They also learn the art of cooperation with other family members and friends, for without them it would be impossible to hold festivals. They learn to see all tasks, even cleaning, to be as important as Deity worship and chanting. But most of all they learn to relate to Kṛṣṇa as a person, as the most special guest in the home. Taking part in a play and wearing costumes is also great fun for children. Festivals help the culture of Kṛṣṇa consciousness become deeply embedded in children's hearts and minds, and the children will carry fond memories of them throughout their lives. Besides, who doesn't like congregational chanting, *prasāda,* plays, and to wear their best clothes?

On our Vaiṣṇava calendar practically every day is a celebration of one type or another. During our homeschooling days, my husband, Ananta-rūpa Prabhu, was particular to celebrate all festivals in a grand way. He encouraged us to make a collective family effort for their success and open our doors to all who came to join us for the celebrations. For days like Janmāṣṭamī, Gaura-Pūrṇimā, Nṛsiṁha-caturdaśī, and Dīpāvalī we took two weeks off from our normal homeschooling routine to prepare. For smaller festivals and the appearance or disappearance days of our *ācāryas* we took a day or two off. During this time we dovetailed our study into learning about the festival, and soon realized the children did more study during those "days off" than during the regular "school days."

For example, for Gaura-Pūrṇimā we would read about Caitanya Mahāprabhu's advent and early childhood pastimes from *Śrī Caitanya-caritāmṛta*. I would also give them writing assignments based on what we read.

We staged plays for most festivals, small or large, which meant the children had to produce a script. We encouraged our children to write

Rādhā Priya (age 4) and her mother Guruvāṇī Devi Dasi paint a Ratha-yātrā cart in Otaki, New Zealand.

these scripts, which always took a tremendous amount of work reading, writing, editing, and summarizing. Then twice a week their friends would come over to practice the play, and my sons would both act in the play and direct it. During the weeks prior to the festival their motivation to learn was stronger than on other days.

How We Celebrated Festivals

My husband guided us through the entire process. For every festival we decorated the altar and dressed the Deities gorgeously with fresh clothes. We produced a play with children of devotees and congregation members, sang special *bhajanas* related to the day, danced, and honored *prasāda*. We designed costumes and made props for the plays, which took care of their school art lessons. For example, just making a bow and arrow for Lord Rāma, or a scenic backdrop, or Govardhana Hill out of paper maché took much planning and tested our craftsmanship.

We also spent a substantial amount of time planning, shopping, and cooking for the Deities' offerings.

We celebrated the appearance and disappearance days of our *ācāryas* in the same manner. In the week prior to the festival we would read the biography of that *ācārya,* and on the festival day itself we would cook him an offering and hold a *puṣpāñjali* and *ārati*. Frankly, this is much of what we did for our homeschooling – plan festivals, temple programs, Deity worship, and preaching activities, and any success we had was a result of this.

Prabhupāda spoke many times on how to celebrate festivals, and we can take guidance from these talks. In a March 11, 1972 room conversation in Vṛndāvana he explained the different festivals on the Vaiṣṇava calendar, their spiritual significance, how they should be celebrated, and how we should fast on those days. He wanted us to celebrate all the festivals that he noted on the calendar, as well as the appearance and disappearance days of our *ācāryas*. An excerpt from that conversation shows how careful Prabhupāda was in celebrating each of these anniversaries: "The next important day is on the 26th, no, 12th September, 12th September, 1970, the advent day of Śrī Jīva Gosvāmī Prabhu. On that day there are three functions. First of all, Ekādaśī, a special Ekādaśī called Pārśvaika Ekādaśī. Then on that day, actually, Ekādaśī according to calendar, Ekādaśī was to be observed on the 11th September, but because the next day is Vāmana Dvādaśī.... Vāmana Dvādaśī means the advent of Lord Vāmanadeva. Therefore we have fast, Ekādaśī fasting, and we observe two fastings in one day, Ekādaśī and Vāmanadeva, Vāmana Dvādaśī. The same process as we observe Ekādaśī, and the evening there should be a meeting discussing on the life and work of Śrīla Jīva Gosvāmī. He is one of the very important *ācāryas* in our *sampradāya,* so especially his *Sandarbhas* should be discussed. If there is no such book, then his life can be discussed."

The question may arise: Should children be encouraged to fast on festival days? Until my boys reached the age of ten, I did not encourage total fasting, but if they wanted to try to fast a little I had food readily available in case they got hungry. Sometimes children want to imitate and try to fast but cannot manage for very long. During such predicaments, giving them food without grains is a good option so that they are performing some austerity but enjoy it.

On Ekādaśīs I kept plenty of food around like buckwheat, potatoes, and other non-grain items so they could fast from grains without difficulty. Gradually their stamina for fasting increased, and as they grew older they were able to do full fasts on days like Janmāṣṭamī.

Children love to play; celebrating festivals is a great way to dovetail this tendency and have them do meaningful service at the same time. They learn valuable practical skills while fixing their minds on Kṛṣṇa. If we don't engage them in these activities they will spend their time playing meaningless games.

The thing I remember most about my own childhood in Allahabad, India is my participation in Holī, Dīpāvalī, and Dassehra. My parents celebrated all festivals with enthusiasm, especially Janmāṣṭamī and Nandotsava, and distributed hundreds of gifts to people every year. I remember fondly the yearly Dassehra in Allahabad, when hundreds of floats depicting Lord Rāma's pastimes were decorated. My father would make prior arrangements so the floats stopped for extra time in front of our house so we could see them to our heart's content. On the last day of the weeklong Dassehra, my father would wake us early and take us to a special place where Lord Rāma was residing. We would touch His feet and perform *ārati*. This was my favorite festival growing up as a child.

Those of us who have these childhood traditions can now pass them on to our children by following Śrīla Prabhupāda's instructions. Let's not be reluctant about celebrating these holidays with our children, for by doing so we help them become more Kṛṣṇa conscious. Festivals require extra work on our part, but the results are lasting. Children love them – but who doesn't?

Vacations and Holidays

Travel was an important component of our homeschooling life. A major advantage of homeschooling was that I could teach my children through the summer and go to India during Kārttika or the winter months when the weather there is more pleasant. Since we were running a preaching center my husband and I would travel to India separately; one of us had to look after the temple. We took our boys to India every year to visit their grandparents and stay in the holy *dhāmas* for some time. This trip was the highlight of their year. Needless to say, they sometimes got sick during the travel, but it was a small price to pay for what they gained both materially and spiritually. When they were very young, they would fall sick easily, so we would stay in the *dhāma* for only a few days. But as they grew older, starting from about eight years old, we were able to stay in Māyāpur and Vṛndāvana longer.

Vraja Maṇḍala Parikrama

When the boys were eight and ten years old I took them on Vraja-maṇḍala *parikrama,* a month-long, 400-kilometer walk around the Vṛndāvana area organized by ISKCON. We walked an average of fifteen kilometers a day, stopping along the way to see the places where Lord Kṛṣṇa performed His pastimes. About two hundred devotees from all over the world participated. A *kīrtana* party from Māyāpur led our group, enlivening the devotees and passersby with beautiful, melodious *bhajanas*. As we walked, we stopped here and there to hear the pastimes of Kṛṣṇa and His devotees or bathe in holy ponds. Lokanātha Mahārāja, Rādhā Ramaṇa Mahārāja, and Bhadra Prabhu managed the *parikrama*, taking care of us and inspiring us with Kṛṣṇa stories and *bhajanas*. We had daily morning and evening programs, with many special classes by guest speakers. A few devotees would get together and improvise a play for the evening program. My children loved participating in the plays, and as soon as each day's walk ended and we had bathed and found our places for the night (generally in a makeshift tent), they would run for play practice. Since they were only two years apart and looked quite similar, they were often given roles of two brothers, perhaps Jagāi and Mādhāi, Lord Caitanya and Lord Nityānanda, or Rāma and Lakṣmaṇa.

The sacred walk helped them appreciate the importance of the holy *dhāma* and the depth of Kṛṣṇa's pastimes. Śrīla Prabhupāda's *Kṛṣṇa* book came alive for them, and they were amazed at the extent of Kṛṣṇa's pastimes, many of which they had never heard before. The *parikrama* also allowed them to associate with older devotees, who offered their wisdom and encouragement. The Vraja area felt endless, and the pleasure was unbounded. We were transported to the spiritual realm for the whole month, even though we had to deal with the inconveniences of fatigue, sore feet, outdoor bathing, mosquitoes, and occasionally, sickness. At night we applied ointments to relieve our muscles, massaged each other's feet, and then fell asleep in our sleeping bags. We took care of each other and our bonds deepened. Every night we slept in makeshift tents or *dharamśālās* (guesthouses), sometimes with no electricity or running water. The water was sometimes rationed, and we had to fill our buckets the night before. The boys especially liked the walks through the sugarcane fields, because the Vraja dust there was so soft and beautiful. They liked bathing in the different holy *kuṇḍas* after a long, hot walk. At Vimāl Kuṇḍa they even got to swim across the holy lake.

The *parikrama* was beneficial for the children both materially and spiritually. They learned the importance of living with only a few facilities. The austerities were sometimes intense, but they gradually began to feel the pleasure that comes from performing austerity. Being in the holy *dhāma* and feeling the presence of Kṛṣṇa and His devotees made a deep impression on their lives. When we repeated this walk a second time, they could appreciate the experience even more.

Other Kinds of Travel

If going on Vraja-maṇḍala *parikrama* is not feasible, one can also participate in other organized visits to the holy places, lasting a week or even just a day. Such tours are organized by the ISKCON temples and often by *sannyāsīs* visiting the *dhāmas*. Organized tours are good for children because the basic necessities such as food and living facilities are taken care of and parents do not have to spend time looking for such conveniences but instead can focus on hearing and chanting about Kṛṣṇa and His pastimes. If participating in such tours is not feasible, a family can stay at the ISKCON guesthouse for a few days and attend the temple programs and immerse themselves in hearing wonderful *kīrtanas* and classes.

I remember one year we attended Radhanātha Mahārāja's ten-day Māyāpur *parikrama*. We happened to be in Māyāpur anyway, and when we found out he would be holding a *parikrama* in a few days, we decided to join. Every day, just after *maṅgala-ārati,* about a thousand devotees boarded buses to a sacred place to spend the day chanting, dancing, and hearing nectarean pastimes. We returned to the temple each night to sleep in our rooms. This kind of *parikrama* was less austere for children, and ours enjoyed it.

During our yearly vacation to India the children spent plenty of time with their grandparents, uncles, aunts, and cousins. Through this they learned about their culture, developed important bonds with grandparents and the extended family, and helped encourage their relatives in Kṛṣṇa consciousness.

Besides our yearly trips to India, we also took smaller vacations to temples, Ratha-yātrā festivals, and national parks in North America. We usually drove to these places over a long weekend. One time, the boys went with my husband to the Badlands in South Dakota and Yellowstone National Park in Wyoming. They had fun together hiking, cooking on their portable burner, and sightseeing in remote places. It was a sweet bonding time with their father. The children loved seeing the national parks and had an official "passport" they stamped each time they visited one. They learned many facts about American geography, and because they helped plan their route, learned to read road maps. They experienced different landscapes and always visited any temples or preaching centers that were nearby.

Visiting Ratha-yātrā Festivals

We attended the Los Angeles Ratha-yātrā every summer. Over time, our trip to Los Angeles grew from a family trip to a group tour. One year we rented two minivans and took many of the Boise devotees and congregation members. For many of our aspiring devotees it was a life-changing experience to see so many Western devotees chanting and dancing, as most of our congregation hails from India. The Ratha-yātrā inspired them to become more serious in their Kṛṣṇa consciousness. For the boys, this was one holiday they looked forward to the most. Seeing a larger temple made a deep impression on them. They brought back new ideas how to dress their Deities, produce better plays, and sing better *kīrtanas*. For instance, when they went to the Los Angeles temple for the first time and saw the *pūjārīs* wearing their *dhotīs* in a special way, they wanted to dress like them while worshiping their own Deities.

Our visits to Los Angeles inspired us to put on our own Ratha-yātrā in Boise, so one year we built a makeshift, hand-drawn rickshaw and seated our small Jagannātha, Baladeva, and Subhadrā deities on it. Another year we joined an old-time fiddlers' parade, where we won third prize for the best float. For a couple of years we participated in the local university's homecoming parade, for which we created a beautiful altar on the back of our pickup truck. My husband put a lot of effort into making these "chariots" with the help of our children and local congregation. Finally, one year we got a full-size chariot and began to participate every year in the city's Independence Day parade.

Ratha-yātrā festivals were dear to Śrīla Prabhupāda, and he was always pleased when he heard about their success throughout the world. He once commented, "I began this Ratha-yātrā festival when I was a young child. I used to take Lord Jagannātha, Subhadrā, and Balarāma in my wagon in front of my father's house. I would hire one *saṅkīrtana* group to follow, and would distribute *prasāda* along the way. My father used to spend Rs.40/-, which at that time was a large expenditure, especially on a child's play. All in all it was a grand affair, and all of the neighborhood used to appreciate. Now by the grace of my childhood Deities, Śrī Śrī Rādhā Govindajī, I have been able to continue this Ratha-yātrā festival even up until this day." (Letter to Vatsala Dāsa, August 16, 1977)

Despite his busy schedule and sometimes poor health Śrīla Prabhupāda went out of his way to attend as many Ratha-yātrās as possible, which his disciples organized in major cities around the world. We should follow in Śrīla Prabhupāda's footsteps and hold Ratha-yātrā festivals in our hometown, or attend Ratha-yātrās with our children in other cities during holidays. This would please Prabhupāda very much. In *The Nectar of Devotion*, Śrīla Prabhupāda writes: "A similar statement is there in the *Bhaviṣya Purāṇa*, in which it is said, 'Even if born of a lowly family, a person who follows the Ratha-yātrā car when the Deities pass in front or from behind will surely be elevated to the position of achieving equal opulence with Viṣṇu.'" (*The Nectar of Devotion*, p. 76)

Many devotee parents ask whether they should take their children to places like Disneyland, theme parks, aquariums, or zoos, since these places are not Kṛṣṇa conscious. We sometimes visited such places if they were on our way, but we generally tried to go on Kṛṣṇa conscious vacations – visiting temples, attending Ratha-yātrās, or going to a place of natural beauty. When my children went to Disneyland they got bored standing in line all day waiting for a few rides. They showed no interest in ever going back. If our children don't watch television or nondevotional movies, they usually have little attraction for such places.

A Student's Perspective on Vacations and Holidays

Rādhikā Ramaṇa shares memories of his vacations while being homeschooled

Parikrama

The Vraja-maṇḍala *parikrama* was a real experience. Basically, you walk about twenty kilometers a day, while an advance party goes ahead and sets up camp, prepares *prasāda*, and gets everything else ready. Along the way you stop at different places where Kṛṣṇa performed his *līlās*, and a senior devotee explains what happened at that location.

There's a form of *parikrama* where you don't walk everywhere but you go by bus. The walking *parikrama* is the extreme-sport version of that type of *yātrā*. You actually walk every day, and then you bathe with a bucket from a hand pump and answer the call of nature in a field. The experience is so valuable because it really helps develop a sense of self-reliance, an "I can" feeling. I remember when I finished the *parikrama* I realized I needed almost nothing to survive. I had a bucket and a few things, and I could lie down anywhere.

I imagine it's a lot like the feeling some people get when they join the army – when they come out they have this feeling, "Okay, I'm a man now. I have some experience under my belt." In the same way, the *parikrama* is devotional boot camp. You go through this experience for a month, and you really come out having some kind of a taste for *tapasya*. You begin to understand why austerity can be so flavorful, so nice. Especially for children who are homeschooled, it's valuable to get a real experience of austerity so that *brahmacārī* life becomes more attractive. The student realizes, "I could actually live like this into the future." Vraja-maṇḍala *parikrama* was one of the most powerful experiences of my life.

Learning About the World Outside

Staying an entire month in the holy *dhāma* – there are very few things that compare with that. But that's one of the wonderful things about homeschooling: one can take time out for special outings like this. Much of true education takes place through unconventional methods. So often we think education means sitting at a desk, getting an assignment, and doing a lesson. We think, "For children to be educated means that from 9 A.M. to 3 P.M. they have to be working at their desks and doing sums, lessons, and writing. Unless our children do that every day, they won't be educated." Deskwork is only one facet of education, and it's a necessary part, of course, but education actually happens in many different ways because there are so many different things to learn about the world.

A friend of mine only half-facetiously says, "Don't let your schoolwork interfere with your education." Sometimes devotees wonder whether a homeschooled child can learn everything he or she needs to know. Aren't homeschooled children disconnected from what's going on in the world? In fact, if we pursue homeschooling in this way, through preaching activities and the right outings and vacations and so on, the homeschooled devotee child ends up knowing more about the way the world works than anyone else.

In other words, by the time the homeschooled devotee student finishes his or her education, he or she will have richer and more varied experiences than the average public or private school child. If you've lived out in the field for a month, if you've been to different places around India, you've seen how people think and act and eat and behave in another part of the world. You've learned about a different culture first-hand and know that what's appropriate in one place isn't appropriate in another, and you understand the world in a way that people learn only after they've become business executives and had the opportunity to travel.

But growing up homeschooled we already experienced such things, because we interacted with so many types of people. Preaching took us into every kind of situation. In our later years of homeschooling we were even going to prison preaching programs. What child gets such an up-close experience of prison? One thing is sure, Gopal and I learned right then that we didn't ever want to commit a crime!

The point is that there are varieties of experience available to our children, and we need to think of homeschooling in the right way. In other words, homeschooling should not be pursued as some kind of a sentence for children: "Sit in this room for eight hours a day and do not come out. You're sentenced to this desk for the next ten years." It shouldn't be like that. Homeschooling actually happens as much outside the home as it does inside it. It's called homeschooling, but don't let the term mislead you – half of it happens outside the home.

Disneyland and Other Vacation Destinations

Disneyland I don't recommend. It was one of the most boring experiences of my life. You stand for hours and hours in a line to get to a five-minute ride, and the ride is not that fun. If you grow up on Mickey Mouse stories and things like that, it's probably more fun, but for the rest of us, Disneyland is overrated in terms of what you get there.

When my family took vacations, our basic plan was that we made a temple or some Kṛṣṇa conscious festival our target, and then along the way, in the neighboring outskirts, we used to see whatever was worth seeing. Mostly we were interested in natural scenery and good exercise, things like trekking, boating, and so forth. In this way we combined Kṛṣṇa conscious goals with a little sightseeing, and we always had fun.

Homeschooling makes the schedule flexible, so when the father has free time, or if the mother has free time, you can go when the opportunity is there. The schedule is all yours.

Book Distribution for Homeschooled Children

Prabhupāda's emphasis on book distribution was founded on his compassion for fallen souls. He asked everyone to preach because people are suffering for want of Kṛṣṇa consciousness. "This, our book distribution is the most important task in our society. Therefore I am giving so much stress and I am working so hard on this. Because this is my life and soul according to the order of my Guru Mahārāja. And by his grace it is to some extent successful. And I took it seriously. I take it seriously still now. That is my life and soul. I never tried in India to construct big temples or even in your country we didn't. I never tried. But I was selling personally books. That is the history. Sometimes they are criticizing, 'What kind of *sannyāsī*? He is doing book business.'" (Lecture, December 31, 1976, Bombay)

He stressed book distribution over street chanting because the effect is wider. A book goes into people's homes and can be read by many, whereas street chanting will be heard only by those in the vicinity. He called book distribution "big *saṅkīrtana*" in contrast to the small *saṅkīrtana* done with a *mṛdaṅga*.

I love book distribution, and learned how to do it from devotees in Los Angeles after I received my initiation. Every day I distributed books with a few other devotees at the local DMV office. When my children were born and I moved to Boise, I could not do as much as I would have liked, so I started devising ways to distribute books. Rādhikā Ramaṇa was four and Gopal two. I put Gopal in a stroller and Rādhikā walked with me to the nearby Boise State University campus. In a bag I hung behind the stroller we carried some of Prabhupāda's books, mostly small and medium. I would distribute books to the students, ask for a donation, and Rādhikā or Gopal would hand them an invitation card to the temple. It used to be a lot of fun for them, and in the evening when my husband came home, they would tell him our scores. If a student came to the temple, we were ecstatic. One time Deborah, a student from BSU, took a copy of *Chant and Be Happy* from us and afterwards began to attend the temple regularly.

Rāgalekhā (age 5) and Hrishikesh (age 8) distribute Śrīla Prabhupāda's books in Winnipeg, Canada.

Book Tables at Colleges

Later, when both my boys were attending Boise State University, they started a Vedic student club and received permission to set up a weekly table to distribute books. The table was very successful, and over the years, by Kṛṣṇa's grace, we distributed hundreds of books. In those days, Gaṇapati Swami came to Boise twice a year and distributed books with us. He taught the boys some techniques and gave them a lot of inspiration. Gopal had a special penchant for book distribution. He would distribute books door to door during his college days. He also distributed many *Śrīmad-Bhāgavatam* sets at the temple.

Besides book distribution we went out on *harināma* in downtown Boise every Wednesday night. Gopal and I would chant – Gopal on his accordion while managing a book table in front of us. He ran into many of his professors during these *harināmas,* but it didn't deter or discourage him. Instead, he offered them books. He was always so ecstatic after the *harināma* that he would say there was nothing more attractive and sublime than *harināma.* He never lost his taste for it, and to this day he frequently visits the London temples to attend their *harināmas.*

Whenever there were events at the university – Earth Day or whatever – we would set up a book table and distribute hundreds of copies of *Bhagavad-gītā As It Is* or other books by Śrīla Prabhupāda. We celebrated World Book Distribution day by going to the local Boise Food Co-op, which was a popular hangout for yuppies and young people. We distributed there in the week before Christmas. It was always cold, but we kept warm by wearing layers of clothing. Our sweetballs were also popular. Sometimes the boys would chant, and the people loved that.

Harināmas

Śrī Caitanya Mahāprabhu showed His mercy to all by giving the following command to Nityānanda Prabhu and Śrīla Haridāsa Ṭhākura.

śuno śuno nityānanda, śuno haridās
sarvatra āmār ājñā koroho prakāś
prati ghare ghare giyā koro ei bhikṣā
bolo 'kṛṣṇa', bhajo kṛṣṇa, koro kṛṣṇa-śikṣā
ihā bai ār nā bolibā, bolāibā
dina-avasāne āsi' āmāre kohibā

"Listen, listen, Nityānanda! Listen, Haridāsa! Make My command known everywhere! Go from house to house and beg

> from all the residents, 'Please chant Kṛṣṇa's name, worship Kṛṣṇa, and teach others to follow Kṛṣṇa's instructions.' Do not speak, or cause anyone to speak, anything other than this." In order to carry out this command, Prabhu Nityānanda and Ṭhākura Haridāsa took the help of other devotees and went from house to house preaching the glories of the holy name. (Śrīla Bhaktivinoda Ṭhākura's *Vaiṣṇava-siddhānta-mālā*, chapter 3, trans. Daśaratha-suta Dāsa)

Going on *harināma* in downtown Boise or at the university was the best part of our homeschooling. We were hardly professional musicians, knowing just enough to keep a nice *kīrtana* going. But really, we were brave. We would contact the people in charge of the Recreation Department at Boise State and ask permission to chant at their outdoor stadium in the summer and indoors at the cafeteria. Even though we were far from perfect performers, the students still became attracted to the *mahā-mantra*, and many would come and sit near us or stand and listen from a little ways away.

Chanting in the cafeteria in the student union building was a bit more challenging. We would notice more uncomfortable looks, and some students would walk away. This would happen especially during times when *sannyāsīs* would visit and we would all go together. Seeing the saffron robes was not something Boise was used to as yet, and we were trying hard to be accepted and appreciated. Still, Hare Kṛṣṇa was slowly becoming known, and we were ecstatic.

As the boys grew older and our devotee community increased, we started to conduct *harināmas* in downtown Boise every Saturday night. So as not to create too much of a stir in the beginning, we chose to walk through the downtown chanting softly with our *mṛdaṅga* and *karatālas* rather than to stand in one place. We would pass nightclubs where young people were drinking and partying. After hearing us, some of them would come outside and dance with us for a few minutes. We would also walk past restaurants with outdoor dining areas, and their customers would be amazed to see our happy faces. We passed out invitation cards to them, and sometimes even small books. I would also try to distribute small books to the passersby while we were chanting.

Going on *harināma* was always an eye-opener for the boys – they had a chance to see the nature of the material world, especially on a Saturday night when people are eating meat, drinking, and behaving loosely with the opposite sex. Even though my children were exposed to this loose behavior they were protected physically and mentally by the holy name and became stronger in their Kṛṣṇa consciousness because of it. It was an adventurous activity for them, and they could dance to their hearts' desire. We felt closer as a family and protected by Kṛṣṇa as well.

Initiation

The boys were initiated when they were fifteen and seventeen years old. It was an auspicious day, the opening day for our new temple in Boise in 1999. We felt as though a major part of our responsibilities as parents was now complete. The larger part of the training had ended, and now our sons would take shelter of their spiritual masters in order to progress further toward the ultimate goal of life. Rādhikā Ramaṇa was ready to leave for Oxford University to pursue his studies in Sanskrit, and Gopal had a year left at Boise State before he completed his undergraduate degree.

This was good timing for their initiation. So far they had been under our shelter in Boise, and now for the first time, at the age of seventeen, my eldest son was leaving home to be on his own. Like any parents, we were nervous about this transition at first, but when our sons decided to seek initiation from their spiritual masters, His Holiness Hanumatpreṣaka Swami and Gopāla Kṛṣṇa Goswami, we felt they were in good hands.

For our children, initiation was a natural result of a Kṛṣṇa conscious upbringing. After watching the initiation of their own parents and many other devotees at our center they were inspired to follow those examples. After associating with and serving their spiritual masters for many years during their yearly trips to Boise, my sons were convinced of the qualifications of their gurus and wanted to dedicate their own lives to their instructions. Śrīla Prabhupāda writes that training children in a *gurukula* atmosphere leads to initiation and success in life:

> In the system of *varṇāśrama-dharma,* which is the beginning of actual human life, small boys after five years of age are sent to become *brahmacārī* at the guru's *āśrama*, where these things are systematically taught to boys, be they king's sons or sons of ordinary citizens. The training was compulsory not only to create good citizens of the state, but also to prepare the boy's future life for spiritual realization. The irresponsible life of sense enjoyment was unknown to the children of the followers of the *varṇāśrama* system ... Without being self-controlled, without being disciplined, and without being fully obedient, no one can become successful in following the instructions of the spiritual master, and without doing so, no one is able to go back to Godhead. (*Bhāgavatam* 1.5.24, purport)

Formal initiation means that the student dedicates his or her life to the service of the chosen guru. Discipleship is a crucial step in life because the guru is a representative of the Lord and surrender to him means willingness to surrender to the Lord. As part of the ceremony, the initiate takes a vow to chant sixteen rounds every day and refrain from illicit sex, gambling, meat-eating, and intoxication. Prabhupāda said that in order to receive initiation, the disciple should be at least ten years old because the student needs to be mature enough to understand the responsibility of initiation and personally convinced of its importance: "Regarding your questions about children at *gurukula,* above ten years old they can be initiated first time, and after one year of perfectly chanting sixteen rounds and observing the other regulative principles, they may receive second initiation." (Letter to Satsvarūpa Dāsa, July 25, 1972)

Of course, there are few actual child initiations these days – most children wait until they are eighteen or nineteen or even older. But in Vedic times children took initiation quite early in life. For example,

Nārada Muni talks about his childhood meeting with the sages and his qualifications for receiving knowledge from them: "I was very much attached to those sages. I was gentle in behavior, and all my sins were eradicated in their service. In my heart I had strong faith in them. I had subjugated the senses, and I was strictly following them with body and mind." (*Bhāgavatam* 1.5.29)

As parents we should make sure our children are qualified before they ask for initiation from a spiritual master. After finding a spiritual master, the aspirant must associate with him for at least a year while both the spiritual master and the disciple examine each other – testing one another's qualifications. The disciple should be sincere and eager to make spiritual advancement under the spiritual master's guidance, and the qualities of the spiritual master should match the qualities of a pure devotee outlined in the scriptures. Prabhupāda comments on Nārada Muni's self-description:

> These are the necessary qualifications of a prospective candidate who can expect to be elevated to the position of a pure unadulterated devotee. Such a candidate must always seek the association of pure devotees. One should not be misled by a pseudodevotee. He himself must be plain and gentle to receive the instructions of such a pure devotee. A pure devotee is a completely surrendered soul unto the Personality of Godhead. He knows the Personality of Godhead as the supreme proprietor and all others as His servitors. And by the association of pure devotees only, one can get rid of all sins accumulated by mundane association. A neophyte devotee must faithfully serve the pure devotee, and he should be very much obedient and strictly follow the instructions. These are the signs of a devotee who is determined to achieve success even in the existing duration of life. (*Bhāgavatam* 1.5.29, purport)

The scriptures say that no one should become a parent unless he or she has the ability to deliver his or her dependents from the cycle of birth and death. We may not be personally qualified to do so, so we place our children under the care of pure souls, who can deliver them. Even to bring our children to the point where they want to surrender to a spiritual master means we have to train them in the basics of Kṛṣṇa consciousness. The first birth is given by the biological father and mother, and if the parents are devotees, the child gets the impetus to become God conscious quickly and easily. Therefore the role of parents is crucial and cannot be underestimated. The second birth is given by the spiritual master, during which time the child's name changes and he or she gets a ticket back to Godhead. Whether the child actually goes back to the spiritual world depends on his or her own sincerity in following the instructions of the spiritual master.

Initiation is just the beginning of spiritual life. The process of purification goes on, and parents may continue teaching their children how to serve and surrender to pure devotees in a submissive way.

Handling Challenges

Flexibility vs. Structure in Homeschooling

Many parents are quite surprised to learn that we did not follow a formal structure in our study, nor did we follow a formal daily time-table. Our structure was loose and would change to accommodate events in the temple or outside. The day always started with a morning program and was followed by a study of the scriptures. However, if we had a preaching program to attend, we would adjust the schedule by waiting to read *Śrīmad-Bhāgavatam* until after the program. Since we were running a temple there were always so many activities going on – festivals and preaching programs – inside and outside the temple. We would participate in all of them, so our homeschooling time would be worked in around them. Sometimes we would try to fit in a couple of hours between two programs, and other times we would make up time on the weekends or in the evenings.

During the Janmāṣṭamī season or leading up to other major festivals we would have no regular school for two weeks, and instead study the activities of Kṛṣṇa from the *Kṛṣṇa* book or the *Śrīmad-Bhāgavatam's* Tenth Canto. We would practice for plays and design costumes and props. We would distribute flyers and books at the university, and sometimes approach teachers to bring their students for the event.

The children studied, but differently than what we did normally, and these times were always exciting for them. They read, wrote scripts for dramas, memorized their parts, and practiced their new *saṅkīrtana* tunes on the harmonium. We were actually working on four out of five Rs (we weren't always doing much math), but in a novel way geared to the needs of the occasion.

Reading the scripture and writing sometimes happened at odd hours depending on which preaching programs were on our schedule. If the programs happened to be first thing in the morning, we would spend the time before the program organizing for it, doing such things as collecting paraphernalia or practicing tunes. When we returned from the program we would eat lunch, rest, and then start our usual homeschooling program. We would read and discuss *Śrīmad-Bhāgavatam,* then work on math, Sanskrit, memorization, and music before my husband came home from work in the evening. If a special event took the entire day, we would skip homeschooling for that day and make up for it another day by doing extra work or studying on the weekend.

We did not have a designated place – a home classroom – in our house. The children moved around, sometimes studying in their rooms, sometimes at the dining room table, and sometimes outside when the weather was good. We always studied *Śrīmad-Bhāgavatam* together, and I always did my main teaching during this time. The remainder of the time I supervised their homework while I worked in the kitchen or did other chores. During breaks between lessons we chanted on beads together or practiced music.

Utility Is the Principle

In another chapter I mentioned the four mottoes on which our homeschooling was based: purity is the force, preaching is the essence, books are the basis, and utility is the principle. We followed the fourth motto by doing whatever was practical rather than following a "standard." Sometimes our boys could play like children and at other times were required to behave like adults, sometimes with serious responsibilities.

Śrīla Prabhupāda exemplified the motto "utility is the principle" in the way he used material things in Kṛṣṇa's service. In the Vedic culture *sannyāsīs* are not encouraged to use modern technology like cars, ships, and machines. However, Prabhupāda used all of these in Kṛṣṇa's service, and he often expressed his opinion on the importance of a practical application of the Kṛṣṇa conscious philosophy. In a letter to Yajñeśvara Dāsa (January 2, 1972) he wrote: "Kṛṣṇa consciousness means practical living, not something utopian or idealistic and vague. We simply do the needful, whatever pleases Kṛṣṇa most, that's all."

To Bṛhaspati Dāsa, November 17, 1971: "Philosophy is the highest, but even higher than philosophy is practice of philosophy."

To Haṁsadūta Dāsa, November 20, 1971: "You should take it to heart as a guiding principle that somehow or other we always please Kṛṣṇa by doing what is practical and necessary, according to time and place."

Time, Place, and Circumstance

Having a loose structure in homeschooling is not something I advocate for all parents. Since we were running a preaching center and my husband was working, the situation demanded it if we wanted to use all the opportunities we had to serve Kṛṣṇa. For some parents, however, a formal structure might work better and be more suited to their natures. Some children also do better with a formal structure. I know many homeschooling parents who adhere to designated times for class and who have created a classroom in their homes where all the children's work takes place. These parents are successful in their efforts. But underlying any structure – loose or formal – we must remember that utility is the principle and do whatever is practical. Spontaneity has its own merits, especially when we are dealing with children, because their restless natures needs constant variety and change.

A Student's Perspective on Flexibility and Structure

Rādhikā Ramaṇa shares his experiences with a flexible study environment and how best to incorporate structure in family situations that need it

Different students function best in different study environments. In our home we didn't have any designated time or space for studies, and our learning took place in an unstructured fashion. Because we were running a temple, there were always many activities, so our policy was that we would study whenever there was time. We would sit and do homework, then attend a preaching program, then when we came back we would sit and study again.

On some days most of our study took place in the evenings, and on other days in the mornings. On some days there would be no study at all – a major festival like Janmāṣṭamī would cancel all of our classes for a week. We weren't "regular students" tied to a schedule, so we would also often make up missed study times on the weekends.

My brother and I had such a full life with all the different and exciting Kṛṣṇa conscious activities going on that we never felt as though there were any intense study periods, even though studying was going on all the time

For some people our way just wouldn't work. They need a structured format. Many homeschoolers are successful mimicking a public school atmosphere: they have a room or a corner of a room with a desk and chairs, pencils and pens, books, designated starting and stopping times for the various subjects, scheduled breaks, and so on.

Either way works as well as it does because children can tell when parents are playing which roles. My brother and I always knew when our mother was being a mother and we could get something out of her by begging, and when she was being a teacher and we had to do what she said with no questions asked! Parents have to learn to play both roles anyway, even if their children attend school – sometimes they are "teachers," scheduling their children's lives and making sure the homework gets done on time, and other times they are "just parents," giving their children what they want and playing with them.

Discipline in Homeschooling

One of the most common questions I'm asked at homeschooling seminars and on my website is about how I disciplined my children. Śrīla Prabhupāda's formula for discipline was love. He said if we can encourage our children to obey through love, that's better than using force or punishment. If there is love and trust between parents and their children, children will automatically obey because they want to please their parents. Of course, the center of that love is Kṛṣṇa, and when we serve Kṛṣṇa together a spiritual bond is established in the family which is much more powerful than the material bonds we already possess. Śrīla Prabhupāda advised that successful discipline arises not from force but from developing a child's loving spirit: "If we train children by developing and encouraging their propensity to love Kṛṣṇa, then we shall be successful in educating them to the topmost standard. Then they shall always very happily agree to do whatever you ask them." (Letter to Rūpa-vilāsa Dāsa, November 18, 1972)

When we raise our children with Kṛṣṇa in the center, they become saintly in character. The transcendental heroes of the *Bhāgavatam* become their heroes. The children emulate these heroes in their play and begin to reflect their character. For example, if one associates with thieves he will become a thief, and if one associates with businessmen he will become a businessman. Similarly, one can become saintly in the association of saintly devotees. Children take seriously whatever they see their parents do, and if we are self-disciplined the children will be the same. We should not teach only by precept but by example, and we should see our children as servants of Kṛṣṇa. This kind of understanding encourages a relationship of love and trust between ourselves and our children. With love and trust, there is obedience. Trusting children want to please their parents, and discipline becomes easy.

The desire to please the parents is natural for children. Pleasing their parents becomes their reward for things done well. From their side parents shower their children with constant encouragement and applause, and show their love by feeding them nice *prasāda* and working with them on all kinds of Kṛṣṇa conscious projects. Parents and children chant and serve the Deities together. In this kind of relationship there is no pressure on the parents to give monetary or any other kind of material rewards to their children, and in turn the children feel happy and proud to be learning from their parents. Material rewards are not good, because children learn that the mark of success is material profit.

Nowadays we see parents who give all material facility to their children but do not encourage or even allow them to read the *Bhagavad-gītā,* go to the temple, or join a spiritual organization. When children are trained only for sense gratification, we should not be surprised if they become disobedient and disrespectful toward their elders.

Real love means giving our children spiritual training so they become Kṛṣṇa conscious. Parents who want to flood their children with material things and allow them to do anything they want without limits will not get good behavior from them. Rather, the children will develop low self-esteem. On the other hand, when parents force their children to obey out of fear of punishment, the children are apt to become rebellious later in life. But when parents give both love and good training, accompanied by their own good example, the children will be disciplined, motivated to learn, and happy. Prabhupāda said that children should both love and fear their teachers.

Prabhupāda did not want teachers to use force or severe punishment to get children to do what was expected of them. Rather, obedience can be generated through proper training. "Simply they should be engaged in such a way that they are somehow or other remembering Kṛṣṇa at every moment, that's all. It is not a mechanical process, that if we force in such a way they will come out like this, no. We are persons, and Kṛṣṇa is a Person, and Kṛṣṇa always leaves our relationship with Him open as a voluntary agreement, and that voluntary attitude – 'Yes, Kṛṣṇa, I shall gladly cooperate whatever you say' – that ready willingness to obey is only possible if there is love." (Letter to Rūpa-vilāsa Dāsa, November 18, 1972) And: "Superficially, strictness may be necessary – some material laws or basic principles – and if they don't follow, they'll be reprimanded. But they should develop the idea of love." (Letter to Jagadīśa Dāsa, July 28, 1974, Dallas)

How to Deal with Misbehavior

One thing that worked well for us in dealing with our children's naughtiness and misbehavior was to keep them always engaged in some Kṛṣṇa conscious activity. If children are not sufficiently engaged it's natural they will create problems and demand attention. We should therefore channel their naughtiness into productive behavior so they can expend their energy and be happy and active. Children are playful by nature; don't try to curb their playfulness. Instead, dovetail it in Kṛṣṇa conscious activities.

The purpose of punishment is to change the heart, not really to instill fear. Prabhupāda often gave the example of the thief who commits theft despite knowing he will be punished, because his heart has not been purified. So the solution is to help children control their senses through Kṛṣṇa consciousness. The *Bhagavad-gītā* (2.59) says that by gaining a higher taste one can give up lower tendencies. The same applies to children. If we engage them properly in Kṛṣṇa conscious activities, they will give up their desires to misbehave, and even if they misbehave accidentally they will understand and reform quickly. If they don't reform, some light discipline may be necessary.

Personally, I did not punish my children but only verbally corrected them and scolded them when they were naughty or did not do what they were supposed to. A firm voice and stern look was usually enough. I tried to use the positive method as far as possible. They understood that neither Kṛṣṇa nor their parents would be pleased with them if they misbehaved. I did not ground my children or use "time out." I felt that denying them any Kṛṣṇa conscious time, food, or association was unnecessary and goes against the principle of helping them become Kṛṣṇa conscious. It seemed to me that these types of punishments would only make them irritable and resentful – and ultimately, they would take it lightly anyway. Śrīla Prabhupāda was against punishing children by withholding *prasāda;* it's important for children to eat to their full satisfaction. He was also against any kind of physical punishment or beating. Using force is not only against Vedic principles but can drive children away from Kṛṣṇa consciousness by giving them a bad taste.

"If there is need you may shake your finger at them but physical punishment is never allowed. Try as far as possible to discipline them with love and affection so that they develop a taste for austerity of life and think it great fun to serve Kṛṣṇa in many ways. Rising early and *maṅgala-ārati,* this is enough austerity. Besides that, let them learn something, chant, dance, eat as much *prasāda* as they like, and do not mind if they have playful nature – let them also play and run, that is natural. It is nice if they eat often – if children overeat it doesn't matter, that is no mistake." (Letter to Aniruddha, January 10, 1972)

Śrīla Prabhupāda wanted children to be so trained that they enjoyed performing austerities for Kṛṣṇa. Good training happens only if there is obedience, and obedience will naturally lead to discipline. Children obey because of affection and respect for their teachers and parents. A respectful environment motivates children to learn, and they then soak up all sorts of knowledge.

A Student's Perspective on Discipline

Rādhikā Ramaṇa shares his thoughts on discipline

The flip side of the discipline coin is giving children plenty of encouragement, and one of the things I remember most when I think back to our homeschooling is that my mother was constantly encouraging us in whatever we did.

We used to go to preaching programs, and the first time I was asked to speak about Kṛṣṇa consciousness to a high school class I was so nervous my legs were shaking, my voice was trembling, and I was sweating. But somehow I got through that half hour. Afterwards, my mother encouraged me, "Oh, you did so well with this – so good! You're a natural!" Looking back I know now that I didn't speak well, but she was still encouraging, "Very good, very good. You did such a nice job." She knew that a little encouragement now – "You made a great effort" – would actually come true later, because encouragement has such power. If you encourage someone by telling them how wonderful they are, they actually become wonderful as a result of the encouragement. Encouragement is a self-fulfilling prophecy, and my mother knew this power, so she would encourage my brother and I a lot. These two things always went side by side: discipline and encouragement.

Another time I had a writing assignment for a *Bhagavad-gītā* correspondence course, and there was one essay question I was stumped on. I couldn't think what to write. I was just sitting there, not producing anything. My mother kept saying, "Why don't you write something?" and I'd say, "I can't figure out what to write." And ultimately she became upset (this is the discipline side of the coin) and said, "Okay, you have ten minutes. I want five pages. You have to write five pages in ten minutes. I'll be back in ten minutes." I said, "Five pages? In ten minutes? That's two minutes a page – I can't even write that fast!" She said, "You have to do it."

She was so serious that I just started writing whatever came to mind. Somehow my writer's block just broke and suddenly all these ideas started coming out of the end of my pencil. I never made it to five pages, of course, but the point was that by being forced to write, whatever was locked was gone thanks to her strictness and discipline.

And right after that there was a lot of encouragement – no criticism that I didn't write five pages. Instead, I heard, "Wow, you wrote! See? I knew you could do it. It's just that something was stopping you. Very good, very good." So these two things were always side by side: discipline and encouragement.

Restrictions

Sometimes parents express concerns about placing too many restrictions on children – forbidding such things as television, unoffered food, and mundane parties, for example. Are these restrictions healthy for children? Will they become resentful? Everyone agrees that some restrictions are good for children. We know, for example, that restricting children from playing with matches or staying up too late is good for them. We also know that children, if allowed, will play all day, and that we need to restrict their playtime so they can be educated.

Just as material restrictions are necessary if we want to maintain a sound mind and healthy body, so spiritual regulations are necessary to keep the soul happy. We are minute spirit souls, part and parcel of Kṛṣṇa, and our happiness lies in reviving our lost relationship with Him. No amount of material assets can make us happy.

To help us revive this lost relationship with Kṛṣṇa the scriptures enjoin that we voluntarily undergo some *tapasya,* or austerity, to cleanse the body, mind, and heart. These austerities include chanting the holy name a fixed number of times every day, eating only food offered to Kṛṣṇa, rising early in the morning, and avoiding the four pillars of sinful life, namely, meat-eating, illicit sex, gambling, and intoxication. Furthermore, any activity that contaminates our minds and discourages us from following these rules – such as watching mundane television, associating closely with nondevotees, and eating unoffered food – should be avoided. Without this basic discipline it is very difficult for us to advance in Kṛṣṇa consciousness. Restrictions like these provide the foundation on which we cultivate our love for Kṛṣṇa.

We should understand that if, in the name of giving them "choices," we do not raise our children in a Kṛṣṇa conscious environment, we are actually training them to a materialistic lifestyle that can harm them. There is no such thing as a "neutral" upbringing. Children who are not trained in a spiritual environment often succumb to the lures of illicit sex and drugs as they grow up. Recently, I met a young woman who was distraught because her twenty-year-old best friend had purposely taken a drug overdose and died. Sadly, this is common today, as evidenced by the suicide rates and the number of young people on prescription anti-depressants. Our youth are disillusioned with life, especially because of bad relationships. The materialistic educational institutions give no information about the soul or the real purpose of life but instead encourage young people to pursue lucrative careers to the exclusion of any higher goal.

Śrīla Prabhupāda wanted our children to be given a Vedic education that would include appropriate restrictions: "So one has to learn this. But they cannot learn because they do not undergo austerity. That is the defect. No education is there how to perform austerity. Therefore Vedic civilization is how to teach small children austerities. That is *brahmacārī*. So we want to start this *brahmacārī-āśrama,* or *gurukula,* to learn austerity from the beginning of life. Then their life will be successful." (Lecture, March 13, 1976, Māyāpur)

Restrictions on Restrictions?

One concern among parents is that too many restrictions will only make their children curious, even rebellious, later on, so that in their adolescence and early adulthood they will indulge in all the "forbidden fruits" they were denied in childhood. A similar example can be seen in a medical patient restricted from eating certain foods while he is sick but who eats them as soon as he is well.

In Vaiṣṇavism, however, the taste for forbidden activities does not remain because we experience a higher taste from the performance of spiritual activities. Śrīla Prabhupāda said,

> Don't say "no," but give a taste for the good, then it will be automatically "no." And if you say "no," then they will rebel. The four "no's" – that is very difficult. Still they are breaking. No illicit sex, they are breaking. But if they develop Kṛṣṇa consciousness, this will be automatically "no." So don't bring many "no's" but give them positive life. Then it will be automatically "no." And if you say "no," that will be a struggle. This is the psychology. Positive engagement is devotional service. So if they are attracted by devotional service, other things will be automatically "no." *Paraṁ dṛṣṭvā nivartate.* Just like Ekādaśī day. Ekādaśī day we observe fasting. And there are many patients in the hospital, they are also fasting. But their "No, no" is not voluntary. They think within the heart, "If I get I shall eat, I shall eat." But those who are devotee, they voluntarily "no." (Lecture, July 31, 1976, New Māyāpur)

The restrictions we recommend are steps toward the ultimate goal of life, and they are actually enjoyable once we grow accustomed to them because they cleanse the body externally and internally. Pure habits are in the mode of goodness, and the mode of goodness makes a person happy and peaceful. The mind becomes clear and free of useless clutter, making it much easier to focus on Kṛṣṇa. Śrīla Prabhupāda explains:

> Children especially are inclined to appreciate Kṛṣṇa's pastimes, so begin by reading to them from *Kṛṣṇa* book. They are not yet covered by false prestige and will very quickly take to *tapasya* as if it were amusing like a game! Just see the young *brahmacārīs* in India. The guru says do this, do that – immediately they do – they go out and beg all day in the hot sun and come back with a little rice, then take rest on the floor with no covering. And they

> are enjoying; it is pleasurable to them to work very hard. So it is very important to train children to endure all sorts of hardships and restrictions at the boyhood stage. Later, no one will renounce what he has accepted as the standard of enjoyment, to accept a standard of less enjoyment." (Letter to Himavatī Dāsī, November 17, 1971)

If children are trained firmly but lovingly, they will enjoy all kinds of austerities, accepting them as play. Austerities such as chanting, rising early in the morning, eating only *prasāda,* and learning the principles of Kṛṣṇa consciousness are easy for children because they have not been conditioned any other way. While avoiding meat may feel like a restriction to us, for a child who has never tasted meat it is only natural. The same is true with avoiding illicit sex, gambling, and intoxication. So when we give them these restrictions from the beginning of their lives, they consider them natural and enjoyable.

When I was homeschooling my children, we did not watch any television. The boys never missed it, and we never thought of turning it on. Missing out on television wasn't an austerity for them because they were satisfied and busy with devotional activities. We didn't go to restaurants or eat other unoffered food, but we didn't miss it because *prasāda* was better. By reading *Śrīmad-Bhāgavatam* they understood the proper way of relating to the opposite sex and the dangers of loose behavior. I did not have to impose restrictions on them in their teens because these habits had already become part of their culture and they understood the reasons behind them from studying scripture.

Sometimes acquaintances thought we were isolating our children or being too harsh with them by not allowing them to eat at restaurants, go to movies, or do other things their own children did. But all those who criticized us were also impressed by our children's bright, happy faces and good behavior. They knew that devotee children were different – clean inside and out. The whole purpose of a Kṛṣṇa conscious education is to teach children how to relate to the wider world – how to properly view the material world and the people who reside in it.

Children learn to see everyone compassionately, as parts and parcels of Kṛṣṇa. Children's exposure to the material world is not without context; instead, they can interpret their experiences through the spiritual knowledge they have gained in their training. They learn to see everyone in a nonsectarian way without bias because the soul has no gender, race, or nationality.

The Importance of Association

Another concern that parents have is what to do when their children do not want to follow these rules. Because of association with friends at school or in the neighborhood, children sometimes want to play video games, watch television, or eat unoffered food.

Good association is essential for spiritual advancement and character formation. Children are very impressionable, and when they watch television or play video games with their friends, they themselves develop desires for these things. Nevertheless, the process of hearing and chanting is powerful, and it can change our hearts by placing us in transcendental association. If we continue with our Kṛṣṇa consciousness at home, by Kṛṣṇa's mercy, our children will overcome such attractions and develop a higher taste.

Our love for our children should not make us blind to what is good for them. That would be misplaced bodily love. We will be their real well-wishers if we make a sincere effort to give them Kṛṣṇa consciousness so they can use all their senses in a way that pleases Kṛṣṇa. As they grow older, our children will appreciate the strong character we have instilled in them. They will use these good values as the basis of a life that is healthy, pleasing to Kṛṣṇa, and beneficial for others.

A Student's Perspective on Restrictions

Rādhikā Ramaṇa shares his thoughts on how to protect our children while still preserving their ability to make their own choices in life

Sometimes, because people think they should not determine what their children believe in or practice, they try to give them a neutral upbringing, thinking that when they grow up they can choose for themselves what path they want to follow – whether they want to be Kṛṣṇa conscious or follow some other religious path or not believe in God at all. But there is no such thing as a neutral upbringing. By not giving our children Kṛṣṇa consciousness we are giving them materialism. There are only two options. If we do not become God conscious, then we become selfish and materialistic, and if we do not give our children God consciousness, then we are giving them materialism.

If we raise our children without values it is not true that when they grow up they will suddenly decide to be Kṛṣṇa conscious. No, we are already pointing them in the direction of materialism because there is no such thing as neutrality; there is no such thing as an objective stance from which they can choose later on.

As devotees we come from certain backgrounds, histories, and karma – all of which have brought us in this direction. It all adds up, and anyone later in life can make a choice for Kṛṣṇa consciousness – even our children. But the question is, are we stacking the odds in their favor or against? If we pile things up high in the department of materialism, then our children can make the choice for Kṛṣṇa consciousness later, but it will be difficult and unlikely. If we pile the cards in favor of Kṛṣṇa consciousness, then of course they might make the choice for materialism later on, but it is also less likely. Ultimately, the choice belongs to our children. Once they have grown up we cannot control what they want, but it is up to us which way we want to stack the deck – where we want to add the favor, the emphasis.

Qualifications of Parents

The teacher is the strength behind any *gurukula* or homeschooling program. Śrīla Prabhupāda therefore emphasized the importance of good Kṛṣṇa consciousness for all his teachers. In a letter to Satsvarūpa Dāsa (February 16, 1972) he wrote: "If [X] is shaky in his Kṛṣṇa consciousness, how he can teach the children? Unless one is firmly convinced about Kṛṣṇa consciousness, I don't think the children will learn properly from such a person." The same applies to parents who are homeschooling their children. If parents want good results, they must set a good devotional example. Children learn mainly by example.

In today's public schools we see that the teachers' academic qualifications are carefully taken into consideration but their personal behavior is rarely examined. They do not follow the four regulative principles, of course, and generally do not know much about God. (And even if they do, they are not allowed to teach God consciousness to their students.) According to *śāstra,* good character and habits are a teacher's primary qualifications. He or she should also know about God. When teachers live according to what they teach, students tend to trust them. When their students respect them, teachers become inspired to teach and students then become more eager to learn.

Śrīla Prabhupāda insisted that devotee teachers follow four rules: no illicit sex, no meat-eating, no intoxication, and no gambling. This would make them real teachers and, because of their dedication to Kṛṣṇa consciousness, they would be able to offer love and guidance to the children by helping them revive their own dormant love for God.

In his purport to *Bhāgavatam* 5.4.8 Prabhupāda writes: "Śrī Caitanya Mahāprabhu has said that in order to preach, one must live a practical life and show people how to do things. *Āpani ācari' bhakti sikhāimu sabāre.* One cannot teach others unless he behaves the same way himself. Ṛṣabhadeva was an ideal king, and He took His education in the *gurukula,* although He was already educated, because the Supreme Lord is omniscient. Although Ṛṣabhadeva had nothing to learn from *gurukula,* He went there just to teach the people in general how to take an education from the right source, from Vedic teachers. He then entered householder life and lived according to the principles of Vedic knowledge – *śruti* and *smṛti.*"

Śrīla Prabhupāda often emphasized good example over precept. "Example is better than precept. You should all be personal examples. If you do not practice what you preach but simply force the children, that will not be very good. If every one of you rises early in the morning, so will the children. You shouldn't think, 'All this austerity is meant for the students, not for us. We are liberated now, so we can sleep until 7:30.' Both teachers and students must perform devotional service." (quoted from *Back to Godhead* Vol. 10, No. 11, 1975)

Again, Śrīla Prabhupāda says, "If you actually follow strictly the rules and regulations and chant sixteen rounds, why they'll not follow? They'll follow. If you are not attending class, if you are not attending *maṅgala-ārati,* if you are not finishing sixteen rounds, then that is bad example." (Lecture, November 2, 1975, Nairobi)

Character formation is one of the main goals of the homeschooling system, and it requires that students have continuous and intimate association with parents who instruct them through their conduct. This system naturally demands a high standard of behavior from the parents. Children are dependent on their parents to show them how to develop strong character, intelligence, and spiritual knowledge. With these they will be equipped to face the challenges that arise when they try to lead disciplined spiritual lives in today's world. They won't easily fall for the lures of drugs, illicit sex, and other things that would cause them misery.

We have to remember that homeschooled children are acquiring not only an education but also a simple and pure culture. Śrīla Prabhupāda said that students trained properly from the beginning of their lives should grow up to be the leaders of the country.

Homeschooling Makes Parents Better Devotees

In Kṛṣṇa conscious homeschooling the parents see themselves as servants of Kṛṣṇa appointed by Him to teach their children without expecting anything in return. Homeschooling helps not only the children become better devotees but the parents as well. By cultivating a Kṛṣṇa conscious atmosphere and an eagerness to make their children devotees, the parents also make spiritual advancement quickly.

From my own experience I can say that even though I was an initiated devotee, I did not have much knowledge of the scriptures, so I felt unqualified to teach my boys. However, as we all participated in the morning program, honored *prasāda,* did some Deity worship, celebrated festivals, read Śrīla Prabhupāda's books, and engaged in preaching activities, my faith and knowledge increased. Not only did our children grow spiritually, but we did too.

By reading Prabhupāda's books daily with our sons – especially *Śrīmad-Bhāgavatam* – my own spiritual conviction became stronger and I became enthused to teach them. My fears about my inabilities disappeared and I became convinced of the necessity of a Kṛṣṇa conscious education. Since I had to constantly preach to my children, I was eager to set the good example that would back up my words, and this too helped my Kṛṣṇa consciousness. I realized that even though we may not have complete faith in Kṛṣṇa consciousness or perfect qualifications to homeschool, as we practice Kṛṣṇa consciousness and teach our children from the scriptures we gain both. Also, I noticed that as we were reading Prabhupāda's books the children were becoming happy and peaceful besides gaining knowledge in all spheres of life.

We learn as they learn. We grow as they grow. Of course, our own understanding and growth in Kṛṣṇa consciousness should be deeper and more mature, so we become more and more qualified to teach our children. Sometimes I would use my personal mistakes or weaknesses as topics for discussion during classes so the children could learn from my shortcomings. They could understand that being a devotee does not mean we are perfect; rather, we are making a sincere effort to *become* perfect in our service to Kṛṣṇa. Examples set by visiting *sannyāsīs* and devotees also guided all of us in proper behavior and practice.

How Important Are the Parents' Academic Qualifications?

There are a number of sincere devotee parents who are hesitant to teach because they feel they lack the necessary academic qualifications – perhaps their language or math skills or knowledge of current affairs or history feels incomplete to them. This is true even among those who have college degrees. They fear they may jeopardize their children's futures. There is a fortunate answer to this quandary for the homeschooling parent: real intelligence is not measured in academic degrees but by the type of knowledge we have and how we apply it in our daily lives. Even those who have only high school diplomas are qualified to teach their children.

Śrīla Prabhupāda tells us what knowledge means from the Vedic perspective: "'The humble sage, by virtue of true knowledge, sees with equal vision a learned and gentle *brāhmaṇa,* a cow, an elephant, a dog, and a dog-eater.' That is a learned man. Not this degree-holder. A degree-holder who has no *tapasya* and no character – Krsna says he is *māyayāpahṛta-jñāna,* 'his knowledge is stolen by illusion.' Although he has learned so many things, nonetheless, *māyā* has taken away his knowledge." (*Civilization and Transcendence*, p. 49)

Elsewhere he says, "*Buddhi* means intelligence. And what is that intelligence? Real intelligence? Real intelligence is to know, to understand that 'Kṛṣṇa is the Supreme, and I am part and parcel.'" (Lecture, January 4, 1967, New York)

Our intelligence comes from scriptures like the *Bhagavad-gītā* and

Śrīmad-Bhāgavatam, which contain all knowledge, both material and spiritual. Parents who read these books and raise their children under their guidance are qualified to teach. Math and other academic subjects can be taught with the help of outside books, which are readily available.

Śrīla Prabhupāda said we are like mailmen; we don't invent our own theories but repeat what our *ācāryas* have said. If we simply read Prabhupāda's books with our children, the books are so spiritually potent that they will do the task of educating the children. We have to pray to Prabhupāda to guide us in this endeavor. By studying the scriptures, our children will develop strong language, critical thinking, and study skills, and in the end will be able to take up any profession they put their minds to and succeed. At the same time, by learning the Vedic conclusion on every subject, they will remain fixed in their Kṛṣṇa consciousness.

Homeschooling trains children to work independently without being spoon-fed by the teacher. In other words, the schooling takes its own shape with the children in the lead. When the children are young, it's not difficult to teach them elementary math and English. By the time their studies are advanced, they are older and capable of learning by themselves using textbooks and requiring only general supervision. So parents need not fear they are academically unqualified to homeschool their children.

Parents are natural teachers. They love and care for their children and are willing to sacrifice more for them than anyone else would do. Parents don't have to go to college to understand what's good for their children. Parents understand their children's nature intimately – both their strengths and weaknesses – so they can help in ways others cannot. As we see our children advance spiritually and academically, we will feel enthusiastic to teach and care for them all the more.

A Student's Perspective on Qualifications for Parents

Rādhikā Ramaṇa shares his thoughts on the relative importance of what parents know and don't know

Some parents worry whether they are academically qualified, but this isn't really a problem. For the first few years of homeschooling, all of us are qualified – there's no doubt. We all have some basic education, we know these subjects, and we can teach them at an elementary level. The nature of homeschooling is that it develops so much self-motivation in the student that soon the child teaches him or herself. This is true of all homeschoolers; by the time they get to the more difficult subjects, all the parents have to do is supervise, oversee work, and suggest assignments. The children study from textbooks, they understand things themselves, they practice, they solve problems, and they can do this almost independently.

In other words, homeschooling becomes a process of self-teaching at a certain level – automatically – because by the time children need advanced instruction they are already quite motivated and don't need anyone to force recitation of formulas and memorization and so forth. Rather, they need someone who can supervise their development. So even if the parents' education level doesn't go up to some arbitrarily high standard, it's okay. By the time the children reach high school they'll be able to study pretty much on their own. If necessary, parents can always hire tutors. In India, for example, it's very common for people to have private tuition despite the fact that they're going to school. So why not just remove the school from the equation, have the parents teach as much as they can, and then have private tuition?

Do Parents Need to Know Everything?

As far as teaching subjects such as history and geography and other such subjects with lots of "facts," those things come easily to children. Basically, when a child reaches a certain level of maturity, the parents can ask the child to read a particular book, say, on World War I or World War II, or study a book on geography, and the child will pick up everything he or she needs to know. The parents don't need to know all those things themselves. Their job is just to make sure the child studies.

Sometimes people think a teacher has to know everything he or she teaches, but in fact teachers more guide and direct study while the students pick up the content themselves. It doesn't hurt for parents to have some basic familiarity with the various subjects in order to teach them, but let me give you a personal example. My brother and I picked up a lot of geography because of a geography contest that was scheduled to come to a shopping mall in Boise. Participants had to submit geography quizzes, and the best answers would be selected for a live talk show, a game show in which the students would answer questions and win prizes. My brother and I found out about this and got excited, and for one month we studied geography. We learned all the countries of the world and their capitals, all on our own, very thoroughly. In the end I was selected as one of the three contestants on the show, and I won second place. Gopal received an honorable mention. It was a lot of fun. That month we studied nothing but geography. We never studied it again. We got what we needed. My parents did not know all the countries and capitals that I was memorizing. They knew some of them, but that was a part of their past education. Because of my personal motivation I was able to do it on my own. And that's the point – the real task of the parents isn't to know everything but to motivate their children to learn.

Possible Pitfalls of Homeschooling

Thanks to the preaching endeavor of sincere devotees, there are now hundreds of devotee families throughout the world – but only a handful of *gurukulas* to accommodate their educational needs. Devotee parents have a desire to pass on spiritual culture to their children, but without devotee schools nearby, they usually have to send their children to public schools. Unfortunately, they often find these public schools academically and spiritually unsatisfying because of weak standards and bad association.

For many of these parents, their only choice has been to educate their children at home. Homeschooling has been especially popular in the United States among families of various religious backgrounds, and today there are over 1.5 million children being homeschooled in America alone. The results have been excellent, both academically and morally, and homeschooled children often go on to very successful careers in college and beyond.

Like with most good things, however, homeschooling has its share of pitfalls and problems, especially if not executed in a balanced manner. Here we will discuss some of the pitfalls parents should guard against.

Overambitious Parents and Psychological Pressure

There is an entire chapter on this topic elsewhere in this book, but it bears repeating because it can be such a serious issue. Nowadays we see many parents with ambitious plans for their children to become doctors, lawyers, engineers, or, in India, IIT graduates working in professional companies. Because of heavy competition in all of these areas many parents induce their children to study hard even at a very young age, leaving them little time for play. Especially in India, schools, teachers, and tutors overload children with lengthy homework assignments. The same phenomena can occur in a homeschool setting when parents make unreasonable demands on their children, pushing them to excel in order to fit into their own ambitious plans. Actually, the purpose of homeschooling is just the opposite – to give children normal, happy childhoods – chanting, dancing, feasting, studying the scriptures, with some reading, math, history, and other subjects included. Until about fifteen, children focus on scriptural study and try to apply what they learn in daily life. Homeschooling can thus be a great blessing and a viable alternative to the educational systems prevalent in today's cultures. I personally know many parents in India who are so frustrated with their children's schools that they are willing to take steps toward home education.

Envy and Imitators

"My child has to be just like them!" I know of an unfortunate case of a homeschooled child who was under a great deal of psychological pressure from his parents to excel beyond his capacity. The parents were trying to get him to compete with another homeschooled child who was excelling academically. In spite of warnings from friends, the parents did not listen, and today the child unfortunately has some psychological scars and is not socially confident. In others words, this boy lost his childhood and grew up too fast because of the personal ambitions of his parents.

Too much competition and pressure is not conducive to a child's growth. Śrīla Prabhupāda was against too much competition for *gurukula* children. Young children should not be under pressure to perform beyond their capacity. At the other extreme, no work or discipline is also bad for a child. As parents, we should recognize the capacity and natural inclination of our children and encourage them accordingly. While some mild competition is natural and even good motivation to perform better, heavy competition or too much comparison can cause both children and parents anxiety. Śrīla Prabhupāda said material life means competition, envy, and the mentality that one can succeed only at the cost of someone else's failure. Spiritual life, on the other hand, is devoid of these qualities. Prabhupāda said that one can be a good teacher only if he or she is a good devotee without bad qualities – especially envy. If we are envious of other people, we will teach our children to become envious.

Overprotecting Your Children

Another possible pitfall in homeschooling is the tendency for parents to overprotect their children and to give them the message that everything "out there" is demonic – in other words, an "us vs. them" or "holier than thou" attitude. If children grow up thinking all nondevotees are bad and that we are the only good people around, it will be detrimental to their spiritual growth since they will be cut off from society at large. Lord Caitanya approached all living entities, even the most sinful, with a mood of compassion. He saw everyone as a servant of Kṛṣṇa, even if they had forgotten that original nature.

Of course, we cannot cultivate this magnanimous vision without protecting our own spiritual life. Lord Caitanya asked us not to associate with nondevotees, and this injunction is especially necessary for children because they are so ready to imitate what they see around them. Devotee children should associate primarily with and be educated by devotees.

So how do we understand this and develop the proper mood? One way to teach our children how we are different from others and why is to share Kṛṣṇa consciousness with those others. When we share Kṛṣṇa with people, it's natural to become compassionate and friendly toward them. When our children witness our compassion rather than our exclusivity, they develop the proper attitude themselves. We can take our children to events in parks, libraries, schools, and churches and encourage them to present Kṛṣṇa consciousness there. When they are small they can serve *prasāda* or help with the chanting, and when they are older they can speak our philosophy and handle questions from the audience. They can also do book distribution and go out on *harināma*, where they will have many opportunities to interact with others. Reading Śrīla Prabhupāda's books at home with lots of discussion will help them develop the broad vision of a devotee and not teach them to become fanatical adherents.

Preaching encourages children to reach out to others, to see everyone as spirit soul, part and parcel of Kṛṣṇa, rather than as a different (sometimes attractive) species. Children will also learn to recognize and appreciate other people's spiritual paths.

So we should give our children opportunities to interact with the outside world, but in a protected way. This protection is necessary in their formative years, because children are so quick to pick up habits from their environment. As long as they have the support of parents and the devotee community, children will be able to take the material world in stride and distinguish right from wrong. As they grow older and attend college, work, or start a family, their ability to deal with the material world will increase. They will be able to stay steady in their spiritual principles and at the same time see others with genuine compassion and friendship.

Isolating Your Children

"My child is too good to associate with anyone." Sometimes parents fear that even devotee association is not good enough for their children because some of the devotees adhere to different standards than they do. Some devotee children have bad habits, and parents with stricter standards want to restrict interaction with them. Even though these problems may be genuine, we have to keep in mind several important points: (1) Devotee association is always better than nondevotee association because Kṛṣṇa is always part of the picture. (2) The solution to unwanted influences is not to isolate our children but to give them strong association at home. By discussing the differing standards openly, we can explain why we live like we do without demonizing others. (3) The greatest quality of a devotee is humility. Raising our children as "pure but proud" is a disservice to them. Instead, we want to cultivate humility while teaching them to discern right from wrong. It is not easy to strike this balance, but by following the process of devotional service, Kṛṣṇa will help us cultivate the proper attitude. Of course, some devotee children may not be practicing their parents' devotional lifestyle, and in such cases we may have to be careful in associating with them.

Problems at Home

If husband and wife have serious relationship issues, the children are exposed to emotional trauma that could be detrimental to their emotional health. Disagreements between parents are normal, but adults should try to resolve these differences peacefully, using the instructions Śrīla Prabhupāda gave, and without creating a volatile situation at home. Parents who suffer from drug or alcohol addictions or other serious negative behaviors should not homeschool, because their children will pick up these behaviors. As Prabhupāda said, children learn mostly by example, and children will do whatever the adults do. If children have good role models, they will become saintly, but if they have parents with unclean habits, they will imbibe the same habits. Usually, parents who are dealing with serious personal problems do not opt for homeschooling.

In general, we should remember that our behavior and the home environment will have a strong effect on our children. (This is true, of course, even if our children go to school.) So for our children's sake we should try to keep the home as happy and secure as possible. Of course, we can't do this artificially; problems are natural, and solving them within the family can serve as lessons for our children, because they too will deal with such issues when they grow up.

No Reason to Fear Homeschooling

Like anything, homeschooling has its potential pitfalls, but there is no reason to be fearful or discouraged. Sometimes people hear about an unhealthy home situation and decide that homeschooling is dangerous. But problems exist for children who attend school, too. Indeed, there are many more cases of school children who become social misfits, immoral, overpressured, or depressed than there are of homeschooled kids with the same problems. So even parents of children who go to school would do well to keep these pitfalls in mind. Any good thing can be misused in the material world, but as long as we're careful we will achieve excellent results. While I know of several problematic cases, the vast majority of parents who are homeschooling their children are successful. Śrīla Prabhupāda's vision for children was that they should not only receive academic education but should develop a godly character.

Overall, homeschooling has many benefits that make it conducive to an academically solid, Kṛṣṇa conscious education, and for many parents it is the only Kṛṣṇa conscious educational option they have. If carried out properly, the benefits of homeschooling far outweigh the pitfalls, and results will be praiseworthy.

A Student's Perspective on the Pitfalls of Homeschooling

Rādhikā Ramaṇa shares his thoughts on how parents can avoid the pitfalls of homeschooling

As Indians we often have the bad habit of comparing our children with other people's children: "My child is this good at math. How's yours doing?" Asking such questions is fine if we're trying to figure out how *we're* doing in our own homeschooling, but if we're trying to make sure our child keeps up with someone else's child, then such questions are detrimental. When children are pitted against one another, they tend to feel inadequate. The parents, in a subtle way, convey this to them.

It's important that children compete only against themselves. Śrīla Prabhupāda often said he was not in favor of heavy competition in education. Rather, teachers and parents should challenge children to do the best they can, expecting the best from them. But "the best they can" does not mean "the best in comparison with others," because that can create a lot of pressure.

Along these same lines, reprimanding children for their failures in front of their peers is humiliating. If children do something wrong, they have to be corrected, but saying something like, "See, you're not doing so well in this subject. Look at him. He's doing so well," damages a child's self-respect. It's so important to preserve that. Again, if children misbehave, especially if they are hurting another child or bullying, that has to be immediately stopped. Children will understand that public misbehavior results in a public reprimand.

But if children are not succeeding in their academic work, then to compare them publicly with someone else is humiliating. Unfortunately, we see it happening. Parents will be talking to another parent and, in front of their own child, complain about the child. The child, of course, can understand what's being said. Children shouldn't suffer because of their parents' competitive spirit.

Don’t Be Too Ambitious to Make Your Children Succeed

Sometimes parents become so ambitious to make their children materially successful that they push them too hard in their studies. In America there’s a saying: “All work and no play makes Jack a dull boy.” Childhood is not meant to be hidden under piles of books and papers.

Śrīla Prabhupāda believed that childhood should be a time to run, play, and eat as much *prasāda* as one likes. Naturally, he wanted children’s play to reflect Kṛṣṇa consciousness, so that even during play they could advance spiritually. Prabhupāda wanted our children to grow into world leaders and good citizens – not seen as illiterate or stupid in worldly things – but first and foremost he wanted them to be good devotees with exemplary character and the desire to share Vedic knowledge with as many people as possible. “The main point,” he once wrote, “is that these children may be given the twofold program of education in Kṛṣṇa consciousness, namely, chanting and performing devotional activities on the one hand, and some knowledge of our philosophy and other subjects of knowledge on the other hand.” (Letter to Stokakṛṣṇa Dāsa, June 20, 1972)

We can see an example of this in Śrīla Prabhupāda’s own childhood. His life at home was steeped in Kṛṣṇa consciousness thanks to the inspiration of his father, Gour Mohan De. Gour Mohan gave the little boy a set of Deities, whom he worshiped playfully in the beginning and more seriously as he grew older. The boy also spent many hours at the nearby Rādhā-Govinda temple, gazing at the beautiful forms of the Deities. He would then imitate Rādhā-Govinda's worship with his Deities at home. His father also encouraged him to celebrate his own Ratha-yātrā every year, and to distribute *prasāda* to his friends.

The Danger of Undue Pressure in Childhood

Some learning in childhood comes without effort and some involves a little work, but undue pressure and competition push children beyond their capabilities. Prabhupāda was not in favor of fierce academic competition between children. Writing in a letter to a disciple, he said: "I beg to acknowledge receipt of your letter regarding the Kṛṣṇa Bowl game, and it should be stopped immediately. This thing will be a taxation on the brain of the young children. Why are you inventing? Why are you not satisfied? You are all only inventing and spoiling money. You should teach the children perfectly Sanskrit and English instead of spoiling time and money. The children cannot pronounce correctly the Sanskrit. Let them read it correctly, that is wanted first. They must pronounce nicely Sanskrit and English. The English is no difficulty. If you can do this, then your education is all right." (Letter to Akṣobhya Dāsa, September 3, 1974)

In India the educational system is faulty insofar as it forces parents to push their children to study harder so they can compete with others. Teachers too often provide minimum instruction in classrooms, passing the responsibility to educate students onto the parents. Some teachers encourage their students to take extra private lessons so they do well on examinations. Paying for these lessons implies that the student will pass the teacher's class, but it also guarantees that the child has hardly any break from studies. Even eight- and nine-year-old children, in school for the full day, head for the teacher's house immediately after school for this additional tutoring. By the time a child comes home it is evening, he or she is tired, and there is barely time for dinner before finishing homework and other school projects. Bedtime comes very late, and children suffer because of their parents' good intentions.

Parents succumb to this faulty system because they worry that their children will not get the good grades that guarantee good jobs in the future. Yes, good jobs mean adequate money, which means a comfortable life, but in pursuit of this dream parents must not allow their children to be turned into robots. Parroting useless facts that are soon forgotten does not increase a child's intelligence. School should not be a burden undertaken for some kind of prosperous future.

Even worse, as children get older the pressure to perform only increases. Too many succumb to the intense stress to succeed and the bitter disappointment of failure. According to the Center for Disease Control, suicide is the second-leading cause of death among US college students, the third-leading cause of death among those aged fifteen to twenty-four, and the fourth-leading cause of death among those aged ten to fourteen. How can we protect our children from an environment that generates this kind of stress?

Academic Alternatives with Room to Grow and Breathe

Homeschooling our children is a practical alternative to the present-day structure of the schools because when done right, homeschooling can accommodate not only good academic goals but spiritual goals as well. All parents worry about their children's future in the material world and know academic success can contribute to something favorable, but homeschooling can easily generate such success while helping the child advance in spiritual life. Because learning in homeschooling is more efficient, it frees up plenty of time for you to teach your children how to chant, write plays, read scripture, engage in Deity worship, and play Kṛṣṇa conscious games.

Homeschooling also allows us to teach our children how to balance spiritual and material life by giving them a taste for Kṛṣṇa consciousness. The drive to succeed is natural, but it must be balanced with activities that relieve the mind from undue stress. My younger son, Gopal, was fortunate to have learned this art. Presently he is working on his doctoral thesis, which requires long sessions of painstaking study, but every hour he removes himself from his work and chants a round or two or plays a devotional song on the harmonium. This way he does not let himself get overwhelmed, but keeps his perspective intact. "All work and no play makes Jack a dull boy" is a saying that is simply true. Those who have to work in the mundane world to earn a living know the meaning of dull, tedious work, and stress-relieving devotional habits come in very handy.

A Different Perspective

As parents we have to think deeply about the purpose of education. Before we became devotees our thinking was materialistic, wanting only material progress for our children, but now we can understand that true happiness comes from knowing and serving Kṛṣṇa. Therefore, if the majority of childhood is spent on useless mundane study and not in chanting, dancing, and reading about Kṛṣṇa, then that time is wasted. By keeping this in mind we can tailor our children's education in such a way that they have enough time to cultivate their spiritual lives. If the local educational system does not allow for that, we should try to find alternatives – perhaps finding schools that don't demand so much, enrolling our children in a *gurukula,* or homeschooling our children.

It's difficult not to be ambitious for our children's success, but don't add excessive academic pressure. Prabhupāda encouraged us instead to be ambitious about making our children devotees of the Lord. It is our duty as parents to bring up our children in such a way that they will never take another birth. If we cannot execute this responsibility we should reconsider having children. However, if we do succeed in this important endeavor, not only will our children go back to Godhead, they will take us with them. Prabhupāda refers to this while discussing the child-saint Dhruva: "Every mother, like Sunīti, must take care of her son and train him to become a *brahmacārī* from the age of five years and to undergo austerities and penances for spiritual realization. The benefit will be that if her son becomes a strong devotee like Dhruva, certainly not only will he be transferred back home, back to Godhead, but she will also be transferred with him to the spiritual world, even though she may be unable to undergo austerities and penances in executing devotional service." (*Bhāgavatam* 4.12.35)

Childhood is definitely not meant for spending all day behind a book. We can see from the example of Kṛṣṇa's own childhood how He played with his friends and tended cows. Even while tending cows He was chanting and dancing. In contrast, today children study many hours a day and for fun sit in front of a computer to play video games. This is not conducive to their spiritual growth. Kṛṣṇa consciousness should grow from the beginning, but if children are overloaded with work they will show little interest in spiritual life.

Appendices

Frequently Asked Questions

Television Cartoons

My child loves to watch cartoons of little Kṛṣṇa. She will take prasāda only when we play the cartoon. Since the cartoon is Kṛṣṇa conscious, is this all right?

Since the cartoons are about Kṛṣṇa, it's all right as long as she doesn't get addicted to watching them. We should also be careful that the cartoon is not leading her to watch more and more television. Too much screentime is not good. We have to be careful about that.

(More on this topic in the chapter "Purity Is the Force.")

Rāmāyaṇa and Mahābhārata Serials

Is it okay for children to watch serials like the Rāmāyaṇa *and* Mahābhārata*?*

The important thing is that watching these programs should not lead to watching television in general. There are some good devotional videos available, such as ITV's "Following Śrīla Prabhupada" as well as the *Mahābhārata* and *Rāmāyaṇa*. And there are times when a diversion seems necessary, so it's okay to sit down as a family and watch some devotional films. But doing so should be an isolated activity, not a habit.

Television is a streaming medium – and the stream never stops. Its content is not devotional. We should never think we are "turning on the television to watch a serial." Rather, we should treat the television as part of the DVD player.

(More on this topic in the chapter "Purity Is the Force.")

Writing Essays and Plays

Can you suggest some topics for essays and clarify the process for writing small scripts for plays?

For essays, you can pick topics from a section the child is currently reading. Suppose the child is reading the story of Prahlāda Mahārāja. Likely topics would be "The Qualities of Prahlāda Mahārāja" or "Prahlāda Mahārāja's School." In the second topic the child could create a story of what it was like when Prahlāda went to school with his friends, who were sons of demons, and his teachers, Ṣaṇḍa and Amarka. (More on essays and typical questions in the chapters "Teaching *Śrīmad-Bhāgavatam* to Children" and "The Five Rs: wRiting.")

As for play scripts, my younger son, Gopal, loved to act, so I encouraged him to write his own plays. Writing was not his favorite subject for a while, so this is how I tricked him into writing. We produced a play for every festival, small or large, and would encourage devotee children and congregation members to participate in them.

To write a play, my children would read a pastime from *Śrīmad-Bhāgavatam, Śrī Caitanya-caritāmṛta,* or *Kṛṣṇa* book, depending on the occasion. This typically took a week or less of daily reading, so instead of our usual *Śrīmad-Bhāgavatam* reading, during that time we would focus on reading about the significance of the festival and the pastime associated with it. For example, for Govardhana-pūjā we would read the pastime from *Kṛṣṇa* book for about a week. Then I would encourage Gopal to start writing the story just the way it had happened – in other words, to create a picture in his mind and to explain it in words.

When you write a script, you first write the title of the play at the top of the page in bold characters. Then under the title you write the author's name (the name of your child). Next, you decide on the cast and how many scenes the play will have. Each scene starts with a small narration of what will come. Scriptwriting requires creating dialogue. The child has to create a picture in his or her mind of what will happen next. Of course, we kept the book open and took some of the dialogue directly from the story.

The parent has to sit with the child during the first few scripts before he or she can write one alone. The play can be very simple – even just a page long – depending on the age and capability of the child.

Once the first draft is finished, the parent lightly edits the script, pointing out different ways to improve the writing, spelling, or explanation. The mood should be very encouraging. The child corrects the mistakes and rewrites until the script is polished. It may take several rough drafts before it is finished. Once the script is written, play practice begins! The child is by now excited, calls friends, and starts rehearsals with the parents' help.

(More on this topic in the chapter "The Five Rs: wRiting.")

Teaching Everything Through Śrīmad-Bhāgavatam

When you talk about teaching different subjects through Śrīmad-Bhāgavatam, *do you mean this to the exclusion of normal teaching of these subjects, or as a way of supplementing those subjects?*

The other subjects can be taught as a supplement to *Śrīmad-Bhāgavatam*. We tend to introduce these additional subjects to our children too early. What children learn about history at the age of seven is pointless. When they get to high school level they have to learn it all again. And when they get to college they have to learn it once more. Instead, our *Bhāgavatam* system gives the child a solid foundation in reading, writing, arithmetic, and so forth, while at the same time creating a solid Kṛṣṇa conscious foundation. We are giving our children the ability to look at the world through the eyes of scripture. Then, gradually, as required, we can introduce the other subjects. By that time they'll be prepared to understand what they read through the understanding of *śāstra*.

(More on this topic in the chapters "Studying History through *Śrīmad-Bhāgavatam*," "Teaching Philosophy to Children," and "Teaching Science from the Vedic Perspective.")

Children Who Aren't Interested in Philosophy

You said children should be introduced to reading through Śrīmad-Bhāgavatam *and other devotional books, but we see many times that children are not interested in spiritual or philosophical things. If a child feels reading is boring, then reading the philosophy in* Śrīmad-Bhāgavatam *is especially boring. What do you recommend in such cases?*

Even if a child is not ready for philosophy, he or she can still be engaged in devotional activities and serve Kṛṣṇa in other ways. Not everyone has the same talents or interests, and different children have different inclinations. It would be a mistake to approach them all in the same way. Some children may not like to read but they love music or art. We can encourage them to take part in dramas or to sing Vaiṣṇava songs. They can learn the philosophy through these songs. My younger son was musically inclined, and thanks to his special attraction for music, he learned so much philosophy just by playing the harmonium and singing *bhajanas*.

If a child finds philosophy boring, we can present the *Bhāgavatam* through stories, because every child is interested in stories, and the *Bhāgavatam* is full of exciting and interesting stories. The philosophical bent may not be there, but the desire to hear stories is universal, and any child appreciates them. There are also other Kṛṣṇa conscious books available for children to read, as I have described in the chapter "Books for Primary and Older Children."

(More on this topic in the chapters "The Five Rs: Reading," "Don't Be Too Ambitious to Make Your Children Succeed," and "Homeschooling in the Early Years.")

Homeschooling Children of Different Ages

Your children are two years apart. How did you teach them Śrīmad-Bhāgavatam *together?*

We took turns reading *Bhāgavatam* translations and then we discussed them together in a way that both boys could understand. If my older son needed more of an intellectual challenge, I would give him more challenging questions while my younger son listened. Gopal may not have been able to grasp as much as Rādhikā Ramaṇa and was listening to things a little ahead of him, but he was learning. It works really well this way.

For subjects such as mathematics, I worked individually with each of them. In the old Vedic system of study, there would be one teacher in a classroom with students of different ages and levels. The teacher would give them assignments and, when they needed help, tutor the students individually. This concept works just as well with homeschooling.

In case children are more than two years apart or there is a third child, the older child can help teach the younger one. This practice is valuable because it reemphasizes the concept being taught for the older child, and the younger child is always happy to learn from a sibling because it's different and fun.

It's not that parents need twice as much time to teach when they have children of different ages. We can manage our time in such a way that we school for the same amount of time and teach two or more children instead of one. A lot of homeschooling families have three or four children.

(More on this topic in the chapters "Starting a Homeschooling Co-op," "Teaching Philosophy to Children," and "Flexibility vs. Structure in Homeschooling.")

Children Learning at Different Rates

We have twins, but one is quicker to understand new material and the other comparatively slower. How do we cope with this while teaching them?

Spend more time with the one who is slower and do more advanced work with the one who is ahead. All mothers know how to make things simpler for a child who is a bit slower in a particular subject. Whenever they deal with children, they know exactly what to say to each child depending on the individual level of understanding – sometimes a little more explanation, sometimes a little less. While homeschooling, then, there may sometimes be more assignments and sometimes less for different children. Finding the balance comes naturally.

(More on this topic in the chapter "Teaching *Śrīmad-Bhāgavatam* to Children.")

Homeschooling for Technical Careers

In the West students can pursue college degrees in religious studies and other humanities, but in India the typical educational system is geared more toward earning bread and butter, so for many people the main career options are engineering or medicine. Getting those degrees means some kind of technical skill becomes necessary. Can this be accomplished by homeschooling?

There is nothing wrong with imparting technical know-how. At the appropriate ages, students can be given science classes. You can even hire a tutor to teach them the technical subjects if you are unable to do it yourself. Any subject can be introduced and taught as necessary and as appropriate. There's no reason to hold anything back. The point here is simply that we give our children the right perspective from which to deal with those subjects should they encounter things that would make them question their faith in Kṛṣṇa.

My own sons went to a science tutor who was tutoring homeschooled students, and he had a laboratory and so forth. He taught several technical subjects. So they learned many things from him. At the same time they were able to take some of it with a grain of salt.

Education in *gurukula* generally means up to fifteen years of age, and then comes higher education. So when we talk about this *Bhāgavatam*-based training, it's for the early part of life, up to fifteen. At that age our children can take up anything they want to – they're sufficiently trained to deal with whatever will come.

Homeschooling doesn't mean we don't become technologists or that there's a limit to what our children can learn. My oldest son, Rādhikā Ramaṇa, chose the humanities track and specialized in philosophy, Sanskrit, and religious studies, but my younger son decided to earn his bachelor's degree in electrical engineering. He completed his master's in electrical engineering as well. He's fully qualified to work as an engineer, but his homeschooling education was the same as Rādhikā Ramaṇa's.

(More on this topic in the chapters "Teaching Science from the Vedic Perspective," "Qualifications of Parents," "The Five Rs: Rote Memorization," "Homeschooling in India," "Starting a Homeschooling Co-op," and "High School and College for Homeschooled Children.")

Reactions to Homeschooling from Friends and Relatives

If someone sees a child who is homeschooled, the typical reaction is, "Oh my God, what have they done to the child's future?" This kind of comment is especially prevalent in India. It is a little difficult – not so much with distant relatives, because we may meet them only once a year – but our own parents and in-laws keep nagging, "Why don't you send them to school? What are you doing to your child's future?" At the same time the child faces a challenge when he tells others he is homeschooled. Please give us some practical tips on how to handle these situations.

The US is not much different than India in this regard. The value and practicality of homeschooling are often questioned here too. But the reputation of homeschooling is gradually shifting in a positive direction. When we were homeschooling our boys, however, we were in a situation much as you've described. Even as Indians living in the US there were always questions from friends and family members: "What are you doing? It's okay for you to have your own ideas, but don't ruin your children's lives!"

There's a saying that no one can argue with success. As long as the results are yet to be seen, people question and argue. This is true for everyone who takes off on a new path. Once success is clear, no one will say anything. Sometimes it's a matter of tolerating, and the process can be a little difficult and painful for both parents and children, but we have to have faith in the instructions Śrīla Prabhupāda gave us. They will carry us through. Prabhupāda said there was no knowledge in the world that is not contained in *Śrīmad-Bhāgavatam,* so someone who studies *Śrīmad-Bhāgavatam* has more than an MA or PhD. We have to keep that faith and tolerate the questions and struggles we go through. Once the success is there, then everyone will say, "Wow! This is a good idea. So nice."

We just have to be determined. When I started homeschooling, I cannot claim I had total faith in everything Prabhupāda said. But my faith developed as time went on. As you homeschool and follow Prabhupāda's instructions, your faith also will grow stronger, so for the child, the backup is the parents. If the student is feeling a little hesitant or nervous about telling others he or she is being home-educated, it is for the parents to support the child and give him or her a moral boost: "No, this is what you are doing and it's good."

Once we accept the premise of *Bhāgavatam*-based homeschooling, it still takes time to develop this faith, but if we look at previous examples of parents and students who have tried it, we will know that it can work. Over time you yourself will also see the results in your own family – how your child is becoming happier and more intelligent and family life is nice. A mother from Bangalore told me, "Ever since I have started homeschooling, all my anxieties have gone away."

(More on this topic in the chapters "Respect for Elders" and "Possible Pitfalls of Homeschooling.")

Eating at School

My son is going to school, where he is exposed to chocolates, biscuits, wafers, and other outside things. How do you control this? At home we eat prasāda, *but when he goes out, he eats at the school canteen because his other friends are also doing it.*

One thing would be to pack his lunch and send it in a lunch box so he doesn't have to eat canteen food. Initially other students may ridicule him, but eventually they will accept his differences and respect him for them. The child has to understand why eating *prasāda* is very important.

(More on this topic in the chapters "Teaching Our Children to Eat Only *Prasāda*," "A Student's Perspective on Eating Only *Prasāda*," and "The Father's Role in Homeschooling.")

Handling Distractions from Younger Siblings

My first child is six years old and my second child is one year old. Whenever I sit to teach the older one, the younger one disturbs. After some time, the older one's enthusiasm goes away in this situation. What should I do?

Rādhikā Ramaṇa responds to this question: I remember when I was a little boy and would get distracted from my studies, my mother would get "heavy" with me. She would say, "Sit down and focus. Why can't you focus?" I can remember several situations where I would lose focus and my mother was firm with me. I would obey her and sit down and focus. So there is an element of discipline. If your child is old enough to focus but is not focusing, then that's an important lesson that needs to be learned. Just because there is an external distraction going on doesn't mean we have to be distracted internally. That's a very valuable lesson to learn, because there will be so many circumstances in life where we will have plenty of distractions but still need to stay focused.

(More on this topic in the chapters "Discipline in Homeschooling" and "Flexibility vs. Structure in Homeschooling.")

Parent as Teacher

Presently my child is in the first grade. If I start homeschooling now, will my child accept me as a teacher?

Definitely! Children accept their parents as teachers because parents are natural teachers. They don't need to go to college to understand their children's wants and needs or to know their children's strengths and weaknesses. It comes naturally to parents. You are already a teacher – you are constantly teaching your children so many things. There is not much of a change when you start homeschooling other than the fact that you are taking on a serious responsibility. But as far as your children are concerned, they are not going to feel much difference.

The mother will be successful playing both roles – teacher and parent – provided there is love and trust between her and her children. It is natural for children to obey and learn from their mother and father because children want to please their parents.

There will be times, of course, when the children won't be obedient – times when they won't accept you in a particular role – but that's okay. Even children who attend school have those moments. It's not that disobedience happens only when parents homeschool.

In fact, homeschooling mothers play at least three different roles: parent, teacher, and spiritual guide. All three roles are natural, and mothers play them anyway. The only difference in the homeschool environment is that the mother plays a particular role for a longer period of time. There will be occasions when this won't work out as perfectly as expected, but that's okay. We don't need perfection to raise or educate children; we simply need to try our best. Kṛṣṇa will do the rest. He takes care of our children.

(More on this topic in the chapters "Qualifications of Parents," "Discipline in Homeschooling," and "The Father's Role in Homeschooling.")

Spoiling the Child

If the child is at home there is every chance the parents will pamper the child. In homeschooling, how do we ensure that parents do not pamper the child, because we are taking the responsibility to give them training?

Obviously it's important not to spoil children. If we pamper children with material facilities, excluding any spiritual training, then the results would be detrimental and destroy the child's self-esteem. At the other extreme, if we become strict and force our children, then they will rebel. Good training requires kind and firm consistency.

The question of spoiling children has ramifications for spiritual life after they mature. Ideally, once children complete their homeschool education, they enter the *brahmacārī-āśrama* in a proper fashion, and at some point later may decide to marry. Śrīla Prabhupāda said at age twenty-five one should make a decision and stick by it. This is what one has to work toward. Because spiritual values are inculcated from the beginning of life by the proper application of Kṛṣṇa conscious education, we can produce fixed *brahmacārīs* and *brahmacāriṇīs* who then make their own decisions about the course of their lives. Even if they become *gṛhasthas* they will understand that *gṛhastha* life has a glorious role in Kṛṣṇa consciousness and that there will come a time to move on and exhibit *vairāgya* at a later stage.

(More on this topic in the chapters "Discipline in Homeschooling" and "Flexibility vs. Structure in Homeschooling.")

Keeping the Child Challenged

How do we make sure our child is academically challenged and not bored with his schoolwork?

Actually, homeschooled children tend to be more challenged than they would be in school because we allow them to work at whatever pace they want. For example, a girl in the first grade is not limited to the first-grade book. She can move on to the second-grade book if she has a special talent in that subject. She can go as fast as she wants. In our homeschooling we kept a flexible structure. If a boy has special musical talent, then there is so much time for him to cultivate that interest, and because of this he will be able to develop confidence and self-esteem by demonstrating expertise in that area. Confident children tend to use their confidence in other areas of study as well.

(More on this topic in the chapters "Flexibility vs. Structure in Homeschooling" and "Why We Homeschooled Our Children.")

Children Too Young for Proper Pūjā

We try to hold a regular maṅgala-ārati, *but when we perform* tulasī-pūjā *my son plucks her leaves. Of course, he offers his obeisance and circumambulates, but in the process Tulasī is getting spoiled. Because of these offenses we stopped* tulasī-pūjā. *Did we do the right thing?*

You should not stop *tulasī-pūjā*. Better to find some way of doing it that avoids the problem. In home *pūjā* there is nothing wrong if your son handles the *pūjā* items, as long as he is not damaging Tulasī. As he grows older, he will learn the boundaries better and understand how to respect Tulasī. But *tulasī-pūjā* should not be stopped. Somehow you have to find a way to conduct *tulasī-pūjā* without allowing him to damage Tulasī in any way. One way to accomplish this might be to not perform the actual worship with the child but simply to sing the song and offer water to Tulasī.

(More on this topic in the chapters "Deity Worship for Children," "Homeschooling in the Early Years," and "Morning Program."

Bilingual (or Multilingual) Education

Should we teach our children in our mother tongue?

If you usually speak a language at home that is different from the language used outside, then both languages are important. For example, suppose the outside language is English. Too often parents worry that if they don't speak English at home their children will fall behind. This worry becomes a self-fulfilling prophecy, especially in India, because the parents often don't know English well themselves, so the children grow up speaking poor English and yet not being able to speak Hindi or Tamil (or the parents' mother tongue).

Children have a natural ability to learn languages and can pick up four or five languages at a time – if several people in the household speak different languages children can communicate with all of them without confusion.

Strive to use both languages in your homeshooling. You may need to teach some of the basic subjects in English or the outside language, but conversation among family members should be in their native language so this important asset is not lost. Language is not just a mode of communication but entrance to an entire culture and a different way of thinking.

If you are able to speak a second language at home, don't forget to encourage your children to read regularly in that language. If they don't, their vocabulary will be severely limited or at worst, they will actually be illiterate in a language they speak well. Books from the Bhaktivedanta Book Trust (including *Śrīmad-Bhāgavatam*) are available in many languages and can be used for this purpose.

(More on this topic in the chapters "The Five Rs: Reading," "The Five Rs: wRiting," "A Student's Perspective on Sanskrit," and "Learning English through *Śrīmad-Bhāgavatam.*")

Mothers Who Work Outside the Home

In most homeschooling families, the typical assumption is that the father earns the bread and the mother is the housewife. In some cases, the mother may be especially materially well qualified and want to pursue her career at least part-time. How would homeschooling work in such a scenario?

There is always some level of Kṛṣṇa conscious education we can give our children. We just have to schedule the time we have available, even if the only available time is in the evenings or on weekends. Some parents work from home using a computer and the Internet and can therefore do some homeschooling during the day.

Even if it is necessary to send children to school, many of the principles we have discussed for creating a Kṛṣṇa conscious home can still be applied. In homeschooling all these activities and practices would be regular (and sometimes intensive) parts of the educational process. If the children are going to school, time for these is much reduced, but they can still be done as extracurricular activities on weekends or at other times.

Sometimes material circumstances require a shift in family

structure. I know of a devotee family where the father (who can't find a job) homeschools the children while the wife works.

(More on this topic in the chapters "Basic Principles of Kṛṣṇa Conscious Homeschooling," "Why We Homeschooled Our Children," and "The Father's Role in Homeschooling.")

Teaching Detachment

In homeschooling, since the child is always with us, how do we teach detachment? In Vedic times teaching detachment was the reason why the child was sent to gurukula *to serve the guru.*

Actually, the reasons for the *gurukula* system are complex enough to fill another book, but let's look at your question of detachment in homeschooling. It is very difficult to be detached in a family.

There is a time for everything. Marriage and raising children is the *gṛhastha-āśrama.* At that time, there will be a certain level of involvement and close interaction between family members. Even if we send our children to *gurukula,* that doesn't mean we feel no attachment for one another. Often "absence makes the heart grow fonder," and attachment is actually increased by separation. Parents might feel they have missed the best years of their children's lives.

The devotional process is to somehow dovetail family attachment toward Kṛṣṇa conscious activity. Then when it's time for *vānaprastha* and the parents know their children are well educated and married, they can focus on *vairāgya.* I am at this stage myself. So there is a time for everything.

Sometimes, a devotee enters *gṛhastha* life and tries to live like a *sannyāsī:* "I won't look at my wife and she won't look at me. I don't care what she thinks." But this is both artificial and harmful. How could such a marriage work? If a person has this attitude, why enter *gṛhastha* life in the first place? Better to remain a *sannyāsī.*

Instead, the *gṛhastha-āśrama* is a time when we take our attachments and desires and try to make them as Kṛṣṇa conscious as possible. When this period is over, you have to have an exit strategy. The *Vedas* are clear about entering the world of attachment with an exit strategy in hand. Śrīla Prabhupāda says that once we reach the age of fifty we have to begin to think about detachment. At that point we voluntarily detach ourselves. Otherwise, our attachments will cause great suffering in the long run.

(More on this topic in the chapters "Basic Principles of Kṛṣṇa Conscious Homeschooling," "Possible Pitfalls of Homeschooling," and "Initiation.")

Homeschooling an Only Child

I have only one daughter. Can I homeschool her?

I know of many devotees who are successfully homeschooling an only child. For your daughter's social needs you could participate in the Sunday temple and Bhakti Vṛkṣā programs. You may even occasionally invite a friend over for a slumber party at your home. Besides daily academics, keep her engaged at home and outside assisting you in all your Kṛṣṇa conscious activities. Let her chant and dance during *ārati,* give her a variety of *prasāda,* and let her experience all the joys of Kṛṣṇa consciousness. You may also try reading *Bhāgavatam* stories to her. Celebrate all the devotional festivals with her by reading relevant material from the scripture.

(More on this topic in the chapters "Social Life for Homeschooled Children," "Possible Pitfalls of Homeschooling," "Book Distribution for Homeschooled Children," "Deity Worship for Children," "Teaching *Śrīmad-Bhāgavatam* to Children," "Festivals," "Morning Program," and "Teaching Our Children to Eat Only *Prasāda.*")

Setting a Good Example

You say one has to create a Kṛṣṇa conscious home environment by chanting, holding a morning program, worshiping the Deity, eating only prasāda, *etc. However, to raise the child's standards in this way I will have to increase my own. Sometimes that may be a fear: "Do I also have to give up eating outside? Do I also have to give up this and that?"*

Yes, that would be necessary. The best teaching is through example. Of course, we are not perfect, so it's good if we can practice our own Kṛṣṇa consciousness along with helping our children, and then make the same advancement. We just need sincerity and faith in Prabhupāda's instructions. One of the important things I have found for those who want to homeschool is good association. With good association giving up bad habits is not so difficult.

(More on this topic in the chapters "Teaching Our Children to Eat Only *Prasāda*," "The Father's Role in Homeschooling," and "Good Association.")

Getting a Break While Homeschooling

Sending kids to regular schools provides some respite to parents. Does homeschooling have an equivalent respite?

I can honestly say that the years I was homeschooling my kids were the best of my life. The homeschooling provided an incentive for me to keep things orderly and clean so I could do the essential thing: train them in Kṛṣṇa consciousness. I was happy and highly motivated. We were running a preaching center. There were so many festivals to celebrate, and I had my children as helpers.

I cannot imagine not having homeschooled the kids. But the rest was there – the children understood if I was sick or just plain tired. I would rest and they would keep themselves busy. In fact, when they were going to a private school it was harder for all of us to keep our energy levels up. They would bring home infections and fall sick. They were healthier when they were home, and my anxiety was less. I became more relaxed and happier as a wife and mother.

(More on this topic in the chapters "Vacations and Holidays" and "Flexibility vs. Structure in Homeschooling.")

Homeschooling Girls

Is Kṛṣṇa conscious homeschooling different for boys and girls? What should a girl learn?

Just as Prabhupāda stressed good *brahmacarya* training for boys, he emphasized qualities like chastity and modesty for girls.

However, he said the main goal was to train each child – male or female – to become a good devotee. For the rest – methodology and curriculum – we do whatever is practical. For example, in Western countries women have to work to survive, so parents need to give their daughters a certain level of education and training so they will be able to take care of their basic material needs.

We must also always take into consideration the variety in children. Some students, whether boys or girls, may excel academically in certain subjects while others may not be that interested in them. We need to look at the circumstances – the nature of the individual child, and certainly not only at the gender. There is no universal formula we can squeeze every student into. The only universal principle is Kṛṣṇa consciousness: whatever training we give a child according to his or her nature should help the child become a good devotee. Applying this principle, we understand that children should have whatever skills they need so they can practice their Kṛṣṇa consciousness without much worry.

Parents sometimes impose their own ambitions on their children. Certain ambitions are forced on girls and others on boys. But that's not the idea. We have to look at each child's nature and adjust accordingly, and be ambitious only in regards to Kṛṣṇa consciousness. Śrīla Prabhupāda's father was like that. Śrīla Prabhupāda always looked back on his father with fond memories, especially because his father's only ambition was that he one day become a servant of Śrīmatī Rādhārāṇī.

(More on this topic in the chapters "Basic Principles of Kṛṣṇa Conscious Homeschooling," "Possible Pitfalls of Homeschooling," and "Flexibility vs. Structure in Homeschooling.")

Encouraging Reluctant Parents

Some parents may feel hesitant to homeschool, particularly those new to Kṛṣṇa consciousness or who lack confidence in their teaching ability. How can we encourage them to homeschool?

The shortcomings on both sides can be overcome as long as parents are motivated. Fortunately, teaching their child is probably one of the most powerful motivations parents might have, so it's definitely possible to find motivation. I have met homeschooling parents from a range of educational and Kṛṣṇa conscious backgrounds. Some are devotees who have been initiated only one or two years.

(More on this topic in the chapter "Qualifications of Parents.")

Disagreements Between Husband and Wife

What if the husband and wife have a disagreement over Kṛṣṇa conscious issues or homeschooling?

Just because we are following a spiritual path does not mean we will all think alike. Variety is the spice of life, and this is especially true of spiritual life. It's natural that as human beings we will have differences of opinion, even if we are devotees. But how we resolve these differences is what counts. If you have differences, take shelter of Śrīla Prabhupāda's instructions and solve them together by finding the answers in his books and purports. You can discuss simple issues in front of your children, but serious issues should not be argued out in front of children.

Rādhikā Ramaṇa adds: In my family things were not always perfect at home. I remember several times my mother came to us and said, "You know, we were in this situation, and we didn't handle it in the best Kṛṣṇa conscious way," or, "You see from this situation how *gṛhastha* life has two sides, and one of them is suffering." From situations like these we got a realistic picture of life, and my mother turned them into teaching moments. Even in times of confusion or error, my mother took advantage of the situation to teach us: "Did you see this? Did you note that?"

We grew up with the clear picture that *gṛhastha* life wouldn't be like a romance movie – find the match of your dreams, ride off into the sunset, and everything will work out nicely. Instead, my mother gave us a real picture, always emphasizing the question of how we can be

Kṛṣṇa conscious in every circumstance. How would a devotee act in this situation?

Our goal as parents and teachers is not to give children a sterile, insulated environment, as if somehow blocking them from the outside world and giving them a picture-perfect life will turn them into "nice devotees." In fact, children grow up to become Kṛṣṇa conscious by dealing with life as it is and realizing how in every situation they can be Kṛṣṇa conscious. Arjuna himself had a problem with his relatives, yet he remained Kṛṣṇa conscious. Dealing with conflict in a devotional way is better training than ignoring or hiding the conflicts we have with those close to us.

(More on this topic in the chapters "Basic Principles of Kṛṣṇa Conscious Homeschooling" and "The Father's Role in Homeschooling.")

Problems in the Gṛhastha-āśrama

In relation to the previous question, gṛhastha *life may not always be good and parents can spill their stress on their children. How should we handle this?*

We are human and sometimes, because of too much stress or work we take our frustrations out on whoever is nearby, which for the homeschooling mother is usually the children. I lost my cool a few times. What I would do in those situations was to sit down with the children and openly tell them, "Look, I was like this and I know I was wrong. You did not deserve the way I acted. I was very tired or frustrated and I'm sorry."

We can be open and honest. The child knows the parents are devotees but also human. We can't expect perfect behavior from everybody. So we can be honest. We can't hide everything, and it's natural sometimes to slip. But we should not make inappropriate behavior the norm. If we are facing a difficult situation, we should try to get help, try to get time away, or try to get someone to take care of the children so we get a little break.

(More on this topic in the chapter "The Father's Role in Homeschooling.")

Homeschooling "Ordinary" Children

I mentioned to a friend how you had taught your sons in such a Kṛṣṇa conscious way that they went on to become very successful both spiritually and materially. My friend was wondering if maybe they were simply geniuses.

My children are definitely not geniuses. They are quite ordinary kids. If my sons did well materially, it was only thanks to Śrīla Prabhupāda's books, which formed the basis of our curriculum. As far as spiritual benefits, again the credit goes to Śrīla Prabhupāda, as he elaborated on every aspect of how to lead a Kṛṣṇa conscious life.

In fact, now there are many examples in ISKCON of devotee children who followed the method of homeschooling based on Prabhupāda's books and have been successful both materially and spiritually. This is true across the board – for Indian families and Western families, for boys and girls.

(More on this topic in the chapters "Why We Homeschooled Our Children" and "The Scriptures as the Basis for Homeschooling.")

Measuring Student Performance

In homeschooling, how can we assess our children's performance?

The United States has standardized examinations children take in school every year depending on their grade level. Some states require homeschooled children to take these examinations only in specific grades. Other states do not require exams but instead ask children to turn in a portfolio of their work, which may or may not need to be reviewed by a licensed teacher. Yet other states have no mandatory requirements for assessment. Parents should check with their local homeschooling association or the state's public school board to find out the specific requirements for where they live.

Even if annual examinations are not required, homeschooling parents can usually arrange to have their children take the exams and in this way measure their children's progress against other children in the state. Some areas even have homeschooling associations that organize these exams for local homeschooled children. Naturally, most homeschoolers come out with scores much higher than the grade level they are competing with, but taking the test seems to create a sense of security among parents, who then know they are doing a good job educating their children.

In India the NIOS, a central government organization, has passed more than a million students so far. NIOS offers examinations on behalf of CBSC or SSC boards for third, fifth, eighth, and tenth standards. Parents have to accompany the child on a designated date for the exam.

(More on this topic in the chapters "Homeschooling in India" and "Starting a Homeschooling Co-op.")

Annual Testing

Did you conduct tests for each grade? How did your sons get credit so they could get into college? Did they skip any grades? How many grades did they complete each year? Did they perform any science experiments? What about physics, social studies, chemistry, and so on?

I homeschooled my children until the eighth grade. They were tested yearly through the Iowa Tests of Basic Skills (ITBS), which are standardized tests provided as a service to schools by the College of Education of the University of Iowa. The tests are administered for grades K–8 in language arts and math. If you are interested, you can find information about this test online. My children skipped grades a couple of times since they scored so high on these tests. However, it is up to the parents whether or not to allow their children to skip grades. Sometimes it's better just to let them progress one grade at a time, even though their test scores may be high.

After eighth grade both my sons skipped high school and went directly to college as part-time students, taking one or two classes each semester. When they had completed enough classes to show their ability, they were admitted as full-time students. During this time they also took their SAT college entrance exams. Public high schools are not a good environment for our children; the college environment is safer and better. In high school there is a lot of peer pressure to conform, whereas college students tend to be more mature and open to differences.

For science, before they began college they were tutored for a couple of months in chemistry and physics to familiarize themselves with these subjects. In many cities there are tutors who have full labs in their homes to help homeschooled children learn science in both theory and practice.

(More on this topic in the chapter "High School and College for Homeschooled Children.")

Preparing for Standardized Tests

Before taking the ITBS test, did your children prepare using locally available materials, or were Bhāgavatam *study and Saxon Math enough for language and math?*

A month before the ITBS exams I ordered some practice tests. These are available at curriculum bookstores or online. My children took these tests while I timed them. The practice tests were helpful and gave us an idea what to expect. The practice tests come with an answer key, and parents can grade their children themselves. The children also get a chance to work under a time constraint. We did not do any other preparation for these exams. The *Bhāgavatam* and Saxon Math seemed sufficient. The practice tests took away most of our anxiety.

(More on this topic in the chapter "Learning English through *Śrīmad-Bhāgavatam*" and "The Five Rs: Rote Memorization.")

Starting College Early

Both your sons started college in their early teens. When do you decide that a child has finished home education and is ready to move on to college?

It's different for different kids. Students who test at a high school or college level academically may not be emotionally ready or even want to go to college early. Starting college early is not the goal; the majority of successful people in the world go through the regular route, and the majority of homeschoolers do that too. When homeschooled children turn eighteen, they apply to a college like everyone else, and pursue whatever degrees they are interested in.

There should definitely be no push in terms of going to college early. We never planned for it; it just happened. So our children did not follow the norm and they don't need to be the standard. Kids' needs vary in terms of when they might want to go to college and when they will feel comfortable there.

(More on this topic in the chapters "High School and College for Homeschooled Children," "Possible Pitfalls of Homeschooling," and "Don't Be Too Ambitious to Make Your Children Succeed.")

Hiding the Outside World

How long can we avoid exposing our children to what's happening in the outside world? They will eventually discover these things and might feel they were left out of certain activities. What clean fun do we have that will overcome these desires?

If children are given a good balance of śāstric reading and practical devotional service they will develop the intelligence to understand and discriminate between good and bad. More often we as parents worry too much that we are denying our children fun. Engage your children as much as possible in Kṛṣṇa consciousness, and they will be able to overcome material desires.

We can only protect our children for so long. When the time comes and they fly out of the nest, our training will be tested. When my children left for graduate school I didn't worry too much. I knew I had given them good training, and now it was up to them to make their lives as they saw fit. And they fared well.

(More on this topic in the chapters "A Student's Perspective on

Television," "Good Association," "Vacations and Holidays," and "Playing for Kṛṣṇa.")

Imparting Worldly Wisdom

The lifestyle you describe is so pure and amazing – keeping śāstra *as the authority – but is such a pure lifestyle suitable only for turning our children into* pūjārīs? *Will they be worldly wise once they are trained according to this method?*

One way I can answer this question is to give my own children as an example. I homeschooled them, but they do not lack anything materially. One of them is married and has a job as a college professor, and the younger one is studying for his PhD. This kind of training does not give them a one-sided education. It trains them both materially and spiritually, because Kṛṣṇa is the creator of this material world as well. Even to live in this world we have to understand Him, and He mercifully gives us the formula for how to live here and be happy. The scriptures cover both sides. There are many stories in *Śrīmad-Bhāgavatam* describing the nature of this material world and the results we reap if we don't act properly.

(More on this topic in the chapter "Studying History through *Śrīmad-Bhāgavatam.*")

Teenage Rebellion and Peer Pressure

My son is fifteen years old, with a good understanding of the philosophy of Kṛṣṇa consciousness. He also reads the Bhagavad-gītā *at home. But now because of his age, he is very much with his friends and likes to party and go out. He says that once his teenage years end, he will come back to Kṛṣṇa consciousness. How should we guide him?*

At this age, as much as he is willing, just engage him in devotional activities in the association of his peers, the children of other devotees, in activities that are fun and keep them busy. Give them projects to do and things like that. At his age, the mind becomes sharp, capable of understanding logical arguments, critical thinking, and noticing detail. Even though he might say he is not interested now but will be later on, his intelligence is hungrily looking at things. He is thirsty to make sense of his world. If somehow you can attract him to study *Śrīmad-Bhāgavatam* with you or other devotees, he will actually enjoy it a lot.

When my sons were that age, I remember those were my nicest years in studying *Śrīmad-Bhāgavatam* with them, because their minds were eagerly looking for some substantial work. Nothing is as satisfying as *Śrīmad-Bhāgavatam*. You can interest him in some kind of study course with other devotees – maybe a Bhakti Śāstrī course going on somewhere – or you can sit down and study with him for half an hour or an hour a day. Study of *śāstra* at his age is crucial to keep him in Kṛṣṇa consciousness, alive and vibrant.

Preaching activities with other devotee children are also important, boosting self-esteem and giving a feeling that life is worthwhile because he is able to contribute. And preaching is also intellectually satisfying and helps build social relationships. "Preaching" in this context means more than just going to the temple and singing *kīrtana*. If there is no organized activity in your area, you can help him set up book distribution or *harināma* engagements to get him involved.

Dealing with teenagers often involves a little bit of pushing in the beginning, but once they are attached to these activities, they really enjoy them. The rest we have to leave up to Kṛṣṇa, as there is only so much we can do. It is ultimately up to the child to develop his own relationship with Kṛṣṇa.

The most important criterion for success at your son's age is association. If he gets in with the wrong association, everything will be finished, but if he finds good association, even though he is not yet fixed in Kṛṣṇa consciousness the good association will carry him through. One day he will wake up with the realization that he wants to be a devotee.

I know a fifteen-year-old child who is a fine example of this. He was just hanging around the temple one day when someone suggested he go to Māyāpur for the Bhakti Śāstrī course. He decided to try it, and when he got back six months later he was a changed boy. He is so serious in Kṛṣṇa consciousness now.

As parents we are fond of believing we "know" our children, but in fact we never know what will ignite that spark of *bhakti*. That spark is there, in your son's heart, because you have already given it to him through his Kṛṣṇa conscious upbringing. Now it is just a matter of time before something fans that spark into a flame, and you as a parent just have to keep pushing buttons to see which one works – and one of them *will* work. As soon as we become devotees, Kṛṣṇa puts a "hook" – a permanent connection – into us. We ourselves may not know what that hook is, but all of a sudden we find ourselves attracted to Kṛṣṇa again.

Both Kṛṣṇa and Māyā have their hooks in us, and Māyā knows how to pull us at just the right time. But there is a big difference between the two: Māyā knows our weakness, but Kṛṣṇa knows our strengths. Māyā can pull us all she likes, but Kṛṣṇa pulls harder and, when we are ready, there is nothing we can do about it – we will come running back to Him.

Our job as parents of teenagers is to keep trying to find Kṛṣṇa's hook. What is it that attracts your son to Kṛṣṇa? Once he finds it, there won't be any problem. It may take a few years, but it will happen. There is no doubt.

(More on this topic in the chapters "Good Association," "Book Distribution for Homeschooled Children," "Social Life for Homeschooled Children," "Preaching Is the Essence," "Festivals," and "Restrictions.")

Advice for Older Children

As children grow older and are about to leave home, is there any particular advice you would give them?

Rādhikā Ramaṇa responds: The whole world follows a standard pattern of life: you play, study, go to college, get a good job, make some money, get married, buy a house, have children, and on and on and on. We all basically follow this herd mentality, but it's hard to believe that the horses in a caravan really enjoy the view of the horse in front.

Most of us do the same because we see everyone else doing it. Here's a possible conversation with a high schooler or college student:

"Why are you studying so hard?"

"So I can get a good job."

"Why do you want a good job?"

"So I can make a lot of money."

"Why do you want to make a lot of money?"

"So I can be happy."

"You think that making a lot of money will make you happy?"

"No."

"Then why are you studying so hard?"

"Well …"

This goal is something we're all taught. Naturally, as members of society we have to do what we have to do, but as devotees – and as devotee children – we have a greater imperative to live up to a much higher standard. Śrīla Prabhupāda asked us to be revolutionaries – he wants us to change the world! The goal is not simply to be "a good person," maintain a family, and then die. That's what the rest of the world is doing. We need to go beyond that and think outside the box.

Kṛṣṇa is unlimited, so our thinking needs to be unlimited when we ask how we can serve Him. Each of us wants to do something unique, something the whole world will remember us by – but even more important is to be remembered by Kṛṣṇa. How wonderful it is if Kṛṣṇa notices and says, "Look at this boy or girl. He or she did this for Me."

Young people have so much energy and drive and ambition, and older people have so much wisdom to tap into. If young people can take advice from parents, grandparents, and senior devotees, they can channel their innate ambition and energy to make a true impact on the world by bringing about the revolution Prabhupāda called for.

(More on this topic in the chapters "Basic Principles of Kṛṣṇa Conscious Homeschooling," "Character Training," and "Respect for Elders.")

Imparting Values to Children Who Aren't Homeschooled

If our child has been in school for many years and we cannot take him out, how can we educate him in proper values?

In the case of children who cannot be homeschooled, we encourage them as far as possible to pursue the devotee lifestyle. The same principles apply as might apply to any other student or even to ourselves: encourage the child to stay in good association, make devotee friends, perform devotional service in the temple at least once a week, attend programs, classes, seminars, and festivals, read and study Śrīla Prabhupāda books, and chant a fixed number of rounds every day.

This encouragement is vitally important, because once children reach a certain age they are virtually adults, and Śrīla Prabhupāda points out that having reached such an age, "stick" discipline no longer works. The only way to reach these children is to become friends with them and to encourage them as much as possible to stay connected to Kṛṣṇa and His devotees. This formula is not different for anyone else; it is the basic formula of Kṛṣṇa conscious preaching.

Adolescence is a difficult and delicate stage of life, and every parent needs to find the balance between being a parent and being a friend. Parents need to be available for help and guidance without being overbearing, for such an approach only breeds rebellion in a teenager.

The best hope is good association, being connected to good devotees, and becoming attached to some kind of devotional activity. Śrīla Rūpa Gosvāmī mentions five forms of devotion as being paricularly potent because even a little attachment to one of them can bring about ecstatic devotion even in a neophyte: Deity worship, devotee association, chanting the holy name, living in the *dhāma,* and hearing the *Bhāgavatam*. If our teenagers are attracted to any one of these five processes, that attachment will lead to the fructification of *bhakti,* just as they would in any adult.

(More on this topic in the chapters "Basic Principles of Kṛṣṇa Conscious Homeschooling," "Deity Worship for Children," "Morning

Program," "Good Association," "Vacations and Holidays," and "The Scriptures as the Basis for Homeschooling.")

Your Own Questions

I love your book so far, but I still have a question. What should I do?

I have started a Yahoo discussion group for parents who are homeschooling their children using Śrīla Prabhupāda's books. As of this printing, there are 540 members, and many have probably experienced a situation similar to the one leading to your question. All are willing to share their insights with you. Sign up at www.krishnahomeschool.com. You can then browse the archives and post your own questions and comments. The group generates a low amount of email traffic – typically about a dozen messages per month.

Reviews of the Methods in Homeschooling Kṛṣṇa's Children

Jayadvaita Swami

On a recent flight from London to New York I read Aruddhā Dāsī's new book *Homeschooling Krishna's Children* – straight through, cover to cover, because it was too good to put down.

The book is chock-full of Kṛṣṇa consciousness, common sense, practical advice, and realized understandings earned from successfully homeschooling her two fine devotee sons. People like me can offer opinions and scriptural citations, but Aruddhā Dāsī offers expertise. Interspersed reflections contributed by her older son Rādhikā Ramaṇa (Dr. Ravi M. Gupta) further brighten the book.

To the extent that raising children in Kṛṣṇa consciousness is important, so too is this book. I wholeheartedly recommend "Homeschooling Krishna's Children" to all devotee parents with school-age children or younger and in fact to all devotee parents, everyone who guides or advises devotee parents, and everyone else who has anything to do with devotee parents or children – that is, I recommend the book to all devotees, everywhere.

Sivarama Swami

I have personally attended Aruddhā Devī Dāsī's course on home schooling Kṛṣṇa's children and consider that it is one of the most important contributions in establishing the social stability and spiritual integrity of ISKCON, which for the most part depends upon the Kṛṣṇa consciousness of its children. Her course gives both techniques and inspiration for any parent to simultaneously educate and deliver Kṛṣṇa to their children.

Rādhānātha Swami

Years ago, I visited a college with two small devotee children. Before my lecture the children sang beautiful prayers. Afterwards, the professor remarked, "I liked your lecture, but what really impresses me is your children." She then spoke words that I never forgot: "Your Society will be successful to the degree that your children find joy in sincerely imbibing your culture."

It is our most important responsibility to inspire stable families and empower our children with good character, effective skills, and happiness in loving Kṛṣṇa. For this purpose Śrīla Prabhupāda appealed to us to educate our children while providing an environment where they will be nourished by the joys of pure *bhakti*.

Aruddhā Devī has dedicated her life to bringing this matchless gift to our children. Wherever she shares her wisdom, lives are transformed. She is an extraordinary devotee with profound academic skills, and beyond that she genuinely cares. The children born from Aruddhā Devī are a testament to her inspired skills. They love Kṛṣṇa and are like jewels of devotional qualities while excelling in their professional careers.

I am overjoyed to see this priceless book being made available. I pray that Śrī Śrī Rādhā-Kṛṣṇa may forever bless and empower Aruddhā Devī, and that all of you readers may gain the precious benefits of this book.

With gratitude,
Rādhānātha Swami

Śeṣa dāsa, ISKCON GBC Minister of Education
This is an excellent resource. I highly recommend it!

Lokādhyakṣa Dāsa and Vidarbha-sutā Devī Dāsī
Maryland, USA

The method taught by Mother Aruddhā is not just a homeschooling system; rather, it provides a complete framework for exciting and thorough Krishna conscious parenting. A few years ago, in the throes of confusion and frustration about the education of our son Nimāi (then six years old), we were contemplating going back to India to provide him a strong Kṛṣṇa conscious education. A month before our scheduled departure we found a newspaper article in the *Hindustan Times* glorifying the achievements of Mother Aruddhā's two boys. We decided to visit Boise, where we found to our surprise a system of education that was innovative, practical, and deeply devotional. We really liked the idea of basing education on Śrīla Prabhupāda's books and spiritual principles. What impressed us most was her gentle and loving approach to educating kids, such that they would feel voluntary enthusiasm for studies while pursuing their individual interests.

We have been homeschooling our son Nimāi in the USA following her method since 2005, and it has worked wonders for him. He has not only developed a deep interest in Kṛṣṇa consciousness but also is doing very well academically and in other areas as well. Aruddhā's method of centering education around Śrīla Prabhupāda's books really works. Nimāi has developed a strong memory, keen skills in logic and argument, and very strong reading and writing skills. This approach has also allowed Nimāi to develop and pursue his interests in other areas like music, art, and writing, and to use those in Kṛṣṇa's service. We would wholeheartedly recommend this book and method to any parents desiring to give a first-class education to their child.

Śrīnivāsācārya Dāsa
Idaho, USA

My wife Sundarī Rādhikā and I have full conviction that we made the right choice to homeschool our daughter, Sugopī. Having been able to receive constant association and guidance from Mother Aruddhā, we started to focus on Sugopī's spiritual life right from the beginning. We even had a *Kṛṣṇa* book story tape playing when she took birth. Now she is five years old, and we already see significant spiritual progress in her. From chanting *japa* to book distribution, she enthusiastically participates in all the spiritual activities a devotee would like to do. And it's not at all surprising to us that she is ahead of non-homeschooled children in her material education. This is possible for anyone, and it's never too late to take up this homeschooling process. A wide variety of tested tools and techniques are available in Mother Aruddhā's homeschooling book to help you begin and succeed in this process.

I recommend that all parents read this book. You will find everything Śrīla Prabhupāda wanted to say about children in one place. Aruddhā teaches you how to apply those teachings in raising your own children.

Acharya Ratna Dāsa and Shyama Vilasini Devī Dāsī
Mauritius

I am indebted to Mātājī Aruddhā for inspiring us and giving us this invaluable gift in the form of her experience in homeschooling her sons in Kṛṣṇa consciousness. What attracted me most is the fact that she used the authorized Vedic scriptures as the basis. The results speak for themselves. She is a true leader to parents who are seeking the best for their children.

Graduating as an electronics engineer and then being exposed to the academic world in various managerial positions, and eventually as a quality consultant, I felt that the present education system did not address the basic questions of human existence as Śrīla Prabhupāda says. Deep in my heart I knew that if we develop faith in the words of Śrīla Prabhupāda and put his teachings into practice, we will raise well cultured, high caliber children with character. However, I had not seen such education translated into real life before Mātājī Aruddhā. Teaching by example and not just precept, she is now an authority in education.

Following in her footsteps I have started homeschooling my two sons using her methodology, and I have within a few months seen a transformation in the performance, behavior, well-being, and attitude of my sons. I will only encourage parents to adopt this methodology with emphasis on the holistic approach as presented by Mātājī Aruddhā. It is our duty as parents to deliver our children from the clutches of *māyā* and guide them on their way home, back to Godhead.

Anantshesh Dāsa and Sundarī Devī Dāsī

Pune, India

When information is loaded with practical realization, it has the full potency to touch hearts and facilitate transformation. That's precisely what happens when prospective parents swim across this book. Undoubtedly, the book is immensely beneficial not only for those who are planning to homeschool their children, but also to all parents who desire to bring up their child spiritually in a wholesome Kṛṣṇa conscious environment in the Age of Kali. A must-read for the new generation of devotee parents!

We seriously started "experimenting" with homeschooling a year back, taking sole inspiration from Her Grace Aruddhā Mātājī's family, who have been a shining example of what wonders homeschooling can do for the child as well as the parents. It's like a dream unfolding, living the enriching Vaiṣṇava lifestyle Bhaktivinoda Ṭhākura mentions in his timeless songs: when I enter my home I feel I am entering Vaikuṇṭha! While there are only a handful of shining live examples within the Indian context, we are sure that if many of the upcoming Kṛṣṇa conscious parents decide to take this up sincerely – especially where the facility of a full-fledged Kṛṣṇa conscious school is not available – it would create a revolution in the coming years within ISKCON communities throughout India and a definite step toward contributing to Śrīla Prabhupāda's vision of bringing up children in a completely Kṛṣṇa conscious environment.

Rādhākaṇṭha Dāsa and Shyameswari Devī Dāsī

Bangalore, India

It is not difficult to understand the problems of current schooling, and we were left with no alternative. We are very much grateful to Aruddhā Mātājī for her motivation and showing us the right direction in terms of our children's education at home. Mātājī took initiative and started guiding many people by conducting seminars.

This book is full of her experiences in homeschooling while following Prabhupāda's instructions. Probably there is no point related to homeschooling that is not discussed in this book, and the topics are on-the-ground reality with practical solutions and full conviction in Kṛṣṇa consciousness. This book will help all devotee parents who want to raise their children in a Kṛṣṇa conscious culture whether they want to homeschool or not.

Kṛṣṇa Kathā Dāsa and Śrī Yaśodā Devī Dāsī

Melbourne, Australia

For a devotee family, considering where to start in the service of bringing up children in Kṛṣṇa consciousness is a bewildering and sometimes intimidating challenge, even before children are conceived! It's a weighty responsibility and a lifetime commitment of parents to offer liberation to their dependents. The question may be asked, "Where do we start?" as we ourselves may also be just beginning and learning at every step. How to be a balanced parent in Kṛṣṇa consciousness? How to best guide our children in a wholesome, sustainable, and natural Kṛṣṇa conscious lifestyle, where they can develop into well-balanced, mature adults, spiritually and materially stable, as per their desire? Is such a holistic parenting choice even an option for families to consider? And if so, could it have been right under our noses the whole time?

In this book Aruddhā Mātājī mercifully shares her great knowledge and realizations in her pioneered development of the Kṛṣṇa conscious homeschool system, offering a wide and flexible range of Kṛṣṇa conscious lifestyle options for parents and children alike to learn and grow from.

Aruddhā Mātājī is empowering families all over the world to deepen their faith in the process of Kṛṣṇa consciousness, as it was so lovingly given to us by Śrīla Prabhupāda and in particular through his books.

Aruddhā Mātājī takes the fear out of homeschooling our children and teaches us how to develop a Kṛṣṇa conscious environment where parents and children alike can learn, grow, and benefit.

Yaśodāmayī Devī Dāsī
Former *gurukula* teacher and preschool reading tutor
Vṛndāvana, India

Her Grace Aruddhā Devī Dāsī has well earned her highly respected position as an authority on homeschooling children in Kṛṣṇa consciousness. As a homeschooling parent, she has successfully trained and educated her own two sons in both spiritual understanding as well as in academic excellence. Both sons are widely recognized in the devotional community as well as in academic circles as exemplary young men of outstanding character and scholarly erudition.

As a dynamic member of the Kṛṣṇa consciousness movement, Aruddhā Devī Dāsī has selflessly reached out to numerous parents and educators. Through personal association, letters, lectures, and seminars, she has deeply inspired and effectively guided them in homeschooling methods based on Śrīla Prabhupāda's teachings and a systematic study of his books.

Now in the spirit of the preceptors of Vaiṣṇava philosophy, Aruddhā Devī Dāsī has compiled a book on homeschooling children in Kṛṣṇa consciousness for the benefit of an even broader audience.

All who by good fortune have received guidance from Aruddhā Devī Dāsī, either through personal association, lectures, seminars, or her book *Homeschooling Kṛṣṇa's Children,* will find their faith in the application of Śrīla Prabhupāda's teachings and books in their personal lives greatly enriched and enhanced.

"A Temple Opens"

The following article, by Tiffany Horan, is reprinted by permission from *The Idaho Statesman,* August 21, 1999:

A culture embraced

On a small street lined with apartments and brick houses near Boise State University, a new Hare Krishna temple has risen.

Constructing the house of worship has been a learning experience for the 30-member congregation, and also for the artists, architect, construction workers, and neighbors who knew little about the eastern faith or Indian culture before the project began.

The Hare Krishna Temple and Vedic Cultural Center opens with a public celebration Sunday. A small temple had previously been located in the home of the Guptas, an Indian family that lives next to the new site.

"The amazing thing about this project is that it's really a project of Idaho by Idahoans," said Ravi Gupta, 17, who called the temple the centerpiece of his life. "They've made their best effort to make it something unique for all of us."

Stained glass master Michael Booth, architect Bruce Poe and artist Mike Baltzell said they enjoyed learning about a new religion and culture and incorporating that knowledge into their work. An added benefit was the cooking of Aruddha Gupta, Ravi's mother, who regularly made special Indian meals for the men. The Guptas used to own Govinda's Restaurant.

"Every time I stopped by food was being handed to me," Poe said. "I think I gained 10 pounds."

Poe said he learned while designing the temple that Hare Krishnas are nonviolent, vegetarian, and unconnected to material things.

The temple sits between two brick duplexes, which had previously been divided by garages. Except for a gold dome, the brick exterior of the temple blends in with the duplexes and the neighborhood – a goal of Poe's design. But inside, the eastern influence is supreme.

"It's a piece of India in Boise," Poe said.

A wooden arch shaped like an inverted lotus flower, marble floors and hand-carved altar are a few of the temple's unique touches. The ceiling and stained glass windows are the others.

The ceiling, which is painted blue, was designed to represent the spiritual sky. Several colorful murals depicting Krishna, or God, in different incarnations grace the ceiling.

Painting the murals was a bit nerve-racking, said Baltzell, an associate professor of Theater Arts at Boise State University. The ceiling isn't very high, so people can look closely at his work for as long as they want – unlike in a theater where the audience is only present for a limited time.

Getting it right

Creating images of someone's faith also is tricky – especially when you are not of that religion, Baltzell said.

But the Guptas helped Baltzell by stopping by his studio about once a week to check on his progress. The family not only helped with the aesthetics of the paintings but made sure the religious symbolism was appropriate, he said.

Working on the project was interesting, Baltzell said.

"It's not often you get a chance to do something like this," he said.

Booth, owner of Kaleidoscope Art Glass Studio in Meridian, also enjoyed the project's uniqueness. Booth often creates Christian scenes for churches, so learning about a different faith was interesting. Translating the spiritual nuances into his work also was challenging, he said.

"I had to make sure I was picking up the right glint in the eye, the tilt of the head, the shape of the shoulder, the drape of the cloth," Booth said.

His pieces are installed in the front window of the temple. The largest piece shows Krishna playing a flute by a river. Ten smaller pieces show the forms Krishna has taken through the ages.

The work is the best of his life, Booth said.

"Not just because of the window, but because of the interaction (with the Guptas), the humor, the learning, the patience," said Booth, whose son Matthew also helped with the project. "I think all of these things came together to make it special."

Guptas share culture, food

Booth and his son also learned to appreciate Indian food during the process. Aruddha Gupta always brought special dishes when the family visited Booth's studio every two weeks.

Matthew Booth was rewarded with more food Tuesday when he finished installing the stained glass at the Temple. Arun Gupta, Ravi's father, told Matthew that Aruddha had something special for him.

Matthew soon was happily eating a big plate of lentils, rice, and vegetables with potato curry in the temple courtyard.

Neighbor Bonnie Bruett, 85, doesn't come over to eat, but to see the progress of the construction. She watches the workers from her front window every day.

"I now know how to lay brick, to put concrete down," she said.

She makes oatmeal cookies for the workers. The workers helped her when a large branch fell on her property.

Bruett likes having the temple across the street.

"I think it's beautiful," she said.

Building the temple

The Guptas moved to Boise 13 years ago for Arun Gupta's new job at Hewlett-Packard Co. There was no Hare Krishna temple in town, so Aruddha Gupta began calling Indian families listed in the phone book.

A week later, a temple was opened in the Gupta home. The family wanted to open a larger temple not only to worship but to share their culture with the community, Aruddha said. Teachers and professors from local schools and colleges often brought classes to the old temple.

Giving back

"Boise has been so nice to us," she said. "I feel very blessed. I have felt very welcome in Boise. I have never felt any bias. Because of that, I have wanted to share everything with the community."

The congregation has been raising money for the new, $250,000 temple for two years, said Arun Gupta, who also is temple president. In addition to the congregation's portion, $50,000 came from the community and the rest from the Gupta family.

Aruddha, who along with other Hare Krishnas marks her forehead with sacred clay from the river Ganges as a sign that her body is a temple of God, was inspired by the *Vedas,* ancient sacred books of Hinduism. The temple will help her share that inspiration with fellow Indians as well as the community at large, she said.

Aruddha used the *Vedas,* along with other academic books, to homeschool her two sons.

Ravi, 17, has a degree from Boise State University in mathematics and philosophy. At the end of September, he leaves for Oxford University in England where he will study Sanskrit, an ancient Indian language. Gopal, 15, will be a junior at BSU. He studies electrical engineering.

The boys will make a lifelong commitment to their faith at opening ceremonies Sunday. Both will vow not to eat meat, gamble, drink or take drugs, and not to have sex outside marriage.

Opening the temple in Boise, where he has lived since age 4, is something Ravi has been anticipating for many years. It will be difficult to leave when he moves to England, Ravi said.

"It's hard in a sense that I won't get to spend time in the temple," he said. "On the other hand, I'm not leaving permanently. (Boise) is a place called home."

"Wise Guys"

The following article, by Emily Simnitt, is reprinted by permission from *The Idaho Statesman,* July 30, 2005:

Ravi and Gopal Gupta are two smart brothers: Ravi has a PhD from Oxford, Gopal is on track to get his Oxford PhD, too.

Inside an immaculate house in Southeast Boise, the Gupta family converses about science and religion.

"Can computers replace life? What is the relationship between artificial intelligence and consciousness?" poses Gopal Gupta, 21. He'll be heading to Oxford University this fall on a prestigious full-ride scholarship to try to answer questions just like those as he works on a PhD in science and religion.

"There are two great forces that influence people," adds Gopal's brother Ravi Gupta, 23. "The most major events in the world, the most important buildings and architecture are either a product of science or religion. It behooves us to see how these work together."

Ravi just returned from Oxford, where he earned a PhD in Hinduism and Sanskrit, and will be heading to the University of Florida this fall to teach in the Religious Studies Department.

"Science is advancing but people are losing spirituality," says father Arun Gupta, who brought the family to Boise about 20 years ago when he took a job at Hewlett Packard. "People don't get relief. That's why the combination is important."

Pretty heady stuff.

But then, this is no ordinary household.

When the Guptas first moved to Boise, they were one of a handful of Indian families. Arun and his wife Aruddha were determined to bring up their boys with a strong sense of their Indian heritage while at the same time drawing from the best of Western culture in raising Ravi and Gopal.

"We knew this was a job we had to do as a family," says Aruddha.

The family created a Hare Krishna temple in their living room and opened it up to interested Boiseans.

And they began homeschooling Ravi and Gopal until the boys reached 13 and entered Boise State University.

High achievers

Yes, BSU at 13.

Ravi has degrees in philosophy and mathematics from BSU. Gopal has bachelors and masters degrees in electrical engineering from BSU.

Clearly, the homeschooling was successful.

Steve Grantham, a math professor at BSU who taught both Guptas, says the two fit in well with older students – and not just because they were intellectually ready for college.

"A lot of students didn't realize there was a young kid in the class," Grantham says. "They had a maturity about them. They didn't seem like some party crashers from junior high. They fit in very well."

Gary Erickson, an electrical engineering professor who was Gopal's advisor, puts it this way: "He's one of the best students I've ever had.

"When he did his masters, he essentially came up with a problem, asked if it was reasonable, then went and solved it, wrote it up, and said here is my thesis."

Most graduate students need a little more hand-holding.

But then, Ravi and Gopal have never been like most students.

Their parents attribute their sons' academic success to a strong sense of cultural heritage and the reverence for the values that were every bit as much of their homeschooling as the traditional reading, writing, and arithmetic.

Ravi lists those values: "Honesty, self-control, compassion, kindness.

"It's about asking 'How can I free myself and others from suffering?' "

"It's about simple living and high thinking," adds Arun. "You minimize your physical needs and maximize your mental capacity."

It's a philosophy the family is working on sharing with others through a presentation on their homeschooling method that they've been presenting throughout the Northwest.

A place of culture

Of course, they've always shared their culture and philosophy with Boiseans since they first arrived here.

After hosting the temple in their house for many years, they built a larger temple next door, which is regularly open to the public.

The design of the gold-domed brick building reflects how the Guptas have lived their lives in Boise. It's designed to be a hybrid of Indian and Boise culture. The dome, the murals inside and the imported teak altar give a taste of India. The outside brick is reminiscent of many buildings on the nearby BSU campus.

The family is as at home in the temple as they are in their living room.

They are proud to show it off and demonstrate the meditation, chanting, and prayer that is part of their daily ritual.

Ravi plays a mridunga, a two-headed drum, and Gopal sits down at the harmonium.

The music starts softly in the incense-filled room and then builds when the young men and then their parents and grandmother who is visiting from India join in.

"Hare Krishna, Hare Krishna," the group chants.

"Music was a big part of our homeschooling," says Aruddha after the chanting is finished. "Music brings people together. It brings our family together."

It will be that music, and the strong family bonds that go with it, that will bring the young men back home again and again to Boise.

Raising kids

Aruddha Gupta knows a thing or two about raising successful kids. Both her sons began coursework at BSU at age 13, after she home-schooled them for their first 12 years.

Here's some of her advice:

Put your heart into it. "A mother is a natural teacher," Aruddha says. "Do what comes naturally."

Focus on the basics. That is, reading, writing, arithmetic, and music. Aruddha's homeschooling method also focused on memorizing skills and developing her children's curiosity.

Be flexible. Aruddha's son Gopal describes a typical day when he was homeschooled: "We used to rise at 5 A.M., come to the temple, do our chanting and meditation for an hour and a half. Then we'd study for three to four hours and spend the rest of the day doing music, art, outdoor sports."

Base the education on your values. For the Guptas, that's meant exploration of the *Vedas* (ancient Indian texts), the *Bhagavad-Gita* and studies in Sanskrit, an ancient Indian language. It's also meant sticking close to their cultural roots (the whole family speaks Hindi in addition to English).

For more information about the Guptas' homeschooling methods – or for more information about the Hare Krishna temple here – e-mail the family at boise_temple@yahoo.com.

Hare Krishna explained

The Guptas are Hare Krishnas, a sect of the much broader Hindu religion.

Here's how the family explains their faith:

The tradition is at least 5,000 years old and it's based on the *Vedas,* which are sacred texts that have been passed down through generations.

The practice was brought to the US in the '60s from India.

"The philosophy follows the belief that all living entities are parts of God. As His children it's our duty to love and serve Him," says Ravi Gupta. "We call Him by the name Krishna, or He who is all attractive."

"God is one and we call Him by many names," adds Gopal. "Chanting His name is how we glorify Him."

CPSIA information can be obtained
at www.ICGtesting.com
Printed in the USA
BVHW030945060822
643953BV00006B/56

9 781736 961094